LOGIC

An Aristotelian Approach

Revised Edition

Mary Michael Spangler, O.P.

Appendixes One and Five by Pierre Conway, O.P.

WIPF & STOCK · Eugene, Oregon

Wipf and Stock Publishers
199 W 8th Ave, Suite 3
Eugene, OR 97401

Logic
An Aristotelian Approach
By Spangler, Mary Michael, OP
Copyright©1993 Rowman & Littlefield Publishing Group
ISBN 13: 978-1-62032-553-7
Publication date 8/31/2012
Previously published by University Press of America, 1993

In gratitude to Pierre Conway, O.P.,
and
Benedict Joseph, O.P.

CONTENTS

PREFACE

PURPOSE

This logic textbook, now in a revised edition, still has one purpose. It has been written in order that the student may learn how to think more effectively. Much has been written in our day about the need for skill in thinking. The fact that the American society is aware of this need is most encouraging. This awareness may surface questions such as the following: Why does the typical student have so much difficulty when he tries to think clearly and what is the remedy for such difficulty? This question cannot be solved by any set of facile procedures. Rather the remedy for untrained minds is simply this: the student must be given both a clear presentation of the rules for correct thinking and numerous exercises applying such rules. This textbook has been written precisely for that purpose.

AUDIENCE

This text is an introductory study of the rules of logic. A deliberate effort was made throughout the book to present only the basic procedures of defining, judging, and reasoning. Constantly the author, aided by many years in the classroom, thought of the beginning student and planned the text accordingly. Therefore this material, already tested on undergraduates, can be taught to college freshmen and even college-bound high school students. Among these individuals, those planning to teach will profit greatly from the text's application to reading skills.

DOCTRINAL BASE

The position in this text is a traditional one. Desiring a logical treatment drawn from everyday thinking, the author chose to follow Aristotle's doctrine, which is based on the natural patterns of the human mind. Since these patterns move from defining through judging to reasoning, the book has this threefold division.

TEACHING TOOLS

Like every other art, the teacher's skill must imitate nature. Therefore it must rely on the various senses, particularly memory, and must proceed either inductively or deductively. For these reasons this text places heavy emphasis on the following teaching tools: (1) familiar illustrations; (2) numerous charts, outlines, summaries, and lists of definitions; (3) many exercises following each chapter.

SPECIAL FEATURES

The following elements in the text should be particularly helpful for the student learning how to think effectively:

1. Since the reasoning process is based on the definition refining the mind's first grasp of the thing's whatness, the text explores very carefully this beginning stage of thinking. All of the various tools needed for a sound definition are presented and applied in numerous exercises. Above all, these tools are interrelated so that the art of defining may be both known and practiced.

2. Both the structure and rules of the basic, categorical syllogism are presented in one chapter. This unified treatment enables the student to understand this logical formation easily and to learn the art of reasoning readily.

3. Every chapter, except the first one, has a section applying its logical rules to the comprehension skills of reading. As the reader can note, there is a striking relationship between these two sets of skills. The author's reasons for making this connection in the text are twofold: (1) If the student sees that the abstract rules of logic are used even in the reading exercises of the primary grades, he may recognize the universal significance of such rules. (2) Those students planning to teach can note that they are learning the theoretical foundations for comprehension skills. (Since the reading section is completely separated from the rest of the text, the book may be taught with or without this section.)

REVISIONS

The author's deeper understanding of Aristotle's doctrine, based both on personal study and numerous classroom explanations, has led to the following revisions:

1. The need to emphasize that the name is the sign of the intellect's first grasp of the thing's whatness has required several changes throughout the text. These revisions can be noted primarily in chapter two.

2. After teaching the methods of division and composition, the author soon realized that the same, elementary example should be used for both methods. This realization led to the revision of most of chapter six.

3. Appendix five is new. In this welcome addition, Pierre Conway, O.P., presents succinctly the connection between the theories of modern science and the fallacy of consequence.

4. A glossary has been added to the text. This is the result of the author's awareness that much of the content is capsulized in its definitions and various rules.

5. Since Joanne Carlisle has a new edition of her *Reasoning and Reading* workbook, appropriate alterations have been made in this logic text.

6. For the sake of clarity, various examples, phrases, and paragraphs have been changed throughout the text.

One final word: the author, as a result of her study, appreciates even more Aristotle's perceptive grasp of reality. Hence she can easily state that his doctrine will be of great benefit to students.

ACKNOWLEDGMENTS

Many individuals have helped to make this textbook a reality, whether by their instruction, advice, or encouragement. Of this group, the author wishes first to thank Pierre H. Conway, O.P., Dominican House of Studies, Washington, D.C., for being a commentator par excellence of Aristotelian Thomism. Secondly, she is grateful for the peace and quiet provided by her congregation so that she could complete the manuscript. Above all, she has treasured the support of her sister and friends. Finally a special word of thanks must be said to her readers, Benedict Joseph, O.P., Mary McCaffrey, O.P., and Raymond Smith, O.P.

The author, in her revision of this text, was helped especially by two individuals. Therefore her appreciation is extended first to Jefferson Glover for his careful line drawings and secondly to Pierre Conway, O.P., for his enlightening appendix.

INTRODUCTION

A. Opening description of logic
B. The outline of logical thinking
C. Logical thinking, an art
D. Some problems for logic

Every human being naturally desires to know the answers to the problems which confront him. Thus the housewife, puzzled by the uneven texture of her cake, wonders if this condition was caused by her ingredients or by a sudden change in her oven. In like manner, the beginning golfer, having sliced his drive along one side of the fairway, will question his coach about the mysterious behavior of his golf ball. Every person, faced with both practical and speculative problems, seeks to know their answers. This basic trait of human nature is underscored by Aristotle at the beginning of his *Metaphysics*. He points out that a sign of this natural desire "is the delight we take in our senses; for even apart from their usefulness they are loved for themselves; and above all others the sense of sight. For not only with a view to action, but even when we are not going to do anything, we prefer seeing (one might say) to everything else. The reason is that this, most of all the senses, makes us know and brings to light many differences between things" (Richard McKeon, ed., *The Basic Works of Aristotle* [New York: Random House, 1941], 1. 1. 980^{a}22–28).

Human knowing, however, cannot be achieved by a rather casual procedure. Rather this highest of human operations demands, like every other rational activity, a vast amount of effort and skill. This need for skill in every human operation is easily seen in the carpenter's trade. Thus the craftsmanship required for a comfortable chair, a usable window, or a sturdy bookcase points out the proficiency needed for every human operation.

Where can the student find the rules to sharpen his skills so that he may more easily undertake the journey toward wisdom? These procedures are commonly found in logic textbooks, just as the rules for proper speech are codified in grammar books. Applications of logical techniques are given in manuals about the best way to study a course, to improve reading comprehension, to write term papers, and even to be a master teacher; but the general guidelines for the art of thinking are explained in logic texts.

A. OPENING DESCRIPTION OF LOGIC

1. ITS DEFINITION

Logic, the art of thinking or reasoning, may be defined as the art of going from the known to the unknown. It may also be described as the art of problem solving. The equivalence between these two definitions is easily noted if one reflects that every problem is an unknown which takes the form of a question to be answered. In order to answer this question, each person must rely on what he knows, must move from the known to the unknown.

If logic is the art of moving from the known to the unknown or of solving problems, is such an art of any use to the human being? Is the solution of problems a part of every human life? If each person reflects on his own personal history, he will readily agree that questions demanding solutions are part of everyday life. Is there enough food for breakfast? Will the children get to school on time? Will things go smoothly at work? Above these daily questions lies the ever-recurring problem about the meaning of life itself. Is there anything beyond the tangible, material world? Is each person his own complete master or is there a Creator of this vast universe? As these questions indicate, the solution of problems is part of human existence. If such is the case, then logic, as the art of solving problems, is essential for the human being.

Granted that the art of solving problems is needed for every human being, what does this art entail? As the following example will indicate, this logical art requires at least the following:

1. an awareness that the problem exists
2. an identification of the particular case under discussion
3. a background of general knowledge or principles

These three requirements will now be illustrated by a common household problem. They will then be treated more explicitly in the following sections.

Early one Saturday morning a householder notices a wet mark on his kitchen ceiling. It goes without saying that he has a problem. In fact, this household crisis triggers at least the two following questions: What is the cause of this sudden leakage? What can be done about it?

To solve this problem, the householder draws constantly upon what he knows about building maintenance. In other words, he is moving from the known to the unknown; i.e., from his identification of the case at hand and from his background of general principles. First, he may remember that the shower drain in the upstairs bathroom is often clogged with hair and may overflow its boundaries. A quick trip to the second floor, however, assures him that all is well in the bathroom. Then he recollects that, since the attic pipes are quite old, one of them may have sprung a leak. A thorough examination of the attic, however, still does not yield the answer. Finally, as the frustrated homeowner stands before the window pondering the problem, he sees the possible answer. Large puddles on the garage driveway indicate that a heavy rain occurred during the night. Since this corner of the kitchen is near a downspout, the wet mark may be the result of a flaw in this pipe. A quick climb up a ladder reveals that the spout is full of leaves. Now the householder is able to solve both of his problems. He not only knows the cause of the wet spot but also is able to do something about it.

2. THE ELEMENTS IN PROBLEM SOLVING

For the solution of any problem, two basic elements are required: the possession of certain general principles and an identification of the particular case at hand. In spite of the fact that the general principles may not be explicitly stated, they are always part of the problem solving process. Thus the householder with the wet ceiling could never have come to the right conclusion without the help of such principles as the following: (1) Whenever a ceiling is near a bathroom drain, it may get wet. (2) Whenever the ceiling is under old pipes, a leak may occur. (3) Whenever the ceiling is near a downspout, it may get wet. These principles are of a general nature because they apply, not just to this particular ceiling, but to any ceiling with identical circumstances.

In addition to having general principles, the problem solver must be able to define the particular case under discussion. Thus the householder may know well the general principle that ceilings near bathroom drains may get wet, but the problem is still unsolved if the bathroom reveals no damage. The fund of general principles is of no avail until the particular situation is defined as falling under one of them. Thus the ceiling must be defined as near a faulty downspout before the problem is solved. It does not suffice to describe the ceiling as near a bathroom or the old pipes (even though both definitions are true), for such a definition does not solve the problem. The particular case must be properly defined; i.e., described as falling under the appropriate general principle.

Therefore two kinds of knowledge are essential for the resolution of a problem: the knowledge of general principles giving needed background for the particular case; the ability to define the case as falling under the fund of principles.

In defining the case, the problem solver must be able to do more than simply give it a name. Rather he should ideally possess an understanding of its nature. Thus the small child may be able to point to the pipe on the outside of the house and call it a downspout. This facility does not mean that the child knows the nature and purpose of such a pipe. It is the person understanding the nature of the case who can more readily solve the problem. Thus the householder with a grasp of the mechanics of the downspout is able to find a substitute, if it still will not drain properly after the leaves are removed. In defining the case, the problem solver needs far more than its name. He must search for its nature.

If the problem solver needs to know both universal principles and the case's definition, which of these elements must he utilize first? Clearly it must be a grasp of the nature of the case, since this understanding dictates which of his principles to use. Thus the salesman may know many techniques about advertising, but he will not know which of them to employ until he analyzes his potential customers. The teacher may know many principles about discipline, but she cannot utilize this knowledge effectively until she studies her pupils carefully. For the solution of a problem, the knowledge of the nature of the case precedes the use of the fund of general principles.

3. THE PRIORITY OF SEEING THE PROBLEM

Granted that the general principles and the case's definition are essential for solving a problem, is there not another factor that precedes both of these elements? Plainly it must be the ability to see the problem in the first place. Just as the case's definition triggers the appropriate principle to use, so the grasp of the problem starts the entire procedure. Thus a scientist can discover why the Dead Sea is the saltiest one only because he first wondered why various bodies of water have different amounts of salt. If he had not seen any incongruity in this situation, he would have had neither a problem nor a solution. The whole procedure can be started only if the problem is well stated first. This ability to see problems is a precious commodity of inventors, who, from seeing something awry, have designed vacuum cleaners, tea strainers, electric hair dryers, and electronic typewriters. Beginning the entire procedure must always be a statement of the problem.

To state the problem is to lay down the goal to be achieved. To begin with one's goal is a proper human activity, which may be illustrated by the opening comments of speeches, the topic sentences of paragraphs, and the chapter outlines of textbooks.

How is the problem stated? In accord with the natural way in which human beings think and talk, the problem is stated as a question which asks whether or not a certain predicate should be said of a given subject. The following examples illustrate this format:

(subject)   (predicate)
Is baseball the favorite American sport?
Are human beings living for a longer period of time?
Is pollution a cause of cancer?

In other words, the problem is stated in the following manner: of a given subject, whether or not to say a certain predicate.

B. THE OUTLINE OF LOGICAL THINKING

The problem solving procedure described in the preceding section is derived from the natural way in which the human intellect operates. What are the steps that reason takes in its search for knowledge? It has three distinct operations: simple apprehension, judgment, and reasoning. These three operations harmonize with each other, building slowly but surely the vast edifice of human knowledge. It is the task of simple apprehension to grasp the nature, essence, or whatness of the simple realities in the material world. Thus the intellect through simple apprehension grasps what dogs, tulips, beetles, kangaroos, fire, water, and all other single material entities are. By the process of judgment the intellect combines or divides the concepts of these various simple realities. Thus the judgment might be made that a kangaroo is not a dog. Finally the reason, utilizing what it already knows, moves to what cannot be known directly (the unknown) by the climactic process of reasoning. This reasoning process is set forth in the syllogism. An example of such syllogistic reasoning follows:

Whatever is an excellent cooling agent will help put out fires.
Water is an excellent cooling agent.
∴ Water will help put out fires.

These three acts of reason are outlined by Thomas Aquinas at the beginning of the first lecture of the *Exposition of the Posterior Analytics of Aristotle* (Quebec, Canada: La Librairie Philosophique M. Doyon, 1956). He states that "there are three acts of reason, of which the first two are of reason as it is a certain understanding. For one act of the understanding (or intellect) is the intelligence of indivisible or incomplex realities, as when it conceives what a thing is.... The second operation of the intellect is the composition or division of the intellect, in which there is now truth or falsehood.... The third act of reason is according to that which is proper to reason, namely, to discourse from one to another, in order that through what is known one may come to a knowledge of the unknown."

By means of the three acts of simple apprehension, judgment, and reasoning, the needed elements for the problem solving procedure are obtained. First, simple apprehension (the grasp of the whatness of simple realities) obtains the needed definition of the subject. Second, judgment (charged with combining and dividing the concepts of these simple realities) formulates the universal principles, as well as all other propositions. Third, reasoning (moving from the known to the unknown) solves the unknown; i.e., the problem which asks whether or not the predicate should be stated of a given subject.

The following outline shows the connection between the three acts of the mind and the elements of problem solving. It also lists the appropriate grammatical expressions of these operations:

<u>Logic</u>

1. act of simple apprehension
   —obtains the universal concept of the essence or whatness of a thing.
   —refines concept into a definition, giving genus and specific difference.
2. act of judgment
   —obtains the proposition by a process of composition and division.
   (Universal principles are one kind of proposition.)
3. act of reasoning
   —reaches the unknown or the solution of the problem by the syllogistic procedure.

<u>Grammar</u>

1. the simple word
   —expressed in a simple word (such as *tulip, lion, horse, fire*) which stands for the whatness, kind, or species.

2. the complex statement
   —expressed in a declarative sentence.

3. the discursive statement
   —expressed in a discursive statement, which gives a cause-effect relationship.
   —uses one or more sentences.

In accord with the three acts of the human mind, this textbook will be divided into the following sections: (1) simple apprehension, (2) judgment, (3) reasoning. The work of each section is illustrated in the following chart:

THE WORK OF THE THREE ACTS OF THE MIND

1. act of simple apprehension	from sensible singulars → to grasp of whatness or nature of simple realities by inductive process (This whatness is refined into a definition.)	from individual bats from individual cases of echolocation from individual cases of darkness what a bat is (a mouselike flying mammal with a furry body and membranous wings)* what echolocation is (the determination of the position of an object by emission of sound waves reflected back to sender as echoes)* what darkness is (the absence of light)*
2. act of judgment	combines or divides the concepts of simple realities, thus obtaining the proposition	Echolocation permits flying in absolute darkness. Bats use echolocation.
3. act of reasoning	moves from known propositions to unknown (to conclusion) by syllogistic procedure	Whatever uses echolocation—can fly in absolute darkness. Every bat-----------uses echolocation. ∴Every bat-----------can fly in absolute darkness.

*The above definitions and all subsequent ones marked with an asterisk (*) are paraphrased from the following source: David B. Guralnik, ed., *Webster's New World Dictionary of the American Language*, Second College Edition (Englewood Cliffs, N.J.: Prentice-Hall, 1970).

C. LOGICAL THINKING, AN ART

1. AN ART IMITATING NATURE

Logic, like every other art, is effective only if it follows the guidelines and limitations set by nature. The reliance of every art upon nature is evident from just a few examples of human artistry. Thus the careful farmer relies upon the natural ways in which plants grow and the proper environment for a bountiful harvest. The master ballet instructor must remember both the purpose of the human body and the limitations of its muscular system. In every case the artistry of human beings must follow the plan of nature and utilize whatever natural materials are available. If any art attempts to go against nature, it cannot succeed.

The skillful logician, imitating nature, must be aware of the following principles about human learning: (1) Every human being has a natural desire to know and therefore has a natural wonder about the unknown. (2) All human knowledge begins with sense knowledge. (3) In knowing the whatness or nature of a material thing, human knowledge moves from its generic or confused to its specific or distinct aspects.

As can be noted, the natural desire of the human being for knowledge was illustrated at the beginning of this text. Why is this desire so basic to each human person? One reason is that understanding is the distinctive and proper work of humankind. In contrast, the proper activity of the lower animals is to sense, while the distinctive operation of the plants is to grow and reproduce. Now the distinctive activity of a thing is naturally sought by it. Thus fire has a natural tendency to make things hot; water has a built-in aptitude to refresh and cool; and the dog has a natural inclination to smell out the newest things in his environment. Therefore, if knowing is indeed the proper work of humankind, it follows that there is a natural desire within each human person to know and understand. This desire to know stands as a great boon to all educators and teachers.

The second principle about human learning is that all knowledge takes its rise from the senses. This principle seems so evident that it may appear rather pointless to discuss it. Nevertheless, such philosophers as Descartes, Hume, and Kant have doubted the veracity of the senses and have consequently postulated a kind of knowing which is independent of them. In other words, the human being, not able to rely on his senses, might know solely by some interior framework independent of sense contact with the outside world. If great thinkers deny the validity of the senses, it is necessary to examine this second principle more closely.

A little reflection enables one to realize that all human knowledge does take its rise from the senses. Even the experience of a small child confirms this fact. If this child sees a strange plant in his yard, he may ask his mother its name. After learning that it is called a dandelion, he may walk around the entire yard and name every other one of these yellow weeds. While walking with his mother on the following day, he may point out and label every dandelion that he sees. In this simple operation the child exemplifies first that he did indeed sense the flower and second, through his giving the same label to each one, that he was able to grasp the universal note common to every one. The direct experience of every person confirms that all human knowledge begins with sensible singulars and rises to the universal thread or whatness common to all of them. The sign of the individual's possession of this universal note is his ability to use the same name for every subsequent case that he encounters. Even though the human being may not be able to describe this nature in detail, he finds no trouble in using the same label for these later similar experiences.

In addition, the ultimate criterion for the soundness of a given piece of information is that it can be verified in sensible reality. This verification may involve more than one sense. Thus the cook, pleased that the guests were satisfied with the pecan pie, may later taste it to be sure that it is as good as described. The shopper, struck by the unusual appearance of a bolt of material, may feel its texture to be sure of its quality. Only when human knowledge is verified from sensible examples is it considered sound and true.

Even in the case of optical illusions, the final court of appeal is found in sense knowledge. Thus two parallel lines, because of a confusing background, may appear to bulge outward from each other. Consequently, it is said that the senses are deceived, that there is an optical illusion. But the interesting fact is that, when confronted with this problem, one uses the senses to discover that the lines are really parallel. This is easily noted if one reflects that the use of a ruler to check this situation demands also the use of one's eyes and hands. Even when faced with the problem of optical illusions, one employs the senses to discover what is the truth of the matter.

The third principle concerning human learning is that, in knowing the whatness of a material thing, the intellect moves from its generic to specific aspects. Thus the first knowledge that one might have about a rabbit is simply that it is a small animal. Only later would one know that it is a mammal with soft fur, long ears, and a short cottony tail. As this example illustrates, all human knowledge moves from the generic to the specific characteristics of a thing, from a confused to a clear understanding of a thing's whatness. Not gifted with angelic insight, the human being moves slowly in his knowledge of the world around him.

In the above respect, the progression of human learning is analogous to the situation of a person watching an object approaching from a distance. At first this object is just a dot on the horizon. Later it appears to be some kind of animal. The object seems too big to be a dog or a sheep; perhaps it is a cow or a horse. Finally one discovers that it is actually a donkey. This gradual bringing into focus of an object approaching from a distance is an excellent analogy of the way in which human learning moves from the generic to the specific, from the confused to the clear.

2. THE ART OF ARTS

Logic has been defined as the art of moving from the known to the unknown. What is meant by the term *art*? A little reflection yields that it is the mind's grasp, aided by the orderly procedures in nature, of both the effective rules and the intermediate steps to follow for a given end. This general definition of art is easily illustrated by the art of medicine. Only if the doctor studies how the body naturally heals itself can he hope to be successful in practicing his profession. Aware of nature's use of sleep, good food, and exercise, the doctor must prescribe remedies which follow and improve upon such natural patterns. From the study of nature's procedures arises the doctor's art, which gives both the efficacious rules and intervening steps leading to a healthy body. In brief, art is a sure method derived from nature for attaining a particular goal well.

Unlike the lower animals which live by instinct, the human being lives by art and reasoning. It is evident that the many kinds of animals have instinctual procedures which aid them in their various activities. Thus the moth larva easily spins a cocoon without being trained in the best way to produce it. Neither the spider nor the bee has had lessons in how to build a home. The human being, on the other hand, must discover from nature the best method for providing for himself. Not living by instinct, he must learn from trial and error the most effective way to build his house, to cook his food, to make his clothes, and even to think. All of these procedures constitute the various arts.

In every art the human mind observes nature, setting down those orderly patterns which bring about a given goal well. Thus the art of horticulture, having noticed the best environment for plant growth, codifies such knowledge for the benefit of all amateur gardeners. Just as reason can observe sound procedures in growing and healing, so it can reflect on its own natural process of thinking and formulate artistic rules. In other words, the mind observes itself at work, notices its most efficient way of thinking, and then records and polishes such procedures. These procedures constitute the art of thinking. This art, perfecting the mind, is defined by Aquinas in the *Exposition of the Posterior Analytics of Aristotle* (ibid., I, 1. 1) as one "by means of which a man may, in the act of reason itself, proceed in a way which is orderly, easy and without error."

Since the mind discovers the various arts, it is most appropriate to call that art guiding the mind the art of arts. If the mind itself is well trained, with how much more ease can it develop the other arts. Just as the all-around athlete can adapt himself easily to a particular sport, so the trained mind can grasp more readily the rules of a specific art. It is well said that logic is the art of arts. If its rules are understood and practiced, logic furnishes the guiding compass for every other art.

Logic, however, only guides the mind toward the possession of the arts and sciences. It is the tool to aid the human being in his search for truth. Its body of knowledge contains true principles about the mind's operations but does not include the various truths about the universe. In other words, logic studies the path to learning, not the actual body of learning itself. In this respect it may be compared to the steel framework of a building. Just as this framework is filled in by bricks and cement, so the thinking framework of logic is completed by the sciences about nature and God. In a word, logic presents the form of thinking, while the various sciences treat the content of thought.

For purposes of clarification, the work of logic may be aligned with that of grammar. The rules of this latter subject guide clarity of speech in every single area of thought. Thus, no matter whether the subject is biology, mathematics, or political science, grammar provides the rules for the proper ways in which to use subjects and predicates. In like manner, logic states the rules of thinking, no matter what the subject may be. Thus it is the work of logic to explain the procedures of defining, but not to give the content of the definition. Logic also shows how true judgments about reality can be adjusted or opposed without wavering from a given truth. Finally, logic lays down the rules for reasoning from two premises to a conclusion, but does not treat the natural or metaphysical truths reached through the reasoning process. Briefly, logic gives only how, not what.

Although logic does not treat the content of the sciences, it has a universal value for every student. The reason is that logic takes the natural thought processes of human beings and refines them to a new artistic level. Among a group of people, it is quite evident that some are naturally more logical than others, just as certain persons have greater musical ability than others. Even these natural logicians, however, would benefit from the increased skill offered by the rules of logic. Just as all persons can profit from training in such arts as dance, music, and drama, so every individual can extend his intellectual talents by practice in the art of thinking.

D. SOME PROBLEMS FOR LOGIC

1. APPARENT REASONING

A basic problem for the art of thinking is that type of reasoning which appears to be sound, but actually is not. A common name for such reasoning is fallacy. It is defined as reasoning which appears to conclude but does not. When one thinks of the fallacy, one may believe that it refers to examples of blatant misreasoning. Such cases, however, are only second-rate or amateur deceptions. The true fallacy is one which appears to be quite orthodox except to the trained logician. Because of its possibility for deception, the fallacy is a serious problem for the field of logic.

Fallacies can arise from two sources, either from the words used in the argument or from the way that the mind combines the things discussed. Because of this division they are called fallacies dependent on language or fallacies independent of language.

The primary type of fallacy dependent on language is that of equivocation. This type arises when the same word has different meanings. As is well known, *ball* may stand for a toy or a dance. In cases such as this, the one word can lead to an appearance of valid reasoning, while the different meanings connect nothing together and lead to no conclusion at all. Why does such a situation arise? The first reason is the human imagination's inability to create enough words for the many things in the universe. The second and greater reason is that a person, forgetting that words are arbitrarily given meaning by human beings, believes and acts as though a given word must always stand for the same thing. This unrealistic position leads to much confusion and unnecessary argument. This fallacy of equivocation may be illustrated as follows:

Whatever requires the law (a hindrance) ------------ *leads to a form of enslavement.*
The life of virtue ---- --- *requires the law (a help).*
∴ The life of virtue --- *leads to a form of enslavement.*

As the above example indicates, the clever use of equivocation makes it quite easy to confuse the listener. Since this fallacy is very common, it is imperative that all students be trained in the rules of sound thinking.

2. LOGIC IN THE CURRICULUM

There is much debate concerning the position of logic in the curriculum. This argumentation revolves chiefly around the following questions: (1) Should logic be a distinct subject in the curriculum? (2) If logic is a distinct subject, when should it be taught?

In relation to the first question, there are individuals who focus on the fact that logic is primarily a skill subject and is found in every area of the curriculum. Just as grammar gives the rules for skillful expression and permeates every kind of subject matter, so logic presents the techniques for thinking and pervades every area where thought occurs. If logic gives only the techniques for thought and is found in every subject, why may it not be learned concomitantly with the presentation of each different subject?

The reason against the above argument is that, while it is true that logic is an all-pervasive skill subject, it is also a distinct subject with its own rules (which are quite abstract and hard). Now experience proves that two different things cannot be learned by the human being at one time. Thus an individual attempting to master voice lessons while he is learning to be a song writer will succeed in neither of these arts. In like manner, the cook who wants to analyze the chemicals in his foodstuffs while he is preparing a tasty dinner will accomplish neither purpose. Because of the limited nature of the human mind, it is impossible for the human being to learn two distinct things at the same time. Therefore, since logic is a subject in its own right, it cannot be mastered as an incidental part of all the other subjects. Just as grammar is taught as a separate entity even though it pervades every area, so logic requires the same careful, distinct presentation. A lack of understanding of this requirement has led to the omission of logic in the curriculum and to the indirect promotion of much slipshod thinking.

The second question in the debate about logic in the curriculum concerns when it should be taught. Since it is abstract and therefore difficult, it is argued that it should be given only to the mature mind, rather than to the young student. The sound reason behind this argument is that the human being must always rely on his senses in the process of learning. Therefore logic, as an extremely abstract subject, should be delayed until the latter part of a pattern of study.

Another attribute of logic, however, must enter into this argument. This subject, giving the techniques for thinking, lays down the method for the mind as it thinks through any problem. But the method or procedure must be mastered before any given project is undertaken. Thus the contractor for a building would never put his plumbers to work before they were proficient in the techniques of plumbing. Also the pianist must master the skills of note reading before he attempts to be an accomplished musician. Therefore, logic, giving the thinker his techniques, must be learned at the beginning of the curriculum. In spite of the fact that it is very abstract, this subject must precede every other academic area. This placement for logic is recognized in the early teaching of reading's comprehension skills.

STUDY QUESTIONS

CHAPTER 1

1. What sign reveals that the human being naturally desires to know?
2. What subject codifies the skills required for clear thinking? Define logic.
3. What are the three requirements for the art of problem solving? In what order are they used?
4. In what format is the problem stated?
5. What are the three operations of human reason? What is the object of each of these operations? What is the grammatical counterpoint for each of these objects?
6. As the logician imitates nature, what three natural principles must he remember?
7. Why does the human being have a natural desire to know?
8. Describe three different situations in knowing which indicate that all knowledge comes from the senses.
9. Illustrate the fact that all human knowing moves from the generic to the specific.
10. Define art.
11. How does the human being differ from the lower animals, which live by instinct?
12. Why is logic called the art of arts?
13. How does the contribution of logic differ from that of the various sciences?
14. List two problems for the art of thinking.
15. Define the fallacy. What are two sources of fallacy?
16. What is meant by the fallacy of equivocation? What are two reasons that this fallacy occurs?
17. Explain the conflicting arguments concerning the need for logic in the curriculum, concerning the placement of logic in the curriculum.

FIRST ACT OF THE MIND: SIMPLE APPREHENSION

The following chart shows the relationship among the chapters treated under simple apprehension.

THE FIRST ACT OF THE MIND: SIMPLE APPREHENSION

ch. 2 — from sensible ------- to whatness or nature
          singular   of simple realities

ch. 6 — by inductive ----------- then clearly
          process using
          division or   first dimly ------- subsequent, divided concept
          composition   initial, unitary concept
          methods

          DEFINITION: 1. genus
                      2. specific difference

EXAMPLE
individual bats ------- A bat: ------- is a mouselike flying mammal with a furry body and membranous wings.*

                        species   genus ----------- mammal ------------- substance (body, wings)
                                         difference   ┌ mouselike --------- form
                                         (inseparable   │ flying ------------- ability   ⟩ qualities
                                         accidents)   │ furry -------------- sense quality
                                                           └ membranous --------- sense quality

                        PREDICABLES   FORMAL CAUSE →

                                                                                  → CATEGORIES

INTERNAL AND EXTERNAL SIGNS OF ABOVE: CONCEPTS AND WORDS

| ch. 3 | ch. 5 | ch. 7 | ch. 4 |

CHAPTER 2

GRASPING SIMPLE REALITIES

A. The human being's knowledge of reality
B. His inductive process
C. His concepts and words
D. His clarified concepts: definitions

Every human being is aware of the fact that he knows many things. His fund of knowledge is demonstrated most graphically in the practical order. Thus, as his practical actions manifest, an individual might hold such facts as the following: (1) Intense cold can kill a human being. (2) Plants will die without water. (3) Aspirin is a good pain reliever. (4) Milk is a valuable food. (5) Electricity should be handled with care. Simple practical information, such as these examples illustrate, is an important part of every person's store of knowledge. In addition, a given individual may possess many theoretical insights, such as why copper tarnishes but gold does not; what causes thunderstorms; what distinguishes an insect from a mammal.

Whether human knowledge is practical or theoretical, it always starts from the sense level and must be lifted to the abstract level of intellectual insight. This dual requirement for human knowledge is easily noted in the following statements: (1) I do not understand any abstract topic unless I have a concrete illustration of it. (2) I failed the test because I could not grasp the abstract questions. Now these two levels of human knowledge, the concrete singular and the abstract universal, are very different. What distinguishes the one from the other? What makes sense knowledge so distinct from intellectual knowledge?

A. THE HUMAN BEING'S KNOWLEDGE OF REALITY

The human being, empowered with his senses and intellect, is able to know the material world both in its sensible, singular aspects and in its essential, universal notes. Each person, reflecting on his own experience, can distinguish both the presence and the difference in these two kinds of knowledge. Thus an individual, knowing this yellow tulip in his garden, is aware not only of its unique singularity but also of its whatness, essence, or nature. More specifically, this person with his five senses knows this tulip as this unique, material thing in this time and place. What is seen is this yellow and green as existing in the here and now. The individual is not seeing the peculiar yellow and green of any other tulip nor even the yellow and green of this tulip as it was yesterday or will be tomorrow. The person sees the yellow and green of this tulip as it is at this minute in this place. This knowledge may be described as follows: It is sensible, singular, and unique. It is a singular and one-time picture presented to the sense of sight, as well as to the other senses.

In contrast to the singular perception obtained by the senses, the intellect knows the nature or whatness of the sensed object. In other words, the senses (through the various sense objects of color, sound, and so forth) know that the material thing is there, but the intellect knows what it is. In reference to the tulip, the senses perceive this singular tulip in all its concreteness, but the intellect grasps the inner core, thread, or note which distinguishes this tulip from every other type of flower. This inner essence, nature, or whatness is common to every single tulip, whether in the past, present, or future; it makes the tulip the kind or type of flower it is. If a trained botanist attempted to describe what type of flower the tulip is, he might give a statement similar to the following: It is a bulb plant of the lily family with long, broad, pointed leaves and a large, cup-shaped, variously colored flower.* In this description the botanist refers to the tulip's type, kind, or nature; he is not presenting a singular picture of a particular sample. This knowledge of a thing's whatness is the proper object of the intellect and is immediately obtained by any functioning intellect working in harmony with the senses.

Does every single reasoning person know immediately the whatness of a material thing, as well as its sensible impression? To know a thing's whatness or essence is indeed the legacy of every human being, but this knowledge is quite dim or obscure when it is first obtained. Then what proof can be given that a person has such knowledge? Returning again to the tulip, one can easily find two indications. First, this individual, having sensed the tulip and been told its name, will readily label every other singular tulip with this same name. He could not do this if he did not know some common thread or nature which prevailed throughout all of these samples. In other words, this action is possible only because this beginning botanist knows dimly the whatness common to every member of the tulip family. Second, the individual, lacking the name of the tulip, is still able to separate all the individual tulips from the other kinds of flowers. This classification activity, found even in small children, occurs only because the person knows the common note, thread, or whatness proper to all the members of a certain type.

Knowledge of the whatness of a simple material thing is obtained in the intellect's first operation of simple apprehension. As the name for this activity indicates, simple apprehension is nothing other than the grasp of the whatness of simple material entities. What is a simple material entity? It is any material thing which is one because it has one form or nature. In other words, it is any of the many distinct things in the physical universe. These distinct things are either of a substantial nature existing on their own or of an accidental nature existing in the different substances. Examples of the former might be bear, pansy, sea gull, and diamond; while illustrations of the latter might be brown, bent, flying, and hard. The essences of these many different things are grasped by the intellect in its first operation of simple apprehension.

B. HIS INDUCTIVE PROCESS

The whatness of a simple material thing, the object of simple apprehension, is obtained by the human being in an inductive process. What is this basic procedure of the human intellect? Induction is defined as a process whereby from sensible singulars, perceived by the senses, one arrives at universal concepts and principles held by the intellect. Thus, from the sense experience of even a single yellow tulip, the intellect arrives at a universal concept of the tulip. In contrast to the singular picture of the senses, the intellect holds in this universal idea or concept that the tulip is a special type or kind. Abstracting from the peculiarities of this yellow tulip, the intellect knows the common thread, essence, or whatness which can be found in any member of the tulip family. Not concerned with any member as a unique singular, the intellect grasps that special note or whatness which is universal or common to every tulip. As this example illustrates, induction is a passage from the singular to the universal, a passage made possible by the abstractive power of the intellect.

As the intellect refines its knowledge of a thing's kind or whatness, it moves from the generic to the specific. In other words, the intellect knows the whatness vaguely before it perceives it clearly. Thus at first this faculty may grasp only that this thing in the garden has the name *tulip*. Later, after more sense experience, the intellect will see this whatness more clearly. Thus it will soon note that this tulip is a pretty plant. Finally, the intellect will perceive the following: The tulip is a bulb plant with long, broad, pointed leaves and a large cup-shaped, variously colored flower.* At every point, however, the intellect knows what kind of thing the tulip is. The distinction lies in the fact that this whatness is known at first very obscurely and then later more clearly or specifically. Said in another way, the intellect's knowledge of the whatness moves from the general outline to the distinctive features.

To illustrate this intellectual movement from the blurred outline to the distinctive features, one may utilize the progressive recognition which occurs in seeing a far-off object. Thus, while driving on the highway, one may see a glistening object at the top of the next hill. It may be recognized first only as a car. Then, as it comes closer, one may see that it is a Plymouth; finally one is able to note that it has a New York license plate. In like manner, the intellect moves from a blurred to a clear knowledge of the whatness or nature of a given thing.

Because of the intellect's movement from the generic to the specific, one can easily see that the more obvious items will require less time and sense experience than the more distinctive items. Thus the realization that this thing in the garden has the name *tulip* is easily obtained after one sense contact with this new flower. In fact, the blurred outline of any simple thing's whatness is grasped each time the functioning intellect is presented with a particular sensation. Thus a small child, sensing a white fluffy cloud in the sky, demonstrates that he has not only the sensible impression but also the obscure whatness by the following statements: "Yes, I see it. I can also tell you what it is. I heard my mother call it a cloud. I saw one just like it yesterday." As this child's statements illustrate, the intellect knows obscurely the whatness in any simple, sensible impression presented to it.

While the obvious outline of a thing's whatness can be grasped in a first sensible impression, the distinct features of this whatness require many more sensible contacts. This is also true of the universal rules or principles which guide one's daily activities. Such a principle might be that an antiseptic condition is produced by tincture of iodine. Since this principle is not an obvious, evident truth (it was first used by a French surgeon in 1839), it can be grasped in its universal significance only after a sufficient amount of sense experience. The stages of this needed sense material from which the intellect grasps a universal judgment are as follows:

1. Memory
   If one will grasp a universal principle applying to many singular cases, one must first collect in the memory enough cases so that the intellect can extract the universal from them. Thus a doctor, using tincture of iodine, needs to remember that this deep scratch, that large bed sore, this sore throat, that nail puncture, and this bullet wound were all made antiseptic by tincture of iodine. If the doctor does not first remember those individual times when tincture of iodine worked well, he can never develop any universal judgment about the efficacy of this medication.

2. Experience
   Out of the memory of a series of like incidents, one puts together a single unified remembrance of these events, which is called experience. Thus the doctor, weaving together his many memories of well-cleaned wounds, might state the following: "My experience tells me to use tincture of iodine for this wound." The important position of this unified sense knowledge is attested by the exhortation to learn from the school of experience.

Experience, however, is not yet a grasp of the universal. Rather it is a unified sense knowledge built from many singular memories. By analogy, it may be compared to the members of a fire department. If one of these firemen extinguishes a strategic spot in a burning building, he stands like the first striking memory preceding experience. As many other firemen join him, their power becomes unified and stronger. These fire fighters may be likened to the unity and power found in experience. Although presenting a unified front, they are still not the whole department or the universal. Only when the entire department arrives, does one have the whole force or the universal.

3. Grasp of the Universal

The grasp of the universal, made possible by the abstractive power of the intellect, implies that one knows the given principle is applicable to every case under it. Thus the doctor, knowing that all wounds are made antiseptic by tincture of iodine, has a truly workable principle, a universal which applies to every type of wound. The sign of the difference between experience and the universal is that, while the experienced man can act well, he cannot explain why or how his actions work. Thus an experienced doctor can handle a given case; but, if he does not truly see the universal behind his experience, he cannot teach a new doctor all that his years have taught him. If one wishes to explain to another how a thing is done, he must really understand what he is talking about. Only the person who sees the entire scope of the problem or who possesses the universal is able to explain his position to another. Therefore the person possessing the universal is easily detected from his ability to explain what he knows.

Whether induction demands little or more sensible contact with the material universe, it always requires two things: a base of sensible knowledge and an insight into the universal. In every case of induction these two essential elements must be present. This is the very nature of this basic procedure: to be a process which moves from the sensible singular to the universal through the abstractive power of the intellect.

In the inductive process, the search for the universal tends toward broader and broader insights. A very basic example of this unifying tendency in the human being might be found in one's experience with squirrels. At first, if one had encountered only tree squirrels, one's universal would include only the tree-climbing type. Later one may discover that there are also squirrels with stripes, such as the antelope squirrel and the chipmunk. At that point one's universal concerning squirrels is extended accordingly. Finally one may learn about all the species of ground squirrels. Now the universal concerning squirrels undergoes another extension. As this illustration indicates, the human being's universalizing tendency moves toward greater and greater unity. The human person is always searching for one final answer concerning the manifold realities in the universe. His mind reaches out, as indicated by his constant unification of related kinds or species, to a single unifying cause.

C. HIS CONCEPTS AND WORDS

It is the intellect's idea or concept which holds the whatness of every simple reality. Just as the sense image retains a singular picture of whatever is sensed, so the mental image or concept holds the universal whatness of the sensed thing. More specifically, it is the sense image which retains the singular, cameralike picture of a swan seen on a peaceful lake, while it is the mental image or concept which retains the whatness of this particular swan. In fact, the concept is defined as that mental mechanism or sign which retains the nature or whatness of a sensed thing. Every concept, holding the nature common to every member, has a universal extension. Thus the concept of swan (defined as a large-bodied, web-footed water bird with a long, graceful neck and, usually, white feathers)* is applicable to each individual swan or is universal in its extension.

This universal concept is given expression in the spoken and written word. If human beings had no reason to communicate with each other, words would not be necessary. In such an extraordinary situation, an individual would be alone with his thoughts, i.e., with his concepts or ideas. Nevertheless, granted that human beings are social by nature, words stand for universal concepts of the various things in the physical universe. Said in another way, words stand for the ideas that people have about things. As such, words also have a universal extension. This extension is evident whenever words are used to designate things. Thus the word *duck* is applicable to any individual duck at any time or place. This universality is true of all words, which function as signs of the concepts had about things.

If words have a universal extension, how does the user of words designate a particular thing, such as one duck? Even the use of the words *one duck* or *this duck* will not suffice; for these expressions, though pointed in their meaning, are applicable to any particular duck. Experience indicates that the person must finally point out in some concrete way the individual duck in question. Only then does one leave the universal world of words and enter the concrete arena of material reality.

Granted that words stand for the concepts of things, it is also true to say that words stand for things. Thus a speaker, using the term *cloud*, is talking about a real cloud in the sky. How is it that the word is truly a sign of the real object? The word is a sign of the thing through the universal concept in the mind, which reflects the universal nature existing in the individual member. Thus the word *cloud* refers to real, individual clouds, but clouds considered in reference to the universal nature found in them. Therefore the word, a sign of the concept, stands for the real thing by means of its whatness known by the mind.

It must be remembered, however, that the word, valuable as it is, is only the sign of the concept. As such, it does not have meaning by itself. Thus the word *addax* is meaningless without the idea corresponding to it. Only when this word can be matched to the meaning or whatness known by the mind, does it have significance. Thus *addax*, as standing for a large antelope with long, twisted horns, becomes valuable or significant. Words alone do not have meaning; it is the concept which holds the meaning. The word must be connected to the proper concept before it can be functional.

D. HIS CLARIFIED CONCEPTS: DEFINITIONS

1. THE MOVEMENT FROM INITIAL TO DIVIDED CONCEPT

The universal concept, expressed by a word, is perceived at first in a very obscure way. Thus the child may know only that her particular kind of pet is named *cat*. At this point the child's concept of her pet (which is revealed only in the name *cat*) is truly a beginning, unrefined idea. In this respect it may be described as an initial, unitary (undivided) concept. Nevertheless, this firm, but vague, notion of the whatness of her pet ("I know that my pet is a cat.") stands as a nominal beginning for all that can be known about the nature of this animal.

Gradually the child begins to refine her initial, unitary concept as she discovers more and more from her own real cat or from the world of books. This clarifying process is none other than the procedure which leads to a definition. In fact, every definition is only the refinement of the unitary beginning. Since this refinement leads to a division of the initial concept into a general class and a distinctive note, the resultant definition may be described as a divided concept. Thus the child is finally able to define her cat as a flesh-eating mammal (general class) which is domesticated and used as a pet or a mouser (distinctive note).* As this illustration indicates, the definition is simply a divided concept which follows the initial, undivided one.

In the defining process, the intellect moves from the better-known generic characteristics to those which are more difficult and specific. Thus the child easily sees that her cat is an animal (general class) before she realizes that it is domesticated and used as a pet or a mouser (distinctive note). As this example illustrates, the intellect moves from the generic characteristics to those which are specific. In logical terminology, the intellect, as it defines, obtains first the genus (general class) and then the specific difference (distinctive note). Because of this movement of the mind, the definition may be described as a clarification of the initial whatness giving the genus and specific difference.

As noted above, the initial, unitary concept of the thing is clarified by a two-stage process into the definition, which states both the genus and the specific difference (or inseparable accidents). This clearer understanding of a thing, such as cat, does not stem from the fact that new characteristics have been added to it. Rather the definition arises from attributes which have always been present, but are now clarified. It must also be noted that, even though the definition is broken into two parts, the object defined is one thing with one nature. Thus the cat, defined as a flesh-eating mammal which is domesticated and used as a pet or a mouser, is not two different things. It is one species or kind with the distinctive nature of catness. Finally, the two-part delineation found in the definition is necessary for the human being because his knowing is such a gradual process, is a progression in which he sees clearly only a little at one time.

As stated in the previous paragraph, the initial, unitary concept is refined into the definition (the subsequent, divided concept), which gives both the genus and the specific difference (or inseparable accidents). These two parts of the definition are easily found in any dictionary. The following illustrations are taken from both a primary and a collegiate dictionary. They indicate clearly that, as human understanding develops, it always retains the same basic pattern.

1. *ant:* *a small insect that lives in the ground*[#]
     a black, brown, or red insect, generally wingless, that lives in
     colonies with a complex division of labor by groups[*]
2. *beaver:* *an animal with sharp teeth and a flat tail*[#]
     a large rodent with soft, brown fur; chisellike teeth; webbed hind
     feet; and a flat, broad tail; that is equally at home on land or the
     water[*]
3. *eagle:* *a large, strong bird with a nest in a high place*[#]
     a large, strong, flesh-eating bird of prey belonging to the falcon
     family, noted for its sharp vision and powerful wings[*]

[#] W. Cabell Greet, William A. Jenkins, and Andrew Schiller, *My First Picture Dictionary* (Glenview, Illinois: Scott, Foresman & Company, 1970).

This section has explained that the initial, unitary concept is refined into the definition giving both the genus and specific difference. The following chart summarizes the movement in human knowing from sense knowledge to the definition:

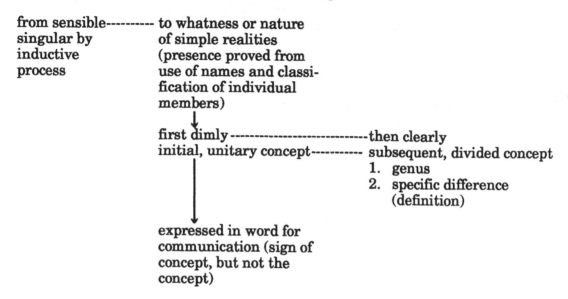

from sensible---------- to whatness or nature
singular by   of simple realities
inductive   (presence proved from
process   use of names and classi-
                     fication of individual
                     members)

first dimly ----------------------------then clearly
initial, unitary concept---------- subsequent, divided concept
                     1. genus
                     2. specific difference
                        (definition)

expressed in word for
communication (sign of
concept, but not the
concept)

2. THE VALUE OF DEFINITION

Is the definition of value to the human being? Each person, by his very nature, desires to know what makes things the way they are. Thus children examine insects to see what they are like, and adults puzzle over strange happenings reported in the newspapers. The human being, because of his intellect, wants to know the essence or whatness of things. Therefore each individual tends naturally toward the clarification of this whatness provided by the definition. This two-part delineation provides the next step in the human being's search for knowledge.

Impelled by his desire to know, the human being moves beyond the evident facts obtained from his surroundings to problems which are not immediately solved. In other words, he moves from the known to the unknown. In this process he must rely on what he knows first; i.e., on the whatness of the material thing clarified by the definition. Thus an Irish householder might wonder why peat is a poor fuel. If he knows that peat can be defined as material with a high water content, he can move from this definition to the solution of his problem. His reasoning might be outlined as follows:

problem	*Why is peat a poor fuel?*
subject defined	*Peat is a material with high water content.*
general principle	*Whatever has a high water content makes a poor fuel.*
conclusion	*∴ Peat is a poor fuel.*

As the above illustration indicates, the finding of the unknown in the reasoning process relies upon the definition of the subject. Without this initial definition of the subject, it is impossible to have any subsequent reasoning about it. Since every conclusion about a subject depends first upon the latter's definition, it is plain that definition sets the direction for all subsequent reasoning. Based on sense knowledge and the initial whatness, definition is the keystone for the vast edifice of knowledge. Therefore, not only because of the initial clarity which it provides but also because of its vital role in reasoning, the definition has great value for the human being.

1. What two kinds of knowledge is a human being able to obtain?
2. Give an original illustration of sensible knowledge, of intellectual knowledge. Give two characteristics which distinguish these two kinds of knowledge.
3. What two actions of the human being prove that he knows the whatness of material things?
4. What is simple apprehension? What is a simple material entity?
5. Define induction. Through what stages does the intellect move in the inductive process? At what stage does the intellect know the whatness of material things? What aspects of a material thing demand less sense contact, more sense experience?
6. Through what stages of knowing does the human being move as he acquires a universal principle? What is the distinction between experience and the universal principle? What sign indicates the possession of the universal?
7. Toward what culmination does the human being's inductive process move?
8. Define the concept or idea. What is the extension of this sign?
9. Human language is a sign of what entity? What is the extension of the word? While using words, how does one designate a particular thing? In what respect is the word a sign of the real object? Has the word any value alone?
10. How is the definition related to the initial concept?
11. In the defining process, through what stages does the intellect move? What are the two needed parts in the definition?
12. Of what value is the definition for the act of simple apprehension, of reasoning?

CHAPTER 3

WORDS AND CONCEPTS: SIGNS IN DEFINITION

A. The sign in general
B. The word
C. The concept

The preceding chapter explained that the human being knows both the sensible singular and the whatness of simple material realities. This whatness, achieved by an inductive process, is signified internally by the concept and externally by the word. Because of the important function of these two signs as the mind moves from the initial whatness to the definition, they must be understood carefully.

A. THE SIGN IN GENERAL

The sign in general is defined as something which, in addition to what it is in itself, also conveys or means something else. Thus smoke is smoke, but it also means fire to one who sees it. A black dress is a black dress, but it also stands for mourning. As is evident from these examples, the sign is basically twofold: it is a given entity, and it also stands for something else.

Signs may be divided into those which are natural and those which are artificial. The natural sign is one in which there is a real connection between the thing and the meaning conveyed. Thus fever is a natural sign of illness; footprints, of an animal or a human being; thunder, of a storm; trembling, of fear; and a shadow, of a body. In contrast, the artificial or conventional sign is one in which the connection between the thing and the meaning conveyed is made by human institution. Thus a wedding ring is an artificial sign of marriage; a red light, of danger; a salute, of respect; a blowing horn, of danger; a scales, of justice; and a flag, of a country.

From another focus, signs may be divided into those which are instrumental and those which are formal. The instrumental sign, retaining the full meaning of sign, is something in itself and also means something else. With an awareness of this definition, one can see that every example in the preceding paragraph is an instrumental sign. In fact, every natural and artificial sign (except the two kinds given in the next paragraph) may also be called instrumental, thus emphasizing that they are instruments leading to something besides their own real identity. Thus fever, a real thing in itself, points to the presence of illness.

In contrast to the instrumental sign, the formal sign retains only one part of the general meaning of sign. Dropping the notion of being a separate thing in itself, the formal sign is only a pointer or indicator of something else. There are only two kinds of formal signs: the sense image and the concept. Both of these signs are only a means of knowing; they are never objects in themselves first, such as flags or fever. Their whole being is to point to something besides themselves. The sense image is only a representation of the material world; the concept is only a mental image of this outer world. They are not something else first, like smoke or footprints. The sense image and concept are well named formal signs, for their whole being, nature, or form is to stand for another thing.

The definitions of sign in general and of its various kinds are summarized in the following listing:

1. sign: something which, in addition to what it is in itself, also conveys or means something else
2. natural sign: a sign in which there is a real connection between the thing and the meaning conveyed
3. artificial sign: a sign in which the connection between the thing and the meaning conveyed is made by human institution
4. instrumental sign: something in itself and also an indicator of something else
5. formal sign: something which only stands for something else

B. THE WORD

1. AN ARTIFICIAL SIGN

The word, whether spoken or written, is an artificial sign. Thus the word *tree* does not naturally convey to the listener or reader the large, green object for which it stands. The connection between the word *tree* and the living object has been established by convention. Hence it is necessary to study the various languages in order to learn the connection between the given vocabulary and the real world.

If the connection between a word and its meaning is established by convention, exactly what human institution decides the meaning of words? It is the usage of the majority of the people which establishes the link between a word and its signification. One could imagine that a given government might decree that a word such as *whopper* would designate only fishburgers. If the people did not choose to use *whopper* in this way, these governmental efforts would be fruitless. Words have the meaning that is used by most people; all other meanings need constant explanation. The influence of the usage of the majority is seen in dictionaries, which simply codify common practice.

2. UNIVOCAL, EQUIVOCAL, AND ANALOGICAL WORDS

If words are artificial signs invented by the human being, it is easy to understand that there may not be enough words for all the kinds of things in the universe. In such a situation, one might easily tend to use the same word for two different things. Thus the word *sage* may mean either a very wise man or a plant of the mint family. The word *fell* may stand for either of the following: an animal's hide or skin; a rocky or barren hill. The word *galley* might mean either a long, single-decked ship or a shallow tray for holding type. Whenever one uses one word to mean two different, unconnected things, one is said to equivocate. Taken from the Latin, *equivocation* literally means equal voice, designating that an equal or same voice is used to express different things. In line with this usage and literal meaning, an equivocal word is defined as a sign which stands for different meanings as applied to different things.

Clearly the use of a word in an equivocal way can lead to confusion. Thus an individual might hear the word *bark* and think that a discussion about trees is taking place, while the conversation might really be about sailing. There is only one solution in such a situation. One must designate the particular meaning belonging to the given word; i.e., one must define the word. Better yet, one should point out an individual case of the meaning designated.

Whenever a given word is restricted to one meaning, it is used univocally. Taken also from the Latin, *univocal* literally stands for one voice. As can be seen, a univocal word is defined as a sign which stands for one meaning as applied to different things. Thus the word *bird* is univocal as used for the robin, the sparrow, and the blue jay. As this example indicates, univocal words are easily found whenever the general classification is given for the particular kinds or species under this class. Thus the word *fish* is univocal as used for bass, trout, and salmon.

The division of words into equivocal and univocal does not mean that some words are always the former, and others, the latter. Rather any word can be either, simply by designating different meanings or only one meaning for its use. Thus *bark* is a univocal word when used for the covering of the maple and elm trees, but it becomes equivocal when used to mean either the covering of trees or a small sailing boat. Since any word can be taken in different senses, it is crucial to explain or define the terms that one is using. If such care is not taken, the speaker may think that he will be understood in a univocal sense, while actually he is taken by the listener in an equivocal manner. Thus the users of the word *law*, although wishing to be understood in a single, positive way, may be heard in both a positive and negative manner.

In addition to the equivocation arising by chance, there is an equivocation by design. This latter type, called analogy, comes about because of some resemblance between two different things. Thus the word *sunny* may stand both for a bright day and for a bright disposition. The analogical word is defined as a sign which stands for a primary meaning and related, secondary meanings when applied to different things. Thus the word *yarn* is used primarily of the material which can unravel and secondarily of a story which unravels in the telling. The connection between these meanings may be close or tenuous. Thus there is a real connection found in the word *healthy* as said of a person and as said of a complexion. In contrast, there is only a slight link between the meanings of *run* as used for a brook and for a tear in a stocking. The following analogical words illustrate this connection, which may be real or farfetched:

1. *precipice:*   *a steep cliff; a greatly hazardous situation**
2. *key:*   *an instrument to open a lock; a translation unlocking a strange language**
3. *posture:*   *the position of the body; an attitude of mind**
4. *steel:*   *a hard, tough metal; great strength**

Since there are different, albeit proportional, meanings for an analogical word, the use of analogy can lead not only to positive but also to negative results. On the advantageous side, analogy permits one to use familiar ideas to shed light on less familiar things. Thus the word *head*, meaning primarily the top part of the body in man and the apes, may be extended to mean a jutting mass of rock or land. On the other hand, analogy, as well as equivocation by chance, can lead to much misunderstanding because of the different meanings signified by one word. Thus the word *love* may signify any of the following meanings, which range from an analogical to a purely equivocal usage: (1) a feeling of good will toward the other person; (2) a passionate affection for another person; (3) a score of zero in tennis.* Because of the possible misunderstanding resulting from the analogical or equivocal usage of a word, it is essential to note how words are used and to state their appropriate definitions.

The definitions of the three kinds of words are summarized as follows:

1. equivocal word: a sign which stands for different meanings as applied to different things

| 2. univocal word: | a sign which stands for one meaning as applied to different things |
| 3. analogical word: | a sign which stands for a primary meaning and related, secondary meanings when applied to different things |

Since any one word can be equivocal, univocal, or analogical, the student must always note its usage or context. Thus the following words are classified in three different ways because of their particular usage:

1. _adder:_	desert adder, mountain adder	(univocal)
2. _adder:_	desert adder, a person who adds*	(equivocal)
3. _adder:_	a person who adds, an adding machine*	(analogical)
4. _brush:_	Australian Outback, American Southwest	(univocal)
5. _brush:_	country covered with scrub growth; a quick, short fight*	(equivocal)
6. _brush:_	country covered with scrub growth; a device with bristles fastened into a hard back*	(analogical)

In addition to noting a word's usage, the student may often need to consult his dictionary. Ordinarily, equivocal meanings are given in two separate entries, while analogical ones are listed as the various shades of meaning under one particular entry. Thus both of the above words, *adder* and *brush*, have two separate entries and also shades of meaning under one given entry.

C. THE CONCEPT

1. ITS UNIVERSALITY

Knowing the signs described in the previous section, one can classify the concept as a natural sign which is formal, rather than instrumental. This classification follows from the fact that the whole being of the concept is to reflect naturally to the knower the whatness found in the individual, sensible thing. Thus one's idea of a kangaroo, a mental reflection of the whatness existing in real, individual kangaroos, enables one to know what kangaroos are like. As also noted previously, the concept is defined as a sign which retains the nature or whatness of the sensed thing.

The whatness or form of things has a true universality about it. In other words, the nature or form can be seen to be common to all the individual members of that type. Thus it is evident that the same nature is found in every individual robin. This common character of form can be noted even if one has perceived only one individual member. Thus, if a person has seen only one robin in one's bird-watching career, one will look expectantly for others. This expectation indicates clearly that nature or form has a universal quality, a quality enabling it to be found in many individual things.

In harmony with the universality proper to form, the concept, as a sign of the form or whatness of things, is universal in its extension. Thus one's concept of robin, even if derived from a single one, is not confined to that robin alone, but is an idea which can be recognized in any number of them. Also this concept is found to be applicable to all the succeeding robins that one encounters. One has, therefore, a universal idea of robin; i.e., a concept able to be perceived in many of them. As exemplified in the idea of robin, the concept, derived from the form of things, is universal in its extension. What is meant by this property of universality found in the concept? It is that attribute of the concept by which it is applicable to many individuals or members.

In this definition of universality, it must be emphasized that the one concept is applicable to many members, rather than actually perceived in many individuals. Thus one's concept of sun is actually perceived in only the single body known to be in existence. One knows, however, that this concept could extend to any other number of suns, should they be found to exist. As this example indicates, the universal is that property by which one concept is *applicable* to many. In other words, the universal concept can be perceived in many, but is not necessarily actually encountered in more than one. This potential multiplicity of the members of a concept may be noted in endangered species, such as the California condor and the American bald eagle. In these cases one has a concept of this type of bird which is applicable to any number of them, but, if only one is left, which is perceived in only one. (See appendix one for a further discussion of the universal concept.)

2. ITS EXTENSION AND COMPREHENSION

The universal concept is a mental image of a nature which is applicable to many members. In logical terminology, the members of the universal are called inferiors in relation to the superior type to which they belong. Thus the robin, the bluebird, and the wheatear are inferiors in relation to the superior thrush family. In addition to this terminology of inferior to superior within a given universal, one should also note that there are levels of universality. Thus carnivore is more universal than bear, mammal is more universal than carnivore, and animal is more universal than mammal. Such gradations of universality can easily be noted in the various concepts about the material world.

Why do gradations of universality exist among the various concepts had about the sensible world? What makes one concept more universal than another? Thus it is evident that the concept, fish, has a greater universality than the concept, shark. Why does one concept have a greater range than another?

An understanding of two characteristics of the universal concept is needed to answer this question about range of universality. These two characteristics are comprehension and extension. The first is defined as the number of qualifications which determines the content of a concept. Thus the comprehension of the concept, carnivore, includes at least the following characteristics: (1) mammals which are primarily meat-eaters; (2) mammals with five toes on the front foot; (3) mammals with large canine teeth. As can be seen from this example, the comprehension of a concept refers to the number of attributes contained within it. In other words, the comprehension of a concept stands for its content.

In contrast, the extension of a concept is defined as the number of inferiors to which the concept is applicable. Thus the concept, carnivore, is applicable to the following inferiors: bears, raccoons, weasels, skunks, dogs, wolves, lions, tigers, cats, and all others with the above characteristics. As this illustration indicates, the extension of a concept refers to the number of inferiors to which it is applicable.

Knowing the meaning of comprehension and extension, one can see that it is the concept's comprehension which determines its extension. Thus, because the concept of carnivore includes the above characteristics in its comprehension, it can extend to every mammal having such attributes, but no further. Granted that comprehension is the determining factor for extension, one can also note that the richer the comprehension the more narrow the extension, and contrariwise. Thus the additional characteristics proper to the cat family restrict this concept to fewer inferiors. Said in another way, the sort of nature held in the concept determines the number of inferiors to which it is applicable. This role of the content in determining the extension of a concept can be noted in the following diagram:

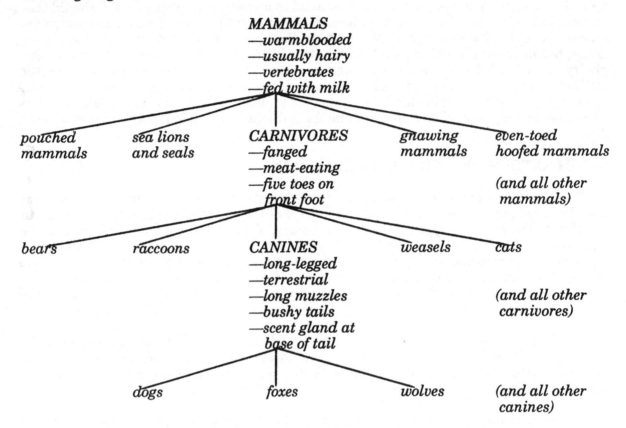

As the above diagram illustrates, concepts, determined by their content, have varying levels of universality or extension. Thus mammal has greater extension than wolf. The reason, as already noted, lies with the content or comprehension of the concept. Therefore the following statements hold:

1. The sparser the comprehension, the greater the extension.
   (The more generic the concept, the greater the extension.)
2. The richer the comprehension, the more limited the extension.
   (The more specific the concept, the more limited the extension.)

Aware of the above principles, the student, remembering that human knowledge moves from the generic to the specific, can immediately see that he first learns concepts with greater extension or universality. Thus the small child knows the concept, food, before he is able to distinguish specific kinds of food, such as fruits, vegetables, or grain products. In accord with the human movement from the generic to the specific, the learner, as he senses the material world, first grasps the simpler concepts with greater extension. Every student of logic must constantly be aware of this natural sequence in human learning. In fact, he will meet it in the treatment of each of the three operations of the human mind. The following list confirms this point:

1. <u>Act of Simple Apprehension, Obtaining the Definition</u>
   In this operation the mind moves from the general class to the specific difference. In other words, it proceeds from the simpler, more extensive concept to the richer,

more exact one. Thus a small child knows that the cat is an animal before she knows that it is a flesh-eating mammal which is domesticated and used as a pet or a mouser.*

2. <u>Act of Judgment, Obtaining the Proposition</u>
In this operation the mind first says simpler, more extensive predicates about the subject. In other words, the predicates are ordinarily more extensive than the given subject. This broader extension of every affirmative predicate can be noted in the following examples:
   a. Every swan is white.
      (All of the swans are some of the white things.)
   b. Every child is lovable.
      (All of the children are some of the lovable things.)
   c. Some of the politicians are trustworthy.
      (Some of the politicians are some of the trustworthy things.)

3. <u>Act of Reasoning, Obtaining the Syllogism</u>
In this operation the mind uses the propositions which have been formed according to the above description.

STUDY QUESTIONS   **CHAPTER 3**

1. Define the following: the sign in general, the natural sign, the artificial sign, the instrumental sign, and the formal sign.
2. What are the two kinds of formal signs? Why are these signs named formal?
3. Why is the word an artificial sign? What human institution decides the meaning of words?
4. Define the equivocal word. How does the equivocal word arise? How does one avoid the confusion arising from equivocal words?
5. Define the univocal word. Can a given word be both equivocal and univocal? How?
6. Define the analogical word. From what source does this type of word arise? Give both a positive and a negative result from the use of analogy.
7. What kind of sign is the concept? Define the concept.
8. What is the extension of the concept? Define universality. In relation to universality, explain why it is defined as applicable to many, rather than actually perceived in many.
9. In relation to the concept, define comprehension and extension. What determines the extension of a given concept? State two principles about the extension of concepts.
10. In relation to comprehension and extension, what types of concepts are known first? Confirm this point in each of the three acts of the mind.

CHAPTER 4

THE CATEGORIES: WHAT IS SAID IN DEFINITION

A. A general treatment
B. Specific categories
C. Summary of the categories
D. Rules for the categories
E. The opposition following the categories

The whole point of the mind's work in simple apprehension is a clear understanding of the distinct things of the sensible universe. In other words, simple apprehension seeks to focus or define its initial concepts of simple realities. In order to arrive at this clear understanding, the mind is helped by a classification or categorization of the various things which it knows. If a housewife wants to expedite her grocery shopping for the week, she will organize her needed foodstuffs into various categories, such as dairy products, meats, vegetables, and fruits. In the same way, the logical thinker will group together the various kinds of things in the universe about which he has ideas or concepts. Just as the housewife is helped if she organizes the materials that she intends to purchase, so the thinker is assisted if he distinguishes the kinds of materials about which he is thinking. Aristotle, the inventor of logic, made such a distinction and called it fittingly the ten categories.

A. A GENERAL TREATMENT

The ten categories may be described as the ten ultimate classifications into which all material things may be placed. In other words, these categories are the ten basic groups of existing things. Thus a dandelion, cutting the grass, and sunburned are very real but different things, which should be grouped accordingly. The ten categories are also called the ten predicaments in that the natures of all existing things may also be predicated or said of their proper subjects. Thus, when one says that the grass is cut, the predicate *cut* is predicated of the subject *grass*. Every predicate can be classified under one or the other of the ten categories or predicaments.

The chief division of the ten categories is into substance and the nine accidents. What is the meaning of substance? A substance is described as a thing which can exist in its own right, not just as a modification of something else. Expressed in a negative way, a substance is a thing which does not exist in something else as in a subject. Thus a lion can exist in its own right, but its color, size, shape, and position can exist only as modifications of the lion. These modifications of the lion, existing only in the lion as in a subject, are called accidents.

As a secondary aspect of a substance, the accident is described as a thing which cannot exist in its own right or which does exist in another thing as in a subject. Thus the various things which inhere in the lion, which cannot exist without him, are his accidents. In this basic division of the categories, substance and the accidents stand in marked contrast, substance being the substantial things of the world and the accidents being the things which exist in the substances. Naturally, then, their descriptions are well taken, for substantial things have a basic existence, while accidental things demand the substance in order to exist at all.

Probably the most famous illustration of the difference between substance and the nine accidents is found in *Alice's Adventures in Wonderland* by Lewis Carroll. When Alice met the cheshire cat, she was disconcerted by the way in which it appeared and vanished so suddenly. She begged it not to play such tricks on her. Then the cat obliged by vanishing very slowly, beginning with the end of its tail and ending with its grin, which remained some time after everything else was gone. This strange behavior of the cat totally puzzled Alice. She thought, "How can this be! I've often seen a cat without a grin, but never a grin without a cat!"

Why had Alice never seen such a sight? The reason is simple. A substance, the cat, is able to exist on its own; but an accident, the grin, is able to exist only in another as in a subject. A color such as purple is definitely a real thing, but one cannot go to the store and ask for a sack of purple. If one wants to purchase some purple, one must buy it in some subject, as in flowers. The reason is that purple is an accident.

The ten categories are divided first into substantial and accidental things. These ten kinds of existing things are divided further according to the following distinctions:

1. category stating whatness or essence -------

SUBSTANCE
What is this thing?
e.g., dog, rose, iron, diamond

2. categories stating accidents
   a. accidents inhering in essence
      1) from material principle ----------------

   QUANTITY
   How many or much of it is there?
   e.g., three, several, quart, pound

      2) from formal or qualifying principle ----------------------------------

   QUALITY
   What sort of thing is it?
   e.g., green, sweet, happy, brave

      3) from relation to another thing ------

   RELATION
   What are its connections?
   e.g., same, similar, equal, father, president, slave

   b. accidents from something extrinsic, but said of essence
      1) as mover or moved ----------------------

   ACTION
   What is it doing?
   e.g., heating, mowing, cutting, plowing

   PASSION
   What is happening to it?
   e.g., being cut, being plowed

      2) as measured
         a) by place -----------------------------

   WHERE
   Where is it?
   e.g., here, there, near, up, down

         b) by position----------------------------

   POSITION
   What is its position?
   e.g., bent, standing, reversed, prone

         c) by time-------------------------------

   WHEN
   When is it operating?
   e.g., yesterday, now, then, before

      3) as having special possessions-------- (only human being)

   POSSESSION
   How is it garbed?
   e.g., dressed, costumed, armored, gloved

As the above chart indicates, the basic distinction within the categories lies between substance and the accidents, between those things which can exist on their own and those which cannot. Thus there is a basic distinction between the mountain lion and its various accidents, such as weight of 150 pounds, tawny color, nocturnal habits, and deer-killing activity. Among the accidents, the primary division is between those accidents which exist in the given substance and those accidents (existing in other substances) which refer to and are said of the given substance. Thus the mountain lion's size and color exist in him, but his nocturnal habits and deer-killing activity extend beyond him to other things, namely the moon and the deers so affected.

B. SPECIFIC CATEGORIES

1. SUBSTANCE

Substance, as described above, is that thing which exists in its own right or which does not exist in something else as in a subject. Thus dogs and cats exist in their own right. Within this category of substance, it is necessary to distinguish individual or primary substance and universal or secondary substance. The former is the existing, individual substance, while the latter is its nature or whatness. Thus the individual dog, Regis, is a primary substance; while his nature, dogness, is a secondary substance.

As can be seen, there is an emphasis in this category on basic existence. In fact, the literal meaning of *substance* is to stand under. What is it that stands under the rest of reality? It is first and foremost the individual substance, which is the actual, existing thing. This is evident from the fact that the nature or universal substance exists only in individual substances. Thus the nature of robin is perceived to be only in individual robins. Also the nine accidents exist only in individual substances. Therefore individual substance, truly called primary substance, stands under the rest of reality. Examples of individual substances are readily found in all natural bodies; i.e., in minerals, plants, animals, and human beings. The various parts of these bodies, such as leaves, trunks, organs, and limbs, also fall in the category of substance.

As the basic existing thing, primary substance stands as the basic subject about which all other things are said or predicated. Thus, of Regis, it can be said that he is a dog and that he is brown. Contrariwise, primary substance is not said about anything else. Thus one does not say that some dog is this Regis. Never a predicate, the individual substance is the basic subject in all predication.

Why is primary substance never a predicate? To be a predicate requires that the thing can be said of another thing, that the thing is applicable to more than just itself. It is for this reason that one does not say that Regis is Fido or Prince. These names, as applicable only to these unique individuals, cannot be said of something else. As these examples indicate, a true predicate can never be the singular, individual thing. Rather a predicate is that which is able to be said of many. Thus the word *dog*, standing for the universal nature existing in individual dogs, can be predicated of Regis, Fido, and Prince. Said in another way, whatever is predicable of a subject must be universal and not singular. It is precisely because primary substance is singular that it cannot be a predicate.

Secondary or universal substance, on the contrary, can always be predicated of some subject. Thus one can say that Regis is a dog. Predicability follows this same pattern in the accidental order. This means that the universal, but not the individual, accident can be a predicate. Thus one can say that Regis is brown, but not this brown on Fido's back.

2. QUANTITY

The quantity of material things is a familiar item to the ordinary layman. Even the small child does not hesitate to inquire about the quantified aspect of his surroundings. Noticing a cake on the kitchen table, he may ask the following: How much? How many? These questions, very common in daily life, refer to quantity, that accident belonging to material things.

Quantity is that accident of material things whereby they are extended into space, measurable by some mathematical standard, and capable of being divided into separate parts. Contrariwise, if things were not extended, it would be possible neither to measure them nor to divide them into separate parts. Quantity, following from the materiality of things, provides the spatial ground floor, so to speak, of extension for the various colors and textures of sensible things. Quantity, however, pertains only to the extension of things, not to their appearance or tangibility.

This extension in space is continuous or discrete, according as its parts have a common boundary or are separated. Thus, before a cake is cut, its parts have a common boundary or are continuous. After it is sliced, however, there are a certain number of discrete pieces or quantities. Continuous quantity admits of three basic types: lines, surfaces, and solids. Discrete quantity, had by the division of continuous quantity, has parts which can be counted. The various number systems, used to count such parts, constitute the basic kinds of discrete quantity.

3. QUALITY

Just as the ordinary layman is very familiar with the quantity of material things, so he is well aware of the qualities of the things around him. Thus he may say that it is not only the quantity of his food but also its quality which is important to him. Again he may declare that one qualified worker is more valuable to him than ten unqualified individuals. About his vacation he may state that he prefers to spend it in a certain kind of place rather than in a great number of spots. In every one of these statements the ordinary person is emphasizing the various qualities of material things.

What is quality? It is that accident by which a thing is a certain sort or kind. In the words of Aristotle, quality is that accident by which a thing is such-and-such. Referring not to the extension of things, quality designates those attributes in a thing which set it apart from other things, which make it such-and-such. These features indicate, not how much nor how many, but how a thing is (its sense qualities and shape) and how it acts (its habits and abilities). In a word, quality is the accident used to describe a thing.

To illustrate quality, the beaver might be described as follows: (1) It is a rodent with soft, brown fur; chisellike teeth; and a naked, scaly tail shaped like a paddle. (2) It is equally at home on land or in the water, feeds on bark and small twigs, and builds dams of mud and twigs.* The description of these parts of the beaver, as well as of his activities using his powers, are all accidents showing what the beaver is like. While these outer characteristics are not the beaver's inner form or nature, they flow from his substantial form. They are such because the nature of the beaver is such. It is from this external, qualifying form that one obtains the first inkling of the inner, substantial form. In brief, the qualities are the external suchness or form.

Quality is divided by Aristotle into four kinds of accidents which make a thing such-and-such, which make it a certain kind or sort. These qualities indicate how a thing is (its sense qualities and shape) and how it acts (its habits and abilities). Their definitions, together with several examples, follow:

1. Habit or Disposition

   These are qualifications of a thing which dispose it well or ill in a durable (habit) or transient (disposition) way.

habits of well-being:	habits for operation:	
to be handsome	to be artistic	to be prudent
to be strong	to be prudent	to be courageous
to be healthy	to be scientific	to be just
to be beautiful	to be wise	to be charitable

2. Ability or Inability

   Ability is the qualification of a thing which is its proximate source of operation. Incapacity is a deficiency in some power or ability. (Ability emphasizes the natural capacity, rather than the acquired habit.)

vegetative powers:	sensitive powers:	intellectual power:
to be nourished	to be observant	to be handy
to be grown	to be sensitive	to be theoretical
to be fertile	to be imaginative	to be contemplative
to be fruitful	to be retentive	to be perceptive

lower and higher appetites:		locomotive power:
to be emotional		to be active
to be loving	to be flexible	to be a swimmer
to be brave	to be agreeable	to be a runner
to be discouraged	to be decisive	to be graceful
	to be joyful	

3. Sense Qualities

   These are qualifications of a thing which affect the powers of sensation. The proper sense objects (color, sound, texture, temperature, odor, and flavor) belong to this division.

to be tanned	to be cold
to be scarlet	to be sharp
to be noisy	to be pungent
to be smooth	to be sour

4. Form or Figure

   These are qualifications of a thing which refer to its shape, whether natural (form) or artificial (figure). As such, form and figure terminate the quantity of substance.

form:	figure:
to be shapely	to be curved
to be humped	to be triangular
to be serpentine	to be circular
to be serrated	to be cubic

In summary, the four qualities given by Aristotle indicate how a thing is (its sense qualities and shape) and how it acts (its habits and abilities). In brief, quality is that accident by which a thing is such-and-such.

4. RELATION

Relation, like quantity and quality, is an accident with which the ordinary person is well acquainted. Thus he speaks very easily of his various relatives or relations, such as his grandparents, parents, uncles, aunts, and cousins. Also he may compare or relate things to each other, noting that they may be the same or different, equal or unequal, similar or dissimilar. In both of these cases, the individual is demonstrating the reality of that accident, relation.

Relation is defined as that accident in a thing which is the bearing or reference of that thing toward another thing. Thus Henry truly has the attribute of being the son of Mr. Babcock, but this accident in Henry is there because of his reference to another thing, his father. Also the number four is double because of its reference to the number two. In like manner, the red of this material is described as similar because of its reference to the red of another material. Again, Mr. Hargrove is an employer because of his reference to those under him, his employees. As these examples indicate, relation is that accident in a thing which consists in the bearing of that thing upon another thing.

What is it about a thing that causes it to be related to another thing? Two basic attributes are a thing's quantity and its action or passion. Examples of the relations following from these attributes are as follows:

1. <u>Relation Based on Quantity</u>

   —based on number
      equal
      unequal: double........half
              triple..........third
              larger........smaller
              more..........less

   —based on unity or oneness
      one in substance
         (same, identical, different)
      one in quality
         (like, similar, unlike)

2. <u>Relation Based on Action or Passion (past, present, or future)</u>

   father............ son
   master........... slave
   chairman.......member
   counselor....... counselee
   leader.............follower

   builder......... building
   barber..........haircut
   digger.......... ditch
   inventor....... invention
   farmer......... crops

As the above examples indicate, a thing has an attribute within it solely because of its reference to another thing. This attribute may stem from the way its quantity is measured by another thing or from the fact that it receives or bestows something on another thing. This attribute or accident is well named relation.

5. ACTION AND PASSION

Action and passion are correlative accidents. The former is defined as the doing of something to something else, while the latter is the receiving of something from something else. Obvious examples of these accidents are as follows:

cutting.............. being cut   *painting........... being painted*
building........... being built   *killing.............. being killed*
hitting.............. being hit   *planting........... being planted*

As the above definitions and examples point out, only transient operations are included under these two accidents. Immanent operations are the use of one's abilities and fall under the accident, quality. The distinction between these two kinds of operations should be clear from the following definitions and examples:

1. Transient operations are those actions which go out from the agent to something else in order to change this latter thing. (Transitive verbs express this kind of operation.)

e.g., *cutting the grass*   *painting the house*
       building the dam   *killing the snake*
       hitting the ball   *planting the seed*

2. Immanent operations are those actions which are the simple use of one's powers. They remain within the agent in order to change or perfect this agent. (Intransitive verbs express this kind of operation.)

e.g., *The man thinks.*   *The bird flies.*
       The child remembers.   *The athlete swims.*
       The boy grows.   *The prima donna sings.*
       The soldier despairs.   *The gymnast exercises.*

As noted above, only transient operations are classified under action and passion. Immanent operations, which are the use of the thing's abilities, fall under that part of quality indicating how a thing acts (habits and abilities).

Finally, the student must note that transient operations (whether action or passion) involve something else. Because of this connection or relation set up between two things, these transient operations can lead to attributes which belong to the accident, relation. (This fact was noted in the section on relation.) Additional examples of relations resulting from action or passion are as follows:

Action	*Passion*	*Relation*
riding	is ridden	rider
tormenting	is tormented	tormentor
baking	is baked	baker
commanding	is commanded	commander
feeding	is fed	feeder
navigating	is navigated	navigator
pitching	is pitched	pitcher
ruling	is ruled	ruler
fathering	is fathered	father

As the above lists indicate, action is expressed by the active voice; passion, by the passive voice; and relation, by the noun. Thus *ruling* expresses the action; *is ruled*, the reception of such an action. Finally, *ruler* signifies the existence of an attribute within the person, an attribute present only because of a relationship between the ruler and ruled.

6. WHERE, POSITION, AND WHEN

Where, position, and when are accidents within the daily experience of every individual. Thus it is quite common to hear the following questions: Where were you yesterday? Were you bent over your desk all day? When did you finish your work? These three accidents, referring to place and time, predicate the external measures of a given thing. Thus the great dane stretched out before the fireplace in the evening is set up or measured by this place, the order of his parts in this place, and the time of this event. He is lined up, so to speak, against time and place, the extrinsic measures of the material world.

Where is that extrinsic accident said of a thing which makes a reference to place. Several examples are as follows: here, there, away, at home, on the stairs, at the airport, in New York.

Position is that extrinsic accident said of a thing which is the order of a thing's parts in a given place. Several examples are as follows: slouched, seated, erect, kneeling, leaning, slanted, curled up.

When is that extrinsic accident said of a thing which makes a reference to time. Several examples are as follows: now, during the day, presently, yesterday, last year, in the Middle Ages.

7. POSSESSION

Possession is that accident peculiar to the human being which includes all the external equipment added to his natural body. This external equipment encompasses his ordinary clothing, his ornaments, and his defensive coverings. This external accident which is said of the human being alone may be exemplified as follows:

dressed	*costumed*	*armored*
shod	*bejeweled*	*padded*
cloaked	*ornamented*	*armed*
bonneted	*crowned*	*bulletproofed*
gloved	*decorated*	*helmeted*

Possession is peculiar to the human being; for all the other animals have built-in equipment, so to speak, such as horns for defense, fangs for killing, furry or scaly skin for covering, and hoofs for walking. The human being, on the other hand, is not restricted to one particular type of covering or defensive mechanism. Rather the human person, with the universal range of his intellect and the versatility of his hands, provides an unbelievable variety in his wearing apparel and in his protective devices. This external equipment falls under the category, possession, and is predicated of the human being alone. If this category is said of the other animals, it is only insofar as these animals are used by human beings. Thus it may be said that a horse is saddled and bridled or that a dog is muzzled.

C. SUMMARY OF THE CATEGORIES

Following the above treatment, the definitions of the ten categories will now be listed.

— ten categories:	the ten ultimate classifications into which all material things can be placed
1. substance:	a thing which can exist in its own right, not just as a modification of something else
— accident:	a thing which cannot exist in its own right; a thing which does exist in another thing as in a subject
2. quantity:	an accident of material things whereby they are extended into space, measurable by some mathematical standard, and capable of being divided into separate parts
3. quality:	an accident by which a thing is a certain sort or kind; an accident indicating how a thing is (its sense qualities and shape) and how a thing acts (its abilities and habits); an accident which is the external, qualifying form
habit or disposition:	a qualification of a thing which disposes it well or ill in a durable or transient way
ability or inability:	a qualification of a thing which is its proximate source of operation or which is a deficiency in some power

	sense qualities:	qualifications of a thing which affect the powers of sensation
	form or figure:	qualifications of a thing which refer to its shape, whether natural (form) or artificial (figure); qualities which terminate the quantity of substance
4.	relation:	an accident in a thing which is the bearing or reference of that thing toward another thing a. from quantity: based on number based on unity or oneness (substance, quality) b. from action or passion
5.	action:	an accident which is the doing of something to something else
6.	passion:	an accident which is the receiving of something from something else
7.	where:	an extrinsic accident said of a thing which makes a reference to place
8.	position:	an extrinsic accident said of a thing which is the order of a thing's parts in a given place
9.	when:	an extrinsic accident said of a thing which makes a reference to time
10.	possession:	an accident peculiar to the human being which includes all external equipment added to his natural body (clothing, ornaments, defensive coverings)

In order to clarify the categories, the opening outline will be utilized again. This outline will list special types under some of the categories, as well as typical examples:

1. category stating whatness	SUBSTANCE		minerals, plants, animals, human being (and parts)

2. categories stating accidents
  a. accidents inhering in essence
    1) from material principle
	QUANTITY	continuous:
		
		discrete:
			lines, planes, solids
			number systems

2) from formal principle
  a) habits/dispositions
 	
  b) ability/inability
 	
  c) sense qualities
 	
  d) form/figure
	QUALITY
	
	how a thing acts
	
	how a thing is
		
		immanent action:
		sense objects:
		shape ending quantity:
			handsome, healthy, artistic, prudent
			fertile, handy, emotional, flexible
			thinking, seeing, growing, walking
			cold, green, loud, tasty, smooth
			curved, angular, circular, humped

3) from relation to another thing (outside) a) based on quantity	RELATION	from number: from unity:	equal/unequal same/different like/unlike

b) based on action or passion		from transient operation:	trader, president, father, leader, baker, slave
b. accidents from outside, but said of essence 1) as mover or moved	ACTION/ PASSION	transient operation:	cutting, planting, milking, making
2) as measured a) by place b) by position c) by time	WHERE POSITION WHEN		here, there, away slouched, erect now, last night
3) as having special possessions (human being)	POSSESSION		clothed, belted, armed, gloved

D. RULES FOR THE CATEGORIES

As already noted, Aristotle divided the simple realities of the material world into ten categories, categories which simplify the defining process. Before one can place a given thing in any one of them, however, one must observe the following rules:

1. Only simple realities can be placed in a given category. This means that, if one has a composite concept, such as *healthy child*, one must reduce this concept to its elements before attempting to utilize the categories. Thus, after such reduction, one could categorize *child* as substance and *healthy* as quality. Said in another way, two kinds of natures cannot be placed in one category.
2. The simple reality must be a whole. The part of something is placed in the same category as the whole to which it belongs. Thus the human foot, as part of the human being, is placed in the category of substance.
3. The simple reality must be natural. An artificial thing, however, may be placed in the same category as the thing which it imitates. Thus an artificial heart may be placed in the category of substance.
4. The simple reality must be signified by a univocal word. If the word is equivocal, two different concepts are implied, as well as the possibility of two different categories. Thus *bark*, as signifying the covering of a tree, is placed in the category of substance. On the other hand, *bark*, as signifying the sound of a dog, is placed in the category of quality.
5. Only the universal nature, not the unique singular, can be placed in the categories. Since the categories are also the ten ultimate kinds of predicates, they must be able to be said about a given subject; i.e., they must be universal in their extension. Thus dog, but not Regis, is placed in the category of substance.

E. THE OPPOSITION FOLLOWING THE CATEGORIES

Various characteristics are common to all or several of the categories of simple reality. As extending across the different categories, these characteristics are explained after them. One of these attributes is opposition. Although there are four kinds of opposition, only two of them will be explained in this text.

The first of these two kinds, contrary opposition, is defined as the opposition existing between the positive extremes of the same subject or genus, each of which excludes the other from that subject. Thus the positive extremes in the subject, water, are hot and cold, which cannot both be present at the same time in that given water. This mutual exclusion sets up a definite opposition. One contrary cannot be present in the subject whenever its opposite is present. The following pairs are clear illustrations of the extremes to be found within a given subject, extremes which mutually exclude each other: black and white, odd and even, good and bad, sick and well, beautiful and ugly, smooth and rough. As each of these pairs illustrates, contraries cannot both be present in the same subject.

Since contrary opposition is between the positive extremes within a given subject, there may be an intermediate or middle position which is neither of these extremes. Thus lukewarm is a middle state between hot and cold, while mediocre is a middle between good and bad. Because a middle may exist between contraries, it is true that neither contrary may be present in a subject, as well as that contraries mutually exclude each other. Thus a given human being, being mediocre, is neither good nor bad. If contraries do not have a middle, however, the subject of the contraries will have either one or the other. Thus all numbers are either odd or even: there is no intermediate between these two contraries.

Contradictory opposition, the second type treated in this text, is defined as the absolute opposition between an affirmation and a negation, an opposition which has no intermediate or middle. Thus the affirmation *Henry is sick* is opposed absolutely by the negation *Henry is not sick*. In like manner, the affirmation *This shoe is black* is opposed absolutely by the negation *This shoe is not black*. In both of these examples, there is an either-or situation. Thus Henry is either sick or not sick. There is no other alternative. In other words, contradictory opposition, consisting of an affirmation and its denial, does not have the possibility of any intermediate or middle position. There are only two choices: either the thing is or the thing is not.

Since contradiction is the only kind of opposition with no middle, it is the only type in which one side must always be true and the other, false. In every other kind of opposition, there is always some kind of middle position, which prevents such a conclusion being drawn. This is evident in the following example of contrariety. The contrary of the statement *Shakespeare is sick* is the statement at the other extreme *Shakespeare is well*. At present neither of these statements is true, since Shakespeare simply isn't. He no longer exists as Shakespeare.

On the other hand, whether the subject exists or not, one side of a contradiction is always true. In relation to the same example, the affirmation *Shakespeare is sick* is opposed by the negation *Shakespeare is not sick*. Whether Shakespeare exists or not, one of these statements must be true. If he exists, he is either sick or he is not. If he does not exist, the negation *Shakespeare is not sick* is true, since, if he does not exist, he certainly is not sick. As this example points out, contradiction is the only type of opposition in which one side must always be true. Such an assertion cannot be made of any other kind of opposition, for in the other kinds some middle, such as the nonexistence of Shakespeare, always intervenes.

1. What is the meaning of the categories? What is their purpose? Why are they called the predicaments?
2. What is the chief division of the categories? Describe substance, accident.
3. List the ten categories and the outline which explains this listing.
4. Distinguish primary and secondary substance. Give two reasons why primary substance is the basic entity in the material universe. Give the basic kinds of material substance.
5. Why is individual substance never a predicate? Why can secondary substance be a predicate? For the accidents, what is the rule for predication?
6. Describe quantity. What are the two types of quantity? Give the basic kinds under these types.
7. Describe quality. Define the four kinds of qualities. Give a summary statement of these four kinds of qualities.
8. Describe relation. What attributes cause a thing to be related to another thing?
9. Describe action and passion. What kind of operations is included in these categories? Which ones are excluded? Define each of these operations.
10. Describe where, position, and when. What external attributes do they predicate?
11. Describe possession and list three kinds. Why is possession restricted to human-kind?
12. State the five rules for the categories.
13. Define contrary and contradictory opposition. What attribute follows from each type?

CHAPTER 5

THE PREDICABLES: MODES IN DEFINITION

A. The natural use of the predicables
B. Definitions of the predicables
C. The purpose of the predicables

The preceding chapter explained the ten categories into which all material things can be placed. These ten categories, divided first of all into substance and the nine accidents, are also called the ten predicaments. The reason is that the natures of all existing things can also be predicated or said of their proper subjects. Thus the following predicates may be said of the given subject:

William—	*is a man.*	*(substance)*
	is six feet tall.	*(quantity)*
	is handsome.	*(quality)*
	is Mr. Harvey's son.	*(relation)*
	is rowing a boat.	*(action)*
	is being rowed home.	*(passion)*
	is in the boat, bent over, at noon.	*(where, position, when)*
	is in a swimsuit.	*(possession)*

As said of a given subject, the ten categories are the ten ultimate kinds of predicates. In this respect the ten categories are called the ten predicaments. These categories or predicaments are what is said about a subject, but not how it is said.

Working hand in hand with the categories, the predicables list how the various kinds of predicates are said of a subject. In other words, the predicables give the way in which the predicate is related to the subject. In general, this way or mode or manner is either essential or accidental. The following sentences point out that one can focus not only on what is said but also on how it is said:

William—	*is rational.*	*(essential connection)*
	is a man.	*(essential connection)*
	is six feet tall.	*(accidental connection)*
	is rowing a boat.	*(accidental connection)*

As these examples indicate, it is possible to consider how a predicate is related to a subject, as well as what kind of predicate is used. This how of predication is called the predicables, while the what of predication is labeled the predicaments. The distinction between these two logical forms is further clarified in the following descriptive statements:

1. The What of Predication
   The predicaments are the ten ultimate kinds of predicates said about a subject. (They are the same as the categories.)
2. The How of Predication
   The predicables are the ways in which the predicate is related to the subject.

The main purpose of studying both the predicaments and the predicables is to be able to define more carefully and clearly. Since these two logical entities treat both the ultimate predicates used in definition and the ways of saying these predicates, they are key instruments for the defining process. In a word, the predicaments and the predicables, giving the ultimate classifications and the types of linkage found in all definitions, are invaluable logical tools. Just as the builder must know both his materials and the ways to use them, so the logician, in defining, must know both the kinds of predicates at his command and the ways in which they can be said of the subject being defined.

A. THE NATURAL USE OF THE PREDICABLES

Together with a brief description, the complete list of the predicables, or ways of predicating, is as follows:

1. genus: the general class for the special thing being defined
   e.g., for the human being: animal
2. specific difference: the identifying characteristic making the thing a special kind within the general class
   e.g., for the human being: rationality
3. species: the special kind of thing being defined
   e.g., the human being
4. property: a characteristic peculiar to the special kind of thing
   e.g., for the human being: ability to laugh
5. accident: a characteristic which is not essential nor peculiar to the special kind of thing
   e.g., for the human being: to be tired

The five predicables listed above are part of the natural procedure followed by everyone who attempts to define anything. What is this natural process? Using the example of a porcupine, one may outline the steps of this process as follows:

1. The existing individual porcupine is a certain kind of thing because of its nature or whatness.
2. This porcupine becomes part of the sense experience of the learner.
3. By means of his intellect, the learner has an idea of the nature or whatness of the porcupine.
4. This concept is very obscure. Nevertheless the learner knows what kind or type of thing (the species) the porcupine is. He proves this by the fact that he can sort out those things which are porcupines and those which are not. The basic name *porcupine* is a typical expression for this kind, type, or species.
5. The learner begins to clarify this obscure concept. To do this, he first searches for the better-known general class (genus) to which the porcupine belongs.
6. Then the learner wants to find out the distinctive mark that makes the porcupine different (specific difference) from everything else in that general class.
7. If the learner is unable to find the intrinsic difference which makes a porcupine a special kind of thing, he will have to settle for characteristics which are not peculiar but are always present in the thing (inseparable accidents). In this situation, the learner does not seek the peculiar characteristics (properties), for such qualities are known to be peculiar to the species only after the species itself is defined.

In harmony with the above outline, the informal thought process of the learner might move through the following stages. As this individual is walking through a forest, he sees a black, stocky, clumsy animal lumbering along in the nearby clearing. Immediately he might say, "I wonder what kind of thing (species) that creature is." Walking very quietly, he moves closer for a careful inspection. After he sees that it is about the size of a small dog, he realizes that it is much too large to be a woodchuck. Then he notices its stiff, coarse hair. This characteristic triggers his memory, causing him to exclaim, "Now I remember! That is a porcupine (species). I've seen pictures of those animals in my nature magazines."

This learner is so fascinated by his find that he decides to observe it more carefully. Soon the porcupine climbs to the top of a tree in the clearing and begins to gnaw at the bark. This latter action makes the learner wonder if the porcupine is a rodent. A good look at the animal's four sharp incisor teeth answers this question. These teeth reveal that the porcupine does indeed belong to the rodent family (genus).

Now pictures of all kinds of rodents run through this individual's memory. What makes the porcupine different from other rodents, such as the woodchuck, the muskrat, and the beaver? The first thought that strikes this person is that most of them are smaller than the porcupine. The mice, the rats, and the squirrels, for example, seem quite diminutive in comparison to this large rodent. Is it size alone, however, that makes a porcupine different from everything else (specific difference)? The learner knows that there is some element which makes a porcupine the special kind of rodent that it is. It might be called porcupineness or spine-pigness, just as the special element in the human being is called humanness or rationality (specific difference). Alas, however, the learner has nothing but a name for that exact element.

Even though the individual does not know the precise difference that makes the porcupine a special rodent, he does not lose heart. He can at least utilize the external characteristics in his attempts to define the porcupine. One of these seems quite peculiar to this rodent and might even be a property of it. This characteristic is its remarkable covering; namely, its coarse hair interlaced with sharp quills.

At this point the learner has an adequate system of definition worked out. He might express it as follows: "I know that I want the general classification (genus) for this animal and its distinctive trademark (specific difference). For this latter element, I may have to settle for nonpeculiar but inseparable characteristics (inseparable accidents)." Such a road map leads this student of the porcupine (species) to work out the following definition:

A porcupine—   *is a rodent,*   *(genus)*
                     about the size of a small dog,   *(inseparable*
                     with coarse black hair overlaid with yellow tipped
                     hairs and thickly set with long sharp quills,
                     with a short-legged, clumsy gait,
                     *at home in trees on which it feeds.**   *accidents)*

As the above example indicates, every definition, clarifying the given subject or species, contains the following elements:

1. the general class   (genus)
2. the identifying difference   (specific difference)
    or an adequate substitution   (inseparable accidents)

These elements in the definition, giving the way the latter is related to the thing defined, are some of the predicables. As noted above, these predicables are five in number and include all the possible connections of the predicate to the given subject. These relationships range through the following connections:

1. the general class   (genus)
2. the identifying characteristic   (specific difference)
3. the special kind of thing being defined   (species)
4. the peculiar characteristic following from the thing   (property)
5. characteristics which are not essential nor peculiar   (accidents)

These five predicables will be treated more precisely in the next section.

B. DEFINITIONS OF THE PREDICABLES

1. PREDICABLES DESCRIBING THE ESSENCE

Three of the five predicables are ways of predicating which describe the essence of a material thing. These are as follows: genus, specific difference, and species. The first one, genus, is defined as that way of predicating which states the essence of the thing in a way common to several different species. Thus each of the following is predicated as a genus of the given subject:

1. Man is an animal.   *4. The rose is a flower.*
2. A triangle is a figure.   *5. Justice is a virtue.*
3. An animal is an organism. *6. The pistol is a weapon.*

Typically the genus or general classification is predicated first in the defining process. Since the human being in knowing moves from the generic to the specific, it is natural for him to state the better-known general class first.

Specific difference is defined as that way of predicating which states the identifying mark within a genus distinguishing one species from another. Thus each of the following is predicated as the specific difference of the given subject:

1. Man is rational.
2. A triangle is three-sided.
3. An animal is sentient.

Species is defined as that way of predicating which states the complete essence of the thing, not just a note common to other things, but that designating it as a special type. Said very simply, species states what type a thing is. If asked what type, one might answer the following: It is a man, a porcupine, a cloud, a rabbit, or a violet.

As predicating the type of thing, species states the whatness held in the mind's concept. This whatness is derived from sensible singulars. Thus the whatness of a cloud is derived from individual clouds. Therefore the species, giving the special type found in individual things, is predicated of singular subjects. Thus, if asked what this individual fluffy thing is, one would say that it is a cloud. (In the logical exercises, the student should note that the species is naturally predicated of a singular subject.)

This whatness, predicated by the species, is clarified by the definition giving the genus and specific difference. Therefore it is evident that the species is clarified by the genus plus the specific difference. This clarification, as well as the species predicated of

45

singulars, is illustrated in the following examples:

Individual	Species	Genus, Specific Difference
1. Brian	is a man.	(rational animal)
2. This figure	is a triangle.	(three-sided figure)
3. This living thing	is an animal.	(sentient organism)

As noted above, *genus* stands for the general category, while *species* refers to the special kind under this general class. Logical usage can apply this relationship of genus to species to any such grouping within a biological classification. Biological usage, on the contrary, restricts the use of *genus* and *species* to a particular section of such classification. The following diagram points out this distinction:

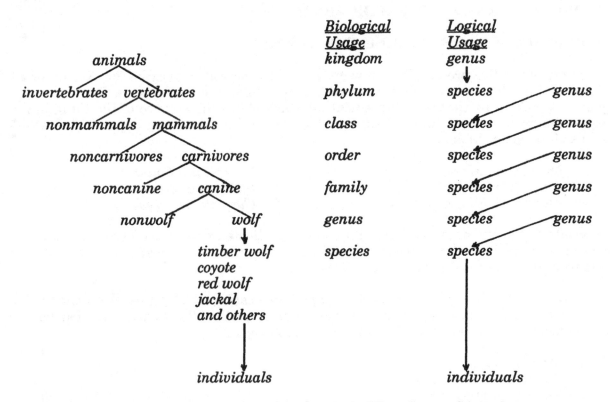

2. PREDICABLES DERIVING FROM OR ADHERING IN ESSENCE

The remaining two of the predicables, property and accident, are ways of predicating which derive from or adhere in the essence of a material thing. The first one, property, is defined as that way of predicating which states some characteristic that follows from and is peculiar to a given essence, in such a manner that the identification of the property leads to the identification of the essence. Thus the ability to laugh is a property of the human being. Clearly this ability does not constitute the human being, as do his rationality and his animality. Nevertheless, given a rational nature, laughter follows. Therefore, wherever laughter is found, one has a rational essence. In the medical field, a yellow cast of the skin would be a property of jaundice, while red spots would be a property of measles. Whenever a doctor identifies such symptoms, he can confidently diagnose the corresponding disease. In brief, a property, deriving from and peculiar to the essence, can be thought of as a trademark of the given thing. If it is present, the thing from which it follows is also present.

Just as *genus* and *species* have different meanings in logic and biology, so *property* is used differently by the logician and the chemist or physicist. While the logical meaning for *property* denotes some one characteristic peculiar to a given thing, the chemical or physical meaning usually designates several general characteristics which together give a particular or peculiar distinction. Thus the properties of oxygen are that it is colorless, odorless, tasteless, gaseous, the most abundant of the elements, and essential to life processes.* Since hydrogen is also colorless and odorless, several general characteristics are required to distinguish oxygen from hydrogen. Rather than being properties, these constant general characteristics are actually inseparable accidents. Since it is very difficult to discover a property, the scientist in identifying a thing uses several general characteristics, which in combination are peculiar to a given thing.

Accident is defined as that way of predicating which states characteristics of a thing which are not part of its essence nor peculiar to it. Such characteristics may be separable or inseparable from the thing. As separable characteristics, these accidents just happen to inhere in the thing and may come and go at any time. Thus the ground may be dry before the rain, but soaked after it; the food may be hot at noon, but cold an hour later.

Other accidents, while inseparable from a given thing, are still not part of its essence nor peculiar to it. Thus odorless is an inseparable accident of oxygen, but it is not peculiar to it. This characteristic is also found in hydrogen. Also, malleable is an inseparable accident of copper, but it is also a constant characteristic of gold. These inseparable accidents, while not part of a given species nor peculiar to it, may be considered as proper to a whole genus. Thus the characteristic of density is only an inseparable accident of gold and copper, but it is a property of the genus embracing both nonliving and living bodies.

Of what value is the accident for the process of definition? As noted before, an aggregate of inseparable accidents is an adequate substitute for the specific difference. The reason is that such a peculiar collection could have been caused only by the given essence. The use of a combination of inseparable accidents is quite common in all the natural sciences. Thus gold is defined as a heavy, yellow, inert, metallic chemical element which has a high degree of ductility and malleability.* Also a tree is defined as a woody perennial plant with one main stem developing many branches, usually at a height above the ground.* Even the wanted bulletin for a criminal uses a combination of fairly permanent accidents such as the following: a man six feet tall, with dark hair and skin, a large mole on right check, one finger missing from right hand. The ideal in this technique for defining is to obtain a satisfactory definition, while using as few inseparable accidents as possible.

At this point it should be noted that *accident* has two meanings in logical terminology. They are as follows:

1. <u>In the Categories or Predicaments</u>
   Here *accident* is distinguished from *substance*. In this context this word means that thing which exists in another thing as in a subject. Thus green is an accident existing in grass.
2. <u>In the Predicables</u>
   Here *accident* is distinguished from *genus, specific difference, species,* and *property*. In this context this word means that characteristic which is neither part of the essence nor peculiar to it. Thus it is accidental that the tomatoes are green.

Because of this twofold meaning of *accident*, it is possible to have a predicamental accident with an accidental predicate said of it. The following example illustrates this twofold usage:

> *The red in that dress*------------ *is faded.*
> *(predicamental*   *(accidental mode*
> *accident)*   *of predicating)*

3. SUMMARY OF THE PREDICABLES

The definitions of the five predicables, as treated in the last two sections, are summarized as follows:

1. <u>Predicables Describing the Essence</u>
   a. genus: that way of predicating which states the essence of the thing in a way common to several different species.
   b. specific difference: that way of predicating which states the identifying mark within a genus distinguishing one species from another.
   c. species: that way of predicating which states the complete essence of the thing, not just a note common to other things, but that designating it as a special type.
2. <u>Predicables Deriving from or Adhering in Essence</u>
   a. property: that way of predicating which states some characteristic that follows from and is peculiar to a given essence, in such a manner that the identification of the property leads to the identification of the essence.
   b. accident: that way of predicating which states characteristics of a thing which are not part of its essence nor peculiar to it.

The above definitions are further clarified by the following example which, using one subject, illustrates all the ways of predicating:

The human being: *(species)*	*is rational.*	*specific difference (identifying mark)*
	is an animal.	*genus (general class)*
(said of individuals, such as Jane, Jim)	*can construct language.*	*property (peculiar trait)*
	is warmblooded, hairy.	*inseparable accidents (not peculiar; always present)*
	is old, sick, happy.	*separable accidents (not always present)*

C. THE PURPOSE OF THE PREDICABLES

What is the point in distinguishing the different ways in which a predicate may be said? The main reason is that the human being seeks knowledge which will always be true. In line with his nature, each person wants to know the answers to things, answers which will have a permanent value. Thus, if one knows that Mr. Collins is at the front door at the present moment, one can state that such a fact is true. What happens, however, if Mr. Collins goes away? This judgment and subsequent statement are no longer true. On the other hand, one might say that Mr. Collins is a rational animal. That statement will always be true, for rational animal states the very nature of Mr. Collins, while his coming and going are only accidental. Therefore the only permanent knowledge one can have is that stating the essence or something inseparable from the essence. Hence it is crucial that one understand which predicates state such essential knowledge and which do not. In other words, one must distinguish between predicates which are always true (genus, species, specific difference, property, and inseparable accident) and predicates which need not be true (separable accident).

But even among those predicates which are always true, one must make a distinction. One wants to know not only that something is always true but also why it is always true. Thus the reason that a human being gets a college degree is not just because he is an animal but because he is a rational animal. Therefore one must be able to distinguish whether a predicate is predicated as a genus or a species. The genus will not give the proper reason why a species behaves the way it does. In order to distinguish between a genus and a species, one must have the notion of specific difference, since it is this difference which, added to a genus, constitutes a species.

Finally, even if an accident is inseparable and therefore always true of a thing, one must distinguish between it and a property. The reason is that a property is always a sure sign of a thing, but an inseparable accident is not such a trademark. Thus laughter always indicates the presence of a human being, but odorless does not immediately signify oxygen.

In summary, the purpose of the predicables is to help the human being in his search for knowledge which will always be true.

STUDY QUESTIONS **CHAPTER 5**

1. Distinguish the predicables from the predicaments.
2. What are the two needed elements in every definition? If the specific difference cannot be found, what substitution can be made?
3. List the predicables which describe the essence.
4. Define genus. Why is the genus predicated first in the defining process?
5. Define specific difference. Define species. What is the proper subject of the species? What two elements clarify the species?
6. Distinguish the usage of *genus* and *species* in logic from that found in biology.
7. List the predicables which derive from or adhere in the essence.
8. Define property. Distinguish the usage of *property* by the logician from that of the chemist or physicist.
9. Define accident. Distinguish the two kinds of accidents.
10. Of what value is the inseparable accident for the definer? What guideline should be followed in compiling a list of inseparable accidents?
11. Explain the two logical meanings of *accident*.
12. By focusing on the distinctions found among the predicables, show how the knowledge of them will aid the human being's search for truth.

CHAPTER 6

THE METHOD FOR DEFINITION

A. The method of division
B. The method of composition
C. The importance of direct perception

The primary reason for the mind's work in simple apprehension is to understand clearly the whatness or essence of simple realities. Thus the mind, having a vague notion of what a giraffe is, wants a clear understanding of the essence or nature of this type of animal. This clear understanding of the nature of a thing is obtained by the mind in its defining process. The preceding chapters have covered the following elements of this defining procedure:

1. The signs used in the defining process: words and concepts
2. the ultimate kinds of things said in definitions: the ten categories
3. how things are said in definitions: the predicables

This chapter will focus on the procedure followed by the mind as it obtains the definition or clear grasp of a thing's whatness. What are the natural steps that the intellect takes as it defines a thing? It is the best of these steps that the art of logic will imitate and codify.

A. THE METHOD OF DIVISION

As the preceding chapter explained, to obtain a definition or clear grasp of a thing's whatness is to secure its genus and specific difference. In other words, a species or kind is clarified by its genus and specific difference. Thus the definition of a porcupine includes that it is a rodent (genus) and that it has coarse, black hair thickly set with long, sharp quills (grouping of inseparable accidents).* What are the steps taken as the human being seeks the genus and specific difference?

1. A PRELIMINARY DESCRIPTION

The first step in the defining process is a preliminary description of the kind of thing to be defined. The purpose of such a description is to single out the thing so that it may be clarified. This first step lays down the goal to be accomplished. Like every other goal it must be known first. If one does not lay down the end or purpose first, one does not know what one intends to accomplish. In such an event one arrives at the given goal only by chance. Such a procedure is similar to a traveler who lays down no end for his journey. Because he has no particular place that he wishes to go, he will arrive at a specific city only by chance.

Since the purpose of this first step is to single out the thing to be defined, it may be achieved by stating its name, if such a name is understandable. Thus, if one is defining the bowl, one might simply say, "Today we are going to learn the meaning of the bowl."

If the meaning of the name is unknown, several other ways to single out the thing are as follows: (1) to point to a real example of the thing; (2) to produce a picture of the thing; (3) to give a verbal description of the external characteristics of the thing. Thus, returning to the bowl, one might produce a real bowl or show a catalog with several pictures of such a container. Finally, one might describe the bowl as follows: It is a container easily found in kitchens. This verbal description of the name of the thing is rightly called a nominal definition. Such a definition, by stating some external characteristics, simply clarifies the name so that one may proceed to define the thing at hand. This subsequent definition of the thing is called, in contrast to this opening description, a real definition.

2. A PERCEPTION OF THE GENERAL CLASS

After one knows the sort of thing to be defined, one tends naturally to seek the general category for the given thing. Thus, in defining a bowl, one easily detects that it is a certain kind of container. In like manner, a peach is easily placed in the general class of fruit; a rose, in the genus of flower; a bear, in the genus of animal; a robin, in the genus of bird. This general category is something seen by the definer: it is evident to him. In picking out the general class, the definer may not immediately see the most proximate genus. In such an event he should state whatever more remote genus is evident to him. Using the example of the bowl, one might begin with a statement such as the following, "Well, I believe that a bowl is some kind of utensil." This general category can then be refined and divided into specific kinds.

The reason that one easily finds the general category first is that all human learning moves from the generic to the specific. In logical terminology, the learner moves from the genus to the specific difference. Thus a beginner in a new job sees first the general outline of his responsibilities before he understands its specific details. Also a newcomer to a city grasps first its main attractions before he has any insight into its fine points. The reason that the human learner always moves from the generic to the specific is that the general outline is a simpler concept. As simpler and therefore easier for the human being, the general level of a thing is always known first.

In finding the general category for the thing to be defined, one is helped by a knowledge of the ten categories. Aware of the fact that there are ten basic kinds of material things, the definer can approach his task with greater assurance. Thus, if one wishes to define prone, one's thinking might proceed as follows: "I know that prone is not a substance. Then what kind of accident is it? It cannot be quantity or relation. I know; it must be position." As the dictionary confirms, prone does indeed fall under this latter category, for it is defined as the position in which the front part of the body lies upon the ground.* The advantage of knowing the ten categories in defining can also be noted in the following definitions:

1. batch: the _quantity_ of anything made in one operation*
2. temperate: a _quality_ of staying within reasonable limits*
3. dexterous: an _ability_ to do things with skill and precision*

As the definer utilizes his knowledge of the ten categories, he avoids the common mistake of placing everything in the categories of where or when. The following examples illustrate this illogical procedure in defining, a procedure which operates as if there were only two kinds of things in the material universe:

1. projectile: _when_ something is hurled or shot forward
2. inventor: _when_ someone devises a new contrivance
3. scarlet fever: _where_ one has a sore throat, fever, and a scarlet rash

51

3. THE DIVISION OF THE GENUS INTO ITS SPECIES

After perceiving the general class for the thing, the definer searches for the distinctive mark which sets the thing apart from all other kinds within this class. In other words, the definer now strives to discover the specific difference (or inseparable accidents) of the thing. In reference to the bowl, the one defining seeks the distinctive notes which make it different from all other containers. What is the procedure that one naturally uses to find such characteristics?

One natural method used to find these distinctive notes is to divide the members of the general class into two opposing groups: the haves and have-nots. In other words, the species or kinds belonging to the general class are divided into contradictory groups. In using this division method, the definer should observe several basic rules. These requirements (illustrated in the pictorial chart below) are as follows:

1. Each member or species must have less extension than the general class. In reference to the chart, one can note that bowl has less extension than container, which includes bowls, frying pans, wastebaskets, and so forth.

2. All the members, taken together, must equal in extension the general class. In other words, one must make a complete or exhaustive division. This important rule is most easily accomplished by using contradictory opposition, which is illustrated on the chart. Here the containers are divided as follows: deep and not-deep; open-at-top and not-open-at-top; rounded and non-rounded.

   As these examples indicate, contradictory opposition is achieved by using *not* or *non-* before the term to be contradicted. These words set up a division between the given term and everything not-that-term. Hence this division comprises all being, since everything must either be or not be that term. Thus any given thing is either a cat or not a cat. Therefore contradictory opposition always creates a complete or exhaustive division.

3. As the definer separates or divides the member to be defined from the other members or kinds, he should focus on the inseparable accidents of this member. Thus the definer easily notes that the bowl is deep. Then he can separate all deep containers from non-deep containers.

4. In working with these inseparable accidents, the definer should utilize the most obvious differences first. Thus he will divide his various containers by deep and non-deep before he attempts rounded and non-rounded.

5. After the definer has made his first division, he must now make every subsequent division fall under each new heading. Thus the first minor general class on the chart is deep containers. Therefore only types of deep containers, such as canisters and bowls, may be found under this heading. (This rule applies through every dividing level and is very easily violated.)

6. After the members are divided through enough levels, the definer can perceive all the distinctive notes belonging to the thing defined. Together these inseparable accidents are an adequate substitute for the specific difference. Thus the distinctive notes of the bowl are as follows: deep, open at top, and rounded.

Following this list of basic rules, both the steps and a pictorial illustration of the division method will now be given.

Steps of the Division Method
1. preliminary description
2. perception of general class
3. division of genus into smaller, opposing groups
4. perception of distinctive notes from dividing groups through enough levels

---

1. We shall define   *THE BOWL*.

2. The bowl belongs to the general class of   *CONTAINERS*.

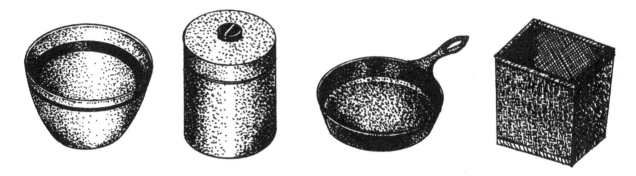

3. Let us find how *THE BOWL* is divided from the other containers.

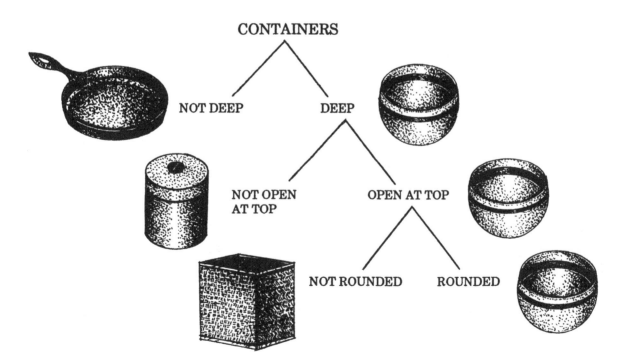

4. THE BOWL IS A CONTAINER WHICH IS DEEP, ROUNDED, AND OPEN AT THE TOP.

(Each of the above groups has only one or a few samples for the needed exhaustive division.)

When the definer perceives not only the genus but also the specific difference (or inseparable accidents) for the thing to be defined, he has attained his goal. In other words, the definer now sees the whatness of the thing clearly, now has a definition of it. Thus the one defining now knows the bowl clearly by perceiving that it is a container (genus) which is deep, rounded, and open at the top (inseparable accidents). The fact that a given member, kind, or species is defined by its genus and specific difference is illustrated by the following definitions:

1. *leash:*   *a cord or strap by which a dog or other animal is held in check**
2. *rice:*   *an aquatic cereal grass grown widely in warm climates**
3. *mural:*   *a large picture painted directly on a wall or ceiling.**

B. THE METHOD OF COMPOSITION

The composition method is the second procedure that the human being follows in his defining process. This procedure differs from the division method in that it focuses on individuals first rather than on the general class. Nevertheless both methods are alike in that they each begin with a preliminary reference to the kind of thing being defined. Thus, if one wished to define the bowl, one might start with the following statement: "Today we shall try to understand the precise meaning of that container which is the bowl."

Having laid down the type of thing to be defined, the composition method now seeks the thing's specific difference by a reverse procedure from that of the division method. As already explained, this latter method proceeds by dividing the general class into contradictory groups and working down to the specific difference. In contrast, the composition method focuses on various individuals with the name of the thing being defined and attempts to discover the common distinctive note for all of them. To carry out this procedure which works up to the specific difference (or inseparable accidents), the definer should observe several basic rules. These requirements (illustrated on the pictorial chart below) are as follows:

1. Each individual examined must have the name of the thing being defined. Thus, if one is defining bowl, every individual container studied must be readily known as a bowl.

2. One begins by examining similar, named individuals in order to perceive their common trait. In reference to the chart, one can note that the similar individuals called mixing bowls have in common that they are deep, open, rounded containers for blending ingredients.

3. Then one examines other named individuals, which form a second group, in order to perceive their common trait. Thus the definer can perceive that the individuals called salad bowls have in common that they are deep, open, rounded containers used for cold side dishes.

4. After sufficient groups of individuals have been examined, one abstracts the distinctive note common to all the specific traits obtained. Thus, from the specific traits belonging to the four groups of bowls, the definer easily abstracts the following common note: deep, open, and rounded. These inseparable accidents for the bowl are an adequate substitute for its specific difference.

5. (A word of caution: If these groups of named individuals do not have a distinctive note in common, they are poorly named and are actually different kinds of things.)

Following this list of basic rules, both the steps and a pictorial illustration of the composition method will now be given.

Steps of the Composition Method
1. preliminary reference to kind
2. perception of general class
3. examination of named individuals for common trait
4. examination of other named individuals for their common trait
5. perception of distinctive notes common to all traits

---

1. We shall define   *THE BOWL*.

2. The bowl belongs to the general class of   *CONTAINERS*.

3,4. Let us examine groups of named individuals for their specific common traits.

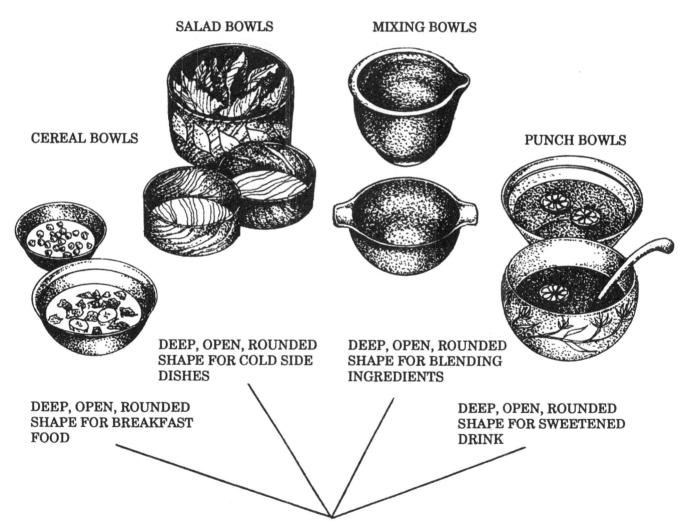

SALAD BOWLS   MIXING BOWLS

CEREAL BOWLS   PUNCH BOWLS

DEEP, OPEN, ROUNDED
SHAPE FOR COLD SIDE
DISHES

DEEP, OPEN, ROUNDED
SHAPE FOR BLENDING
INGREDIENTS

DEEP, OPEN, ROUNDED
SHAPE FOR BREAKFAST
FOOD

DEEP, OPEN, ROUNDED
SHAPE FOR SWEETENED
DRINK

5. THE BOWL IS A CONTAINER WHICH IS DEEP, ROUNDED, AND OPEN AT THE TOP.

(The above groups of named individuals have only one or a few samples.)

As the above pictorial chart illustrates, the composition method begins with individuals having the name of the thing to be defined. Having perceived the specific traits for sufficient groups of these individuals, this method searches for the distinctive note common to all these traits. This note will be the specific difference (or inseparable accidents) for the thing being defined. Thus the specific difference for the bowl is the following: deep, open, and rounded. As this method arrives at the specific difference, it already is in possession of the general class or genus. The reason is that the mind moves from the generic to the specific aspects of a thing. Thus the definer, in his search for the specific difference, perceives first that the bowl is a certain kind of container.

C. THE IMPORTANCE OF DIRECT PERCEPTION

Both of the above methods for arriving at a definition rest on a direct, if progressive, perception of the elements involved. As the clarification of the initial concept obtained by the intellect, definition is not reasoned about; rather it is something accepted or admitted as the definer follows either of the above methods. Thus the definer does not reason that the bowl is a container; rather he accepts this genus because of the evident examples that he sees before him. In addition, he also accepts each successive division of the genus, container. Thus he sees that the bowl is deep, that it is open at the top, that it is rounded. Utilizing a sufficient number of examples, the definer holds each step of his given method because the insight obtained is obvious to him. In a word, the definer, through the examples before him, perceives directly the elements obtained.

Why are the elements of definition obvious to the definer? The reason is simple. The definer is relying on both sensible examples and his intellectual insight. In other words, he is making full use of the inductive method. Thus the definer knows that the bowl is a container both because he has a given sample before him and because he has a mind which can grasp the whatness or kind. This method, defined as the process of moving from the sensible singular to the universal, is anchored in sensible reality and relies on the abstractive power of the intellect. Utilizing this basic method, the definer rests his case on the examples he sees before him and on his ability to know the kinds of things these examples are.

In defining any given thing, the definer moves from the more obvious elements to those which are more obscure. Throughout this movement, however, he relies both on sense knowledge and his intellectual insight. The distinction in this process is found in the fact that the more obvious characteristics of a thing may require only one piece of sense data, while the more obscure attributes may require lengthy sense experience. Thus the tulip may be defined as a plant in the very first sense contact with it. On the other hand, the following distinguishing characteristics may demand more observations:

1. bulb plant of the lily family
2. spring blooming
3. long, broad, pointed leaves
4. single, large, cup-shaped, variously colored flower*

As this example indicates, the amount of required sense contact is that which is sufficient for the given insight to occur. This sufficient sense background may vary from one example to years of observation and experimentation.

It is imperative for the definer to recognize the base on which his definition rests; i.e., a direct perception of the whatness from a sufficient number of examples. He need not look for any complicated way to prove what is evident before him. His examples and his intellectual ability are the anchor for what he knows. Thus a little child, having learned that two is one more than one, might state the following: "I know what two is. It is one more than one. Can't you see? Just look at my fingers." As this example indicates, the definer perceives his definition directly through enough examples. He need not hunt for a more complicated proof.

In the impossible situation in which the beginnings of knowledge did not rest on the obvious illustrated by examples, then one would have all knowing begin with what is not evident. In such an event, one would have to prove this beginning. But how could one find a proof to precede what one wishes to hold first? If one needs a proof for the beginnings of knowledge and it is impossible to find it, then one automatically has no further knowledge. In other words, the demand for proof at the beginning leads to the impossibility of any knowledge at all. But this conclusion is proved false by the fact that every person has at least some practical knowledge, such as that fire burns and that water is necessary for life. Therefore it is evident that definition, as the clarification of the initial grasp of a thing's whatness, is perceived directly. It cannot rest ultimately on some type of proof.

To illustrate the importance of direct perception in the defining process, the following example is given. Throughout this example, the teacher moves to the next step of the procedure only because the student perceives clearly the step before it.

T. *Today we shall learn about the fox. First I shall show you a picture of it. Then we shall try to find out what kind of animal it is. Finally we shall list its special characteristics.*

S. *I think I know what kind of animal it is. It looks like a dog. I know that the dog nurses its young, because I've seen my own pet nurse her new babies. I'll bet that the fox is a mammal, just as the dog is.*

T. *You are absolutely right. The fox is a mammal, but it is a special kind of mammal. If you remember what kind of food your dog eats, you might be able to tell me what makes the fox a special kind of mammal.*

S. *I certainly know what kind of food my dog likes best. She always wants meat to eat. Could you say that the fox is a flesh-eating mammal?*

T. *Indeed you can say that the fox is a flesh-eating mammal. Technically we call him a carnivore, which is only a larger word for flesh-eating. There are many kinds of carnivores, such as bears, raccoons, weasels, skunks, dogs, wolves, foxes, and cats. Some of these carnivores look very different, but some look alike. Do any of those I mentioned look quite similar?*

S. *Well, I know that the dog and fox look alike. Even the wolf might be a cousin of the two that I mentioned. Could these three be a special kind of carnivore?*

T. *Yes. The dog, fox, and wolf are put in a special class called doglike or canine. Well, we already know a lot about the fox. It belongs to the canine family under the carnivores, which are part of the large grouping called mammals. Now we have one more task. We must find what makes the fox different from the dog.*

S. *Let me see your picture again. The fox certainly is different from the dog. If I could list some characteristics which make the fox special, they might be the following: his bushy tail, his sharp pointed nose, his large erect ears, and his handsome reddish coat trimmed with black and white. Will this description do?*

T. *Very well indeed. You understand a lot about the fox. You know both his general class and his distinguishing characteristics. You can easily formulate this knowledge into a sound definition.*

1. What is the primary purpose of simple apprehension? What logical structure is the result of this purpose? List three tools aiding this purpose.
2. State the first step in the division method. What is its purpose and why is this step first? Give four ways to achieve this first step.
3. What is a nominal definition? How is it distinguished from a real definition?
4. What is the second step in the division method? How is it known by the definer? Why is this step in the second position?
5. Give two original examples which show that the categories aid in perceiving the genus. The categories of where and when are often misused in defining. Give two examples of this mistake and then correct them.
6. What is the third step in the division method? What natural procedure is used to achieve this step?
7. List five rules to be observed in the division method.
8. What two elements clarify the species?
9. What is the first step in the composition method?
10. For the composition method, list the four rules to be observed in finding the specific difference.
11. List all the steps for the division method, for the composition method.
12. Why are the various elements of the definition directly perceived by the definer?
13. As the definer moves from the generic to the specific, how does this movement affect the amount of needed sense data?
14. Show that it is impossible to begin human knowing from the nonevident.

CHAPTER 7

DEFINITION: A STATEMENT OF CAUSES

A. The meaning of the four causes
B. The causes as found in definitions
C. Basic rules for definitions
D. Undefined terms
E. Summary

In the preceding chapters the student learned that the human being is able to abstract the whatness from a given sensible singular, such as this yellow tulip. This initial whatness is held in a concept and expressed in a word. As this initial, unitary concept is clarified, one arrives by the method of division or composition at the divided concept or the definition. This definition is given most clearly by means of the genus and the specific difference (or inseparable accidents). Thus the tulip is defined as a bulb plant of the lily family with long, broad, pointed leaves and a single, large, cup-shaped, variously colored flower.*

The definition, giving both the genus and the specific difference, clarifies the initial concept. In other words, it expresses what the given thing is. As an expression of what the thing is, the definition automatically gives some cause of this given thing. Said in another way, the definition, stating what makes the thing what it is, is at once a statement of the causes of that thing. This fact can be seen in the following definition of steel: It is a hard, tough metal composed of iron alloyed with carbon and often other metals to produce hardness, resistance to rusting, and so forth.* This definition of steel, telling what it is, gives at the same time both its material and final causes. As a statement of what the thing is, the definition is automatically an expression of the causes of a thing.

Since definition is a statement of the causes of a given thing, this chapter will examine the meaning of the four causes and then clarify how these four factors are present in all definitions.

A. THE MEANING OF THE FOUR CAUSES

Causality is at the very heart of the material universe. Thus an eclipse of the sun is caused when the moon is directly between the earth and the sun. A tornado causes great destruction wherever it touches down. Weathering is a process which causes the earth's bedrock to be changed into soil. As these examples indicate, causes and their effects are constantly present in the various changes in the physical universe. Causality is also seen wherever the human being is at work. Thus the hard work of the baker is the cause of the daily supply of bread. In addition, the blueprint of the architect causes the chain of activity which results in a finished building. Also the coal furnished by the miner is one of the reasons that homes have heat. As is evident from these illustrations, causality is an important part of the human being's daily life.

What is the general meaning of cause? It can be defined very simply as any factor from which another thing follows with dependence. Thus growing roots are a factor in the breaking up of the earth's rocks. Boiling of water is a factor bringing about the purification of this liquid. Eating proper food is a factor leading to good health. In this general definition of cause, there is a reference both to the cause itself and its effect, as well as to the connection between them. Without that thing which follows it with dependence, a cause cannot exist as a cause.

There are four causes which play a part before any material thing can exist. These causes, together with their definitions, are as follows:

1. end: that for the sake of which a thing is accomplished; the goal
2. agent: that by which the thing is accomplished; the mover
3. form: that which makes the thing to be what it is; the determiner
4. matter: that from which the thing comes to be; the receiver

To illustrate these four causes, one might use the example of a split-level house. The dream of Mr. Hastings, a more comfortable home for his family, is the goal, plan, or objective which started the building of the house in the first place. As can be seen, this dream is that for the sake of which the house is finally built. After Mr. Hastings presents his plan to the Jiffy Construction Company, they must first haul in all the needed materials. As is evident, these materials are that from which the house comes to be. With reference to the four causes, these building materials are the matter or the material cause. Provided with the needed materials, the Jiffy Company can set to work building the house. Their labors are the efforts by means of which the house is actually built or accomplished. This company is the mover leading to the actual house; it is an example of the agent or efficient cause.

Finally the house itself is finished. As a split-level house, it is a certain kind of family dwelling. This distinct outer shape is its artificial form. It is the split-level character of this house which makes Mr. Hastings' home to be the kind of thing it is, which determines his home to be this kind and no other. This outer shape is an example of the formal cause. Various synonyms of the formal cause are as follows: identifying mark, specifying note, qualifying element, and trademark. The house itself is twofold: it is composed of matter and form. In other words, the house is a composite of materials formed in a certain way. The finished thing is not just a form; it is a form embodied in matter. Form, on the other hand, is the determining element in the house. As defined, form is that which makes the thing to be what it is.

Among these four causes, the form and matter are intrinsic to the given thing, while the end and agent are extrinsic. Using the same example, one can see that the split-level form and the various materials are the internal components of the finished home of Mr. Hastings. On the other hand, the Jiffy Construction Company is no longer needed after the house is produced. This agent, as an outside force, can pack up its equipment after its work is finished and no longer return to the scene. As the mover, the agent is an external cause. In addition, the end or plan is not the actual thing. Rather it is the thing as proposed or intended. Thus Mr. Hastings' dream is not the actual house; it is the house as only planned and unexecuted. As only the plan, the end is an extrinsic cause. In summary, the form and matter are intrinsic causes, while the end and agent are extrinsic factors.

The four causes have a definite hierarchy among themselves in that one given cause, by its very nature, is the reason for another one. This order in value or importance, stemming from the relationship among the causes, is as follows: (1) end, (2) agent, (3) form, and (4) matter. As this list indicates, the end is the first of all the causes. This means that the agent begins to operate only because of some end or plan set before it. Thus the Jiffy Company could not undertake the particular task of building this split-level house for Mr. Hastings unless his plan were first placed before them. Without Mr. Hastings' plan, the company would not know what to do and could not exercise its proper part in the causal picture, i.e., to be the builder or mover.

As the mover, the agent brings forth from the potential character of the materials the desired formation. Thus the Jiffy Company must first have materials able to be formed into a permanent dwelling, such as reinforced concrete and properly fired bricks. Given satisfactory materials, the company is then the moving force whereby the actual split-level form arises from them. Without the hard work or causality of the company, the concrete and bricks could stay in large piles or stacks forever. It is only because of the Jiffy Company that the actual split-level form is educed from the given amount of bricks and concrete. Because of the need for the agent to educe the form from matter, the mover has a priority in causality over these two intrinsic causes.

Of the two intrinsic causes, it is the form which gives the actual identity to the materials used. Thus the split-level design of Mr. Hastings' home is that attribute which identifies it for what it is. As the determining element, form has a priority in causality over the materials used, which function as receivers rather than determiners.

In summary, then, the four causes have a definite hierarchy among themselves in that one given cause, by its very nature, is the reason for another one. This order in value or importance, stemming from the relationship among the causes, is as follows: (1) end, (2) agent, (3) form, and (4) matter.

In addition to giving identity to the given thing, form is also the fulfillment of the end or plan first intended. Thus the actual formed house, if completed carefully, is the fulfillment or the realization of Mr. Hastings' dream. At first there is only Mr. Hastings' dream or intention. In other words, there is only the end or goal which is unfulfilled in any concrete way. Later the materials are formed into the actual house. This formed thing stands as the fulfillment or realization of the initial dream or plan. As this example indicates, form is truly the fulfillment of the end. Said in another way, the formed thing is identical with the end realized.

The end realized in the formed thing is called the end of production, of constructive labor. Thus the formed split-level house is the end of production. More briefly, form is the end of production. There is also a further end, which is called the end of the product or of the thing formed. This further end is the use of that product. In other words, the end of the product is its use. Thus the end of that product, Mr. Hastings' house, is its use as a dwelling for his family. In summary, the following two ends exist:

1. the end of production, which is the product
2. the end of the product, which is its use

B. THE CAUSES AS FOUND IN DEFINITIONS

The previous chapters have stressed that the definition, in clarifying the initial whatness, gives the genus and specific difference. Such a definition, in stating what the thing is, also gives the causes of this thing. As the preceding section pointed out, these causes are the end, agent, form, and matter. Stated more simply, these factors are the why, the who, the what, and the materials. Among these four causes, it is the form (the what) which is naturally and ordinarily used in defining a given thing. Thus, if asked what a balcony is, the definer might give the following answer: It is a platform (genus) projecting from the wall of a building and enclosed with a railing (difference).* As is evident, this definition gives the artificial form which makes the balcony a special kind of platform. This same emphasis on form is seen in the following definitions:

1. *snake:*   *a limbless reptile with an elongated, scaly body; lidless eyes; and a tapering tail**

2. *starfish:*   *an echinoderm with a hard, spiny skeleton and five or more arms arranged like the points of a star**

3. *orangutan:* *a manlike ape with shaggy, reddish-brown hair; very long arms; small ears; and a hairless face**

4. *rake:*   *a long-handled tool with teeth or prongs at one end**

5. *umbrella:* *a screen stretched over a folding radial frame**

6. *cardigan:* *a sweater that opens down the front and is usually collarless and long-sleeved**

Why is the formal cause ordinarily found in a given definition? The answer lies in the fact that form is the terminal point or realization of all the other causes. This is seen first in that form is the fulfillment of the end. Thus, in reference to the balcony, this formed platform is the realization in matter of a certain plan, goal, or end. Secondly, since the agent moves only under the guidance of the given end, all of its activity is fulfilled as this goal is realized, i.e., in the form. Thus the work of the balcony construction crew is completed in the actual, formed balcony. Finally, the whole purpose of the matter is for the form. Thus the only reason for the sturdy materials chosen is that they can sustain the projecting form of the balcony. Therefore, if one knows the type of form, one can deduce the general kind of material needed. In summary, then, form is indeed the terminal point or realization of the other three causes. It is for this reason that form is commonly given in the defining process.

As the terminal point of the other three causes, form is that cause which first strikes the onlooker. As the cause which presents itself to the learner, it is the obvious factor to be used in the defining process. Paving the way to the form, the other three causes may not be so evident to the definer. Thus a hill may be defined as a natural raised part of the earth's surface, frequently rounded and smaller than a mountain.* As is evident, this definition stresses that which is first observed by the onlooker, i.e., the shape or form of the hill. While referring to the hill's origin from nature, this explanation makes no mention of its materials or its purpose. As this example indicates, form, as the cause before the observer, is the obvious factor to be found in the definition.

In the observation of the form of a given thing, the definer sees first its outer appearance (sense qualities and form/figure) and its activities (stemming from abilities and habits). Thus, noting the appearance and behavior of the beaver, the learner is able to define it as follows: It is a rodent with soft, brown fur; chisellike teeth; and a naked, scaly tail shaped like a paddle. This rodent is equally at home on land or in the water, feeds on bark and small twigs, and builds dams of mud and twigs.* This same use of the outer form or qualities of a thing can be noted in the following definitions:

1. *apple:*   *a round, firm, fleshy, edible fruit which has small seeds and green, yellow, or red skin**

2. *bear:*   *a large, heavy mammal that eats any sort of food, walks flat on the soles of its feet, and has shaggy fur and a very short tail**

3. *beagle:* *a small hound with a smooth coat, short legs, and drooping ears**

4. *nail:*   *a tapered piece of metal, usually pointed and having a flattened head**

5. *junk:*   *a Chinese flat-bottomed ship which has battened sails and a high poop**

6. *fork:*   *an instrument of greatly varying size which has a handle at one end and two or more pointed prongs at the other**

The definer does well to use the outer form of a given thing; for this inseparable, qualifying form is an external effect of the thing's inner, substantial form or essence. Thus the human being's abilities to create a language, to make tools for himself, and to laugh at the world's incongruities are external effects of his inner rational form. These external effects, if inseparable from the thing, are excellent means of clarification in the defining process. Naturally the definer desires to know the inner nature or form. In the meantime, he makes good use of the thing's external form, i.e., of its appearance and behavior.

Although it is always true that form is the fulfillment of the end, it must also be pointed out that the formed things of this world are ordained to some end beyond themselves. Said again, the forms of this world are ordered to some further end, even beyond their operations. This final cause is the Creator of this universe. He is well named the Final Cause of all the forms of this world. He is also the First Form, of which all created forms are an image or representation. In summary, then, it is true that form is the fulfillment of the end, but it must also be noted that created forms are ordained to the final end of the universe.

As has been explained, the formal cause is the most frequent and most natural one used in definitions. In other words, the definer tends to say what the given thing is, rather than why it is, what it is made of, or who or what made it. Nevertheless, one of the other three causes may be more appropriate for the definer's purposes. This varying usage can easily be noted in connection with artificial things, of which the human being is the master. In defining such things, one can emphasize the purpose of the artifact, the need for a certain kind of material, or the type of agent required. These distinctions can be noted in the following definitions:

1. *purpose*
   door: *a movable structure for opening or closing an entrance**
   bridle: *a head harness for guiding a horse**
2. *matter*
   beret: *a flat, round cap made of felt, wool, and so forth**
   cement: *a powdered substance made of burned lime and clay**
3. *agent*
   furrow: *a narrow groove made in the earth by a plow**
   scratch: *a mark or tear made in a surface by a sharp or rough thing**

Even though the formal cause is most frequently found in definitions, the perfect definition naturally would embrace all four causes. The reason is that, just as all four factors are needed for the existence of a material thing, so all four are required for a complete understanding of this same thing. Thus the person, seeking to understand a cloud, wants to know everything about it; i.e., he wants to know what it is, out of what it is made, what brought it about, and for what purpose it exists. The following definitions are illustrations of the use of all four causes:

1. *vinegar:*   *a sour liquid with a pungent odor, which contains acetic acid and is made by fermenting dilute alcoholic liquids, such as cider, wine, and malt: it is used as a condiment and preservative.**

2. *soap:*   *a substance which with water produces suds for washing or cleaning: soaps are usually sodium or potassium salts of fatty acids, made by the action of an alkali (such as caustic soda or potash) on fats or oils.**

C. BASIC RULES FOR DEFINITIONS

Rule 1: The definition should contain both the genus and the specific difference (or inseparable accidents).

As already explained, the definition, clarifying the initial whatness, moves from the generic to the specific aspects of the thing. In other words, the definer discovers first the genus and then the identifying differences. Granted this process, the good definition should contain both of these elements. This means that the definer should be careful to find the proximate general class and also a difference which adequately distinguishes the given thing from the other members in this class. The following examples, citing three species of the same class, illustrate the need for both elements in the process of defining:

1. *tiger:*   *a fierce, flesh-eating animal of the cat family, with males averaging 9 feet and weighing 450 pounds. It has a fawn coat striped with black.*
2. *leopard:*   *a fierce, flesh-eating animal of the cat family, with males averaging 7 feet and weighing 150 pounds. It has a tawny coat with black spots mainly arranged in rosettes.*
3. *jaguar:*   *a fierce, flesh-eating animal of the cat family, with males averaging 7 feet and weighing 300 pounds. It has a yellow coat with black spots arranged in rosettes of 4 to 5 around a central spot.*

Rule 2: The definition should be clearer than the thing defined.

Since the whole purpose of the definition is to clarify the initial whatness obtained by the intellect, it should present the meaning as clearly as possible. Therefore the following aspects of language should be avoided:

1. strange, difficult, or excessively technical words
2. figurative or metaphorical expressions
3. equivocal usage of words
4. repetition of the word signifying the thing defined

These aspects of language to be avoided are illustrated in the following examples:

1. *lantern:*   *a pellucid receptacle for a luminous substance*
2. *rose:*   *a flower with the breath of love upon it*
3. *match:*   *an arrangement which is struck between two parties*
4. *ruler:*   *the person who rules a nation*

Rule 3: The definition and the thing defined should be equivalent to each other.

Since the definition is to give a clear picture of the thing defined, it should also express as completely as possible what the thing is. In other words, the definition should not present only half of the whatness of the thing. Rather the definition, clarifying the whatness, should give a complete picture of the given object. If such is the case, the definition and the thing defined will be equivalent. As equivalent, these two elements can be interchanged or are convertible. Thus the complete definition of the human being is rational animal. As such, it is an equivalent expression and can be interchanged with the concept, human being.

An awareness of this rule will enable the definer easily to detect inadequate definitions. The following are examples of such inadequacy:

1. *table:*   *a piece of furniture with a horizontal top*
2. *desk:*   *a piece of furniture with a horizontal top*
3. *chair:*   *a piece of furniture having a back*
4. *rocker:*   *a piece of furniture having a back*

D. UNDEFINED TERMS

Having completed the treatment of the definition's components, its procedures, and its rules, this text must face the position that every definition is finally resolved into some opening undefined term. Thus it is said that every definition in modern mathematics rests ultimately on some basic undefined terms, such as *point* and *line*. Then this position, emphasizing that anything undefined certainly cannot be known, concludes that definitions rest ultimately on the unknown. In other words, the conclusion of the undefined-term position is that the beginnings of knowledge are unknown. A syllogistic outline of this reasoning is as follows:

minor premise	The source of all definitions--------------- is an undefined term.
major premise	But whatever is undefined ---------------- is unknown.
conclusion	∴ The source of all definitions ----------- is unknown.

What are the intellectual consequences which easily follow from such a conclusion? First, the learner, beginning with undefined terms, starts from a meaningless beginning and builds all his knowledge on such a foundation. This means that the learner from beginning to end has no sound knowledge, i.e., no truth nor certitude. Then, with no knowledge of the real world, he can easily retreat into some imaginary or mental world. Finally the learner may hold that neither his knowledge nor his actions need correspond to anything real. In a word, the undefined-term position attempts to establish that there is no objective knowledge and no need to be accountable to the limitations of the real world.

As the succeeding paragraphs will show, the above conclusion and its intellectual consequences are unsound. Nevertheless, the minor premise is in full accord with the way that the human mind operates. This premise states that the source of all definitions is an undefined term. This position concerning the base of all definitions is also expressed in the following quotation: "We must use some terms without definitions, while all other terms may be defined ultimately in terms of these *undefined terms.* That is, all our definitions must involve some terms which are taken without definition" (Moses Richardson, *Fundamentals of Mathematics*, 3d ed. [New York: The Macmillan Company, 1966], p. 25).

What is the reason that the most basic terms, which are the source of all definitions, are undefinable? The reason for such a situation is simple. Every definition demands a genus (or general class) and specific difference. But the most basic terms cannot be classified in any broader, more general class, for they have the broadest extension. Thus the word *being* is the most general term applicable to any material thing. There is no more general term to stand as the genus for being; for, whatever it is, it would fall in the class of being. As having the greatest extension, the most basic terms cannot be classified in any more general class and are properly undefinable. Clear examples of such terms are those designating substance and the nine accidents, which are the ten ultimate genera of material things.

Are these most basic terms, properly undefinable, therefore unknowable? No, for they designate the most obvious things. Thus *being* or *thing* is one of the most commonly used words in the English language. As meaning something which exists, *thing* is most basic and obvious. Any person can easily point out an example of *thing*, for it might be anything. If then these basic terms are so obvious that they have no proper definitions, how is their meaning delineated? In addition to pointing out examples of them, the definer, having no more general class, will simply describe such basic terms by their effects. Thus *good* is described as that which all things desire. In summary, then, the most basic terms, although lacking proper definitions, are most obvious and can be described by their effects.

As noted in the two preceding paragraphs, the most basic terms are undefined. This presence of undefined terms has led some thinkers to assume that whatever is undefined (together with whatever follows) is unknown. This assumption is clearly stated in the following quotation: "Bertrand Russell [*International Monthly*, Vol. 4, 1901, p. 84] once described mathematics as 'the subject in which we never know what we are talking about nor whether what we are saying is true.' Many students heartily agree with this, in a mood of personal confession. But it is correct literally. We never know what we are talking about since all our definitions rest ultimately on some undefined terms; we never know whether what we are saying is true because all our proofs rest ultimately on some meaningless un-proved statements or assumptions involving these undefined terms. Moreover, this situation must come about if you take any subject and try to give it a logical structure" (ibid., p. 26).

Is it true that whatever is undefined is unknown? This assumption cannot stand, for it completely ignores a basic step in the defining process. This step is the intellect's grasp from the sensible singular of the whatness or initial meaning of a given thing. This whatness is the basic intellectual knowledge from which the refinement called definition proceeds. As already explained, the defining process moves through the following stages:

1. The senses experience a given thing, such as a daisy.
2. The intellect grasps the whatness or initial meaning of the daisy. (The learner proves that he knows what a daisy is by the fact that he can point to others of the same kind.)
3. This initial knowledge, although grasped firmly, is very obscure, except in the case of simple, obvious things.
4. Moving from the generic to the specific, the learner refines this initial meaning into a definition, which gives both the genus and specific difference.
5. The following should be noted about the definition: (a) It is only the clarification of the initial knowledge grasped by the intellect. (b) As the clarification of the basic whatness, the definition always presupposes this first basic understanding.

If the learner recognizes the above steps in the defining process, he cannot hold that whatever is undefined is unknown. The reason is that there is a step in intellectual knowledge which precedes all definition and which can exist without definition's refining process. This step is the intellect's initial grasp of the thing's whatness. This knowledge is then followed by the refinement called definition. The relationship here is between an initial grasp and a subsequent refinement, between the intellectual kernel and its development.

To clarify this relationship, an analogy might be made with a rosebud and its blossoming. While both are needed for complete growth, the rosebud is the core and can exist alone. On the contrary, there can be no blossoming without the initial bud. The lack of the full-blown flower, however, does not simultaneously indicate the absence of a bud. The cause precedes the effect. In like manner, the core of initial knowledge can stand alone. On the contrary, there can be no clarification or definition without this initial core of meaning. Finally, contrary to the undefined-term position, the lack of a definition does not indicate the absence of all meaning. Rather the core of initial knowledge always precedes the definition and can exist without this clarifying element.

Granted the above relationship between the initial whatness and its refinement, one can see that the absence of definition does not cancel all meaning. Rather the initial core of meaning can always be present, even if the precise definition is never found. Thus the unlettered people of a given primitive tribe may have no definitions nor dictionaries, but they know what they mean when they converse together. Therefore it is false that the absence of definition cancels all meaning. In other words, it cannot be held that whatever is undefined is unknown. In addition, it cannot be assumed that the presence of undefined terms at the beginning of a subject leads to only the unknown.

E. SUMMARY

With this explanation about undefined terms, this text completes its logical treatment of the first act of the mind, simple apprehension. The primary object of the mind's simple apprehension is the initial whatness or essence of a material thing, an object derived from sensible experience. The whole purpose of simple apprehension, from the logical viewpoint, is the actual construction of a good definition from this initial whatness. To achieve this purpose the logician needs the following tools:

1. words and concepts, which are the signs used in definition
2. the ten categories, which are the ultimate predicates found in definition
3. the five predicables, which are the modes used in defining
4. the methods of division and composition, which proceed inductively
5. a knowledge of the four causes, which are the content of definition

As the logician works toward a good definition, he always proceeds from the generic to the specific, from the vague to the distinct. To achieve this good definition, the logician should heed the following rules:

1. The definition should contain both the genus and specific difference (or inseparable accidents).
2. The definition should be clearer than the thing defined.
3. The definition should be equivalent to the thing defined.

The following chart, while indicating the content of the six preceding chapters, clarifies the relationship existing among the various logical tools needed for a good definition:

THE FIRST ACT OF THE MIND: SIMPLE APPREHENSION

ch. 2
from sensible singular --------- to whatness or nature of simple realities

ch. 6
by inductive process using division or composition methods
first dimly --------- then clearly
initial, unitary concept --------- subsequent, divided concept

DEFINITION: 1. genus
2. specific difference

EXAMPLE
individual bats --------- A bat:
species --------- is a mouselike flying mammal with a furry body and membranous wings.*

genus --------- mammal
difference (inseparable accidents) --------- mouselike, flying, furry, membranous

substance (body, wings)
form
ability
sense quality
sense quality
} qualities → **CATEGORIES**

mammal → **FORMAL CAUSE**
membranous

PREDICABLES

INTERNAL AND EXTERNAL SIGNS OF ABOVE: CONCEPTS AND WORDS

ch. 3   ch. 5   ch. 7   ch. 4

1. Why is definition a statement of the causes of a thing?
2. Give the general definition of cause. Define each of the four causes. Give an original example which illustrates each of these causes. Distinguish the formal cause from the actual material thing.
3. List the intrinsic and extrinsic causes.
4. What is the causal hierarchy existing among the four causes? Explain why this hierarchy is so placed.
5. Show that form is the fulfillment of the end.
6. Distinguish between the end of production and the end of the product.
7. Using the other three causes, show why the formal cause is ordinarily found in a given definition.
8. Which cause is seen first by the observer? In the observation of this cause, what aspect of it is first known? Why is this aspect helpful to the definer?
9. Clarify how form is the fulfillment of the end, and yet is ordained to an end.
10. When may the other three causes be found in a given definition?
11. Why does the perfect definition include all four causes?
12. State the three rules for definitions. For each of these rules, give a procedure which aids its implementation.
13. Outline the argument of the undefined-term position concerning the beginnings of knowledge. What intellectual consequences follow from such argumentation?
14. Why must the source of all definitions be an undefined term? What are the ten kinds of most basic terms? How are these basic terms made known?
15. Some thinkers hold that whatever is undefined is unknown. What step in the defining process do these thinkers ignore? List the various stages of the defining process.
16. Give an analogy showing that the core of initial knowledge can exist without the definition.
17. In relation to simple apprehension, state the primary object, the chief purpose, the logical tools, and the basic intellectual movement.

SECOND ACT OF THE MIND: JUDGMENT

CHAPTER 8

THE PROPOSITION: THE RESULT OF JUDGMENT

A. Judgment: its definition and elements
B. Characteristics of the proposition
C. Types of propositions

As noted in the first chapter of this text, the human intellect has three operations: simple apprehension, judgment, and reasoning. Thus the intellect first grasps the whatness of the various simple material realities, such as a giraffe, a scorpion, water, fire, coolness, and awkwardness. Then it judges whether or not the concepts of these various simple realities belong together. In other words, the mind judges if it should combine or divide its ideas of these different objects. It might, for example, assert or propose the following:

1. *The giraffe is awkward.*
2. *The scorpion is not a giraffe.*
3. *The water is cool.*
4. *Fire is not water.*

Finally, the intellect reasons to a valid conclusion as a result of seeing the connection between certain judgments. For example, building on its acts of apprehension and judgment, the intellect moves on to reach the following conclusion:

Whatever is an excellent cooling agent will help put out fires.

Water is an excellent cooling agent.

∴ Water will help put out fires.

As the above examples indicate, the three acts of the human intellect work harmoniously together, building slowly but surely the vast edifice of the arts and sciences. From its initial apprehension of the whatness of sensible things, the mind is able to move forward, now judging whether to combine or divide its concepts of simple realities. Then, having in hand the judgments gained, the mind climaxes its work by reasoning carefully to conclusions which are known only through the appropriate apprehensions and judgments on which they are built. The human intellect does not reach the fullness of its knowledge in one operation. Rather it has three acts which, working together, form a strong chain enabling the human being to lay hold of the causes of things.

A. JUDGMENT: ITS DEFINITION AND ELEMENTS

The human being makes many judgments daily about his surroundings and circumstances. Thus he may assert or declare such statements as the following:

1. *The weather is depressing.*
2. *The potatoes are cold.*
3. *The children are not home.*
4. *The traffic is not moving.*

Each of the above assertions is the result of the mind's operation of judgment. This second act of the mind is defined as follows: It is a mental process which obtains the proposition by combining or dividing the concepts of simple realities. This proposition, if conformed to the real world, is pronounced true. If not, it is pronounced false. Possible variations in this proposition may be illustrated as follows:

1. *The ice is slippery.*   *(a combination by affirming which is true)*
2. *The turtle is fast.*   *(a combination by affirming which is false)*
3. *The gold is not tarnished.*   *(a division by denying which is true)*
4. *The diamond is not useful.*   *(a division by denying which is false)*

As the above definition and examples already indicate, the basic elements of the proposition resulting from the judgmental process are twofold:

1. The simple reality which now stands as the subject
2. The simple reality which is predicated of this subject

Of these elements, the subject functions as the foundation in the proposition. In fact, the etymological meaning of *subject* is that which is placed or put under. Of what entity is the subject the foundation? It is the underlying element for the predicate which is asserted of it. Just as the basement stands as the foundation for a house, so the subject is the base for the various things said of it. Thus the subject *turtle* stands as the base for various predicates, such as *slow*, *small*, and *clumsy*.

The predicate, the second element of the proposition, is that which is asserted or said about the subject. In other words, the predicate is that reality which is asserted to inhere in the subject as in a base. Thus *swift* may be predicated of the tiger. As is evident, this predicate is a quality which inheres in the tiger as in a base. Whatever the predicate may be, it can finally be classified under one of the ten categories or predicaments. As the ten basic kinds of simple material realities, these categories can function as predicates. For this reason their second name, the ten predicaments, is well taken. The following propositions illustrate not only that the predicate inheres in the subject as in a base but also that the predicates fall under the ten categories:

1. *The locust is a grasshopper.*   *(substance)*
2. *The locust is two inches long.*   *(quantity)*
3. *The rattlesnake is dangerous.*   *(quality)*
4. *The boa constrictor is enormous.*   *(relation)*

Among the various predicates said of a subject, the following distinction can be found:

1. Some predicates are a sign both of the combination of the subject and predicate and of the time of this combination.
   e.g.: William walked.
2. Some predicates indicate neither of the above signs.
   e.g., William----------walking
   In this case, one still needs a way to learn if *walking* is combined with *William* and when it is done.

Since some predicates indicate neither the combination nor its time, the copula or linking verb serves this necessary function in such cases. This verb is expressed by the various forms of *to be*. Thus *is* stands as the copula in the following sentence: *The stork is eating.*

The term *copula* was originally a Latin word meaning a band or link. What is its purpose in the proposition? The copula serves as a time-bearing link for the predicates signifying neither of these elements. This purpose is evident in the following propositions:

1. *William is walking.*
2. *William was walking.*
3. *William has been walking.*

In summary, then, the copula is a time-bearing link between the subject and predicate for those propositions requiring such a sign.

For the sake of clarity it may sometimes be necessary to change the predicate from the noncopula to the copula form. Illustrations of this change are as follows:

1. *The policeman dragged the pond.*
   The policeman is one who dragged the pond.
2. *The monkey climbed up the tree.*
   The monkey is one which climbed up the tree.

It should also be noted that the various forms of *to be* indicate only a time-bearing linkage in the above usage. They do not carry the meaning of existence. Like all words, it is possible for *to be* to have different or equivocal meanings. These differing meanings can easily be noted in the following examples:

1. *The ostrich feather is valuable.*   *(linkage)*
2. *You can believe me or not! I tell you that ghosts are.*   *(existence)*

In addition to the copula for some predicates, a negative sign is always needed to indicate that the subject and predicate are divided, rather than combined. Ordinarily *not* or its equivalent serves this function. This use of negative signs is illustrated in the following propositions:

1. *Some hyenas are not silent.*
2. *Not every hyena is silent.*
3. *No hyena is silent.*

B. CHARACTERISTICS OF THE PROPOSITION

As the result of the mind's act of judgment, the logical proposition is obtained. As noted above, its elements are the subject and the predicate. Strictly speaking, this logical proposition is called a categorical proposition. Its grammatical counterpart is the declarative sentence. This categorical proposition is defined as a composite statement which is judged true or false if it conforms or does not conform to reality. Therefore this proposition has the following characteristics:

1. It is an actual affirmation or denial.
2. It is a simple proposition with only one subject and one predicate.
3. It can be judged as true or false.

This list of characteristics states more plainly what is implied in the definition of the proposition. As a complex statement which can be judged true or false, it automatically has the two qualities not mentioned in the definition. Thus the proposition must actually assert or deny some predicate of some subject. Next it must stay with the point at hand; i.e., it must not add extra subjects or predicates. Then, and only then, can the proposition be judged true or false. Therefore the concise summary or definition of the proposition is that it is a complex statement which is judged true or false if it conforms or does not conform to reality. Nevertheless the other qualities are implicit in this definition.

For a better understanding of the proposition, all three characteristics will now be treated.

1. AN ACTUAL AFFIRMATION OR DENIAL

To be a categorical proposition, the combination or division must actually affirm or deny something. This requirement finds grammatical expression only in the declarative sentence which affirms or denies that a subject and predicate belong together. The following declarative sentences illustrate this fact: (1) *The porcupine is clumsy.* (2) *The jaguar is not timid.*

Now there are several kinds of complex expressions which have no actual affirmation or denial. Automatically, such complexities cannot stand as grammatical expressions for the categorical proposition. It is true that this proposition is a composite statement, but it is also one which actually affirms or denies. The basic types of complex expressions with no actual affirmation or denial are as follows:

1. *The Phrase*
   --*eating the apple*
   --*a large, red tomato*
2. *The Clause*
   --*which cost five dollars*
   --*who fell down the stairs*
3. *The Nondeclarative Sentences*
   --*My dear, please cook the dinner.*   *(imperative sentence)*
   --*Is the dinner cooked?*   *(interrogative sentence)*
   --*What a well-cooked dinner this is!*   *(exclamatory sentence)*

The first of the above complex expressions, the phrase, does indeed combine several simple realities. Nevertheless it has no actual affirmation or denial. The second of the above types, the clause, does have a subject and predicate. These elements, however, are not intended to express a complete thought which can stand alone or be independent. As such, their affirmation or denial is not actually independent. Rather it is conditioned by the expression on which it depends or to which it is connected.

Even the third type of complex expressions, the nondeclarative sentences, does not actually affirm or deny the combination or division of simple realities. Rather they request, inquire after, or exclaim about such a combination or division. They do not express an actual state of affairs, but rather conditions which lead up to it. Thus the imperative sentence requests a state which does not yet exist; the interrogation asks if the situation has happened. Finally, the exclamation expresses one's feelings about the matter, rather than the actual state of affairs.

Granted the above explanation, one can see that the categorical proposition can never be given grammatical expression in the phrase, clause, or nondeclarative sentences. Rather this proposition is expressed only in the declarative sentence which actually affirms or denies some predicate of some subject. If the proposition is an affirmation or denial, it cannot be expressed by a complexity which gives only a hint of what is needed. It must be given expression by a grammatical entity which actually declares such a state.

2. A SIMPLE PROPOSITION

In addition to being an actual affirmation or denial, the categorical proposition must be simple. In other words, the proposition must have only one predicate said of one subject. The reason for this ruling is evident. As a complex expression actually affirming or denying, the proposition can be judged true or false. If one introduces several predicates or subjects, the possibility of making a straightforward judgment becomes impossible unless the proposition is pared down to one predicate of one subject. This is easily seen in the following dialogue:

A. *The fox is cunning, handsome, and vegetarian.*
B. *That is false.*
A. *Do you mean that the fox is not cunning?*
B. *No, I mean that the fox is not vegetarian.*
A. *Is it also false that the fox is handsome?*
B. *No, that is true.*
A. *Now I'm confused. Should we start over and say one thing at a time about the fox?*
B. *That might help. Then we will know what point we have in mind.*

As the above dialogue indicates, only a simple proposition can be judged easily and accurately as true or false.

The ruling that the proposition must have only one subject and one predicate can be rephrased as follows: one thing of one thing. To what does this limitation refer? This rule applies only to the simple reality, not to the number of words needed to express it. In addition, all essentially related attributes of one reality are counted as one. The reason is that these attributes are all inseparable qualities of the one thing. If one of these qualities is present, the others are also found in it. In listing such attributes, one must be careful that there is no overlapping. The following propositions illustrate the use or misuse of the rule requiring one thing of one thing:

1. *The human being is a rational animal.*   *(one S--one P)*
2. *The maple tree is abundant.*   *(one S--one P)*
3. *The rattlesnake is a scaly, limbless reptile.*   *(one S--one P)*
4. *The octopus is extremely dangerous.*   *(one S--two P)*
5. *The muskrat is huge and old.*   *(one S--two P)*
6. *Jim and Joe are obedient.*   *(two S--one P)*

3. THE PROPOSITION: TRUE OR FALSE

The categorical proposition, actually affirming or denying one predicate of one subject, can be pronounced true or false. This evaluation of the proposition is noted in the following examples:

1. *The swan is graceful.*   *(true)*
2. *The beaver is not valuable.*   *(false)*

What does the evaluator mean when he says that one of the above propositions is true, while the other one is false? Plainly he means that the statements do or do not correspond to the way things are in the real world. Thus he knows that the proposition about swans is true only if the actual swans are really graceful. This realization about truth and falsity is well summarized in the basic definition of truth. It is defined as the conformity or correspondence between the thing and the intellect. As the above examples indicate, truth exists when there is an equation between the external reality and the mind's judgment about it. Put very simply, if the actual coffee is hot, one can say that such a fact is true.

Now it is evident that all categorical propositions can be pronounced true or false. One's daily experience confirms this fact. Thus, if one says that the weather is fine, he must be prepared to have his listener look up at the sky and agree or disagree. Any outright judgment that an individual might make is subject to a comparison with the actual state of things and the immediate pronouncement, true or false. The following examples illustrate this point:

1. *The traveling is risky.*   *Yes, it is.*
2. *The bedroom is cold.*   *No, it's not.*

As these examples indicate, the categorical proposition has all the elements for truth (or falsity). These elements, as the preceding definition states, are three: (1) external reality, (2) the judgment of the intellect about such reality, (3) the conformity (or nonconformity) between the thing and the intellect. Since the categorical proposition is a judgment either corresponding or not to reality, it can indeed be pronounced true or false.

As noted above, truth is defined as the conformity between the intellect and the thing. Thus the intellect holding that the house is cold can be pronounced true only if this judgment conforms to the actual house. In brief, truth consists in the equation between the intellect and the thing. If the intellect conforms to the actual state of things, it has truth. If it fails in such correspondence, it is pronounced false.

Granted that truth is the conformity between the intellect and the thing, this power will know truth only when it knows such conformity. Thus the intellect, perceiving the correspondence between its judgment about the cold house and the actual house, knows the truth about this given topic. Now the intellect's consciousness of its conformity occurs in its second act of judgment, rather than in its first act of simple apprehension. Why is this power conscious of its correspondence with the real world through its judgment, rather than in its initial grasp of the whatness of a material thing?

To answer the above question, one must note two facts. First, both the human senses and intellect, having the likeness of the known thing, are thus pronounced true or conformed to the real object. Thus the human intellect's idea of a dog is true as it conforms to real individual dogs. Second, while the senses are not aware of such conformity with reality, the intellect is conscious of it. Thus this power is aware that its statement *Dolphins are playful* is in accord with a characteristic of real dolphins. As this example indicates, the human intellect is conscious that it is true or conformed with the real world.

Now the intellect's awareness of its conformity does not occur in its initial grasp of the likenesses of simple realities. The work of this first operation is to grasp these various likenesses. Its task is not to reflect upon them and combine or separate them. That is the work of judgment. The stages of this second operation, leading to the intellect's awareness of its conformity, are as follows:

1. In its second work of judgment, the intellect, reflecting upon the concepts grasped in its first act, combines or divides them as the occasion demands. For example, reflecting upon its concepts of dolphins and playfulness, the intellect combines these two ideas. This means that it states or judges that dolphins are playful.
2. Having combined or divided its concepts, the judging intellect now compares its combination or division with the real world. Thus the proposition *Dolphins are playful* is compared with a characteristic of real dolphins.
3. If its combination or division is perceived as conformed to the combination or division in reality, the intellect now knows the truth about a given topic. Since truth is defined as the conformity between the intellect and the thing, one can see that this power, knowing such conformity, knows truth. Thus the intellect, perceiving the correspondence between its proposition *Dolphins are playful* and an attribute of real dolphins, knows the truth about them.

As the above explanation reveals, the human intellect knows truth in its second act of judgment, rather than in its first act of simple apprehension. This first operation, through which the intellect grasps the whatness of any material thing, is naturally correct or conformed with reality. In other words, simple apprehension is always true or never deceived when it obtains its proper object. Just as the eye naturally sees color, so the intellect naturally knows the thing's whatness.

Accidentally, however, the act of simple apprehension can lead to falsity or error. This can occur if this act makes an incorrect combination or division as it refines the initial, unitary concept into the subsequent, two-part definition. Thus one might define a computer as a machine which is able to think. In addition, this first act of the mind results in error if one combines a given definition with the wrong thing. Thus one might maintain that the definition of a porcupine (a rodent with sharp quills) belongs to the beaver. (Since the combinations or divisions made as the one species is refined into its two-part definition can lead accidentally to truth or falsity, the propositions in this text may concern either two different realities or the defining parts of one reality).

The fact that the intellect knows truth or falsity primarily in the act of judgment, rather than in the act of simple apprehension, is easily illustrated from daily experience. The following dialogue points out that the simple concept is not judged as true or false. Rather it is the combination or division of such simple concepts. Even there, the focus of the judgment is on the combination or division, not on the subjects or predicates being combined or divided.

A. *(looking at the blue sky)   green*   *(simple concept)*
B. *That is false.*
A. *I did not say anything about anything. I was just*   *(simple apprehension)*
   thinking. In fact, I was thinking about grass.
B. *Well, now that we're talking about grass, what*
   can you tell me about it?
A. *Let me see. I haven't reflected on it much.*   *(judgment)*
   Oh, I know. The grass is wet. Will that do?   *(proposition)*
B. *Indeed. At least I can say that it is true.*   *(truth)*
A. *What do you mean? Are you referring to grass*   *(subject, predicate)*
   or wet?
B. *Of course not! I mean that it is true that*   *(combination)*
   the grass is wet.

As the above dialogue illustrates, truth or falsity is a property, not of isolated concepts, but of the combination or division of these concepts in the act of judgment. When such propositions conform to reality, they can be pronounced true. If they do not conform, these propositions have the property of falsity. In summary, it is primarily the proposition, an actual combination or division of simple concepts, which is matched against the real world and thus pronounced true or false.

At this point the treatment of the three characteristics of the proposition has been completed. As the above treatment explained, the categorical proposition must be an actual affirmation or denial in which one predicate is said of one subject. Such a proposition can be pronounced true or false. In other words, it has the property of truth or falsity. Such a proposition is very valuable to the logician, for it aids him in his search for scientific or certain knowledge.

C. TYPES OF PROPOSITIONS

There are four basic types of propositions. In order to know what they are, it is necessary first to divide the proposition in the following two ways:

1. according to its form, quality, or kind
2. according to its matter, quantity, or extension of the subject

Each of these divisions will be given a brief explanation; then the four basic types of propositions will be listed.

1. THE QUALITY: AFFIRMATIVE OR NEGATIVE

If one will divide the proposition according to its form, quality, or kind, one will have the two basic kinds of assertions possible in the act of judgment. These assertions are that the thing either is or is not. Therefore the two kinds of propositions, qualitatively speaking, are as follows:

1. *affirmative:*   *This plant is watered.*
2. *negative:*   *This plant is not watered.*

It should be noted that it is always the main verb (or the copula) with or without its negative element which determines the quality of the proposition. If there are any clauses in a given proposition, their affirmation or denial does not constitute the quality of the entire proposition. The use of the main verb (or the copula) as the determiner of quality is illustrated as follows:

1. *Every horse is an animal.*   (affirmative)
2. *No panther is vegetarian.*   (negative)
3. *All boys who are not finished are detained.* (affirmative)
4. *James did not like the ice cream.*   (negative)

In addition, a negative subject or predicate in no way indicates that the proposition itself is negative. Only the main verb (or the copula) and its negative element perform this function. The need to be careful concerning the placement of negatives is illustrated in the following examples:

1. *All workers who are not interested are non-partisan.* (affirmative)
2. *The non-profiteers are able to make trouble.*   (affirmative)
3. *The non-unionists are non-acceptable.*   (affirmative)

79

2. THE QUANTITY: UNIVERSAL OR PARTICULAR

The division of the proposition according to its quantity is a division based on the extension of its subject. As chapter three explained, every idea or concept is universal or applicable to many individuals or members. Thus the concept of robin is applicable to every individual robin. As such, the concept of robin is universal.

Now it is possible to take a given idea or concept in its full extent or universality. It is also possible to consider a concept in less than its full extension. The following phrases indicate this distinction.

1. *universal:*   *every apple, every rose, every tiger*
2. *particular:*   *some apples, some roses, some tigers*

As noted above, the quantitative division of the proposition is according to the extension or universality of its subject. If the subject is taken in its full extent, the proposition is classified as universal. In the following examples of universal propositions, the student should note that *every* and *no* are the terms used to indicate strict logical universality:

1. *Every eagle is powerful.*
2. *No eagle is weak.*
3. *Every beaver is sharp-toothed.*
4. *No beaver is toothless.*

If the subject is taken in less than its full extent, the proposition is classified as particular. In the following examples of particular propositions, the student should note that the meaning of *not every* is that some are missing. Therefore *not every* always designates a particular proposition. This meaning prevails even if the two terms are separated in a given proposition.

1. *Some children are tired.*
2. *Some apples are rotten.*
3. *Some books are not open.*
4. *Not every book is open.*   *(Some books are not open.)*
5. *Every book is not open.*   *(Not every book is open.)*

If the subject is a specific individual falling under the universal concept, then the proposition is called singular. It is true that this type belongs to the general division of particular propositions. Nevertheless it is still designated as singular. Note the following examples of singular propositions:

1. *Mary is tall.*
2. *This man is not coming.*
3. *That book is expensive.*

Finally, if the extension of the subject is not actually expressed, the proposition is classified as indefinite. Since every subject is taken either in its full extent or in less than its full extent, such an indefinite subject must truly be universal or particular. Since this extension is not expressed, the proposition is classified as indefinite. Its real meaning must be decided from the context. Examples of indefinite propositions follow:

1. *Women are fickle.*
2. *Politicians cannot be trusted.*
3. *Tigers are dangerous.*

In summary, the kinds of propositions, quantitatively speaking, are as follows: universal, particular, singular, and indefinite.

3. TYPES OF PROPOSITIONS

The four types of propositions are derived from the combination of the above divisions. In other words, they are the result of the combination of affirmative and negative with universal and particular. These combinations are named A, I, E, and O from the first two vowels in *affirmo* ("I affirm") and the two vowels in *nego* ("I deny"). The following are examples of these types of propositions:

1. *Every bird is beautiful.*   *universal affirmative*   *(A)*
2. *Some bird is beautiful.*   *particular affirmative*   *(I)*
3. *No bird is beautiful.*   *universal negative*   *(E)*
4. *Some bird is not beautiful.*   *particular negative*   *(O)*

As can be readily noted, the above four types of propositions utilize only two kinds under the quantitative division of the proposition, i.e., the universal and particular. Neither the singular nor the indefinite is utilized. The reasons for such reduction are as follows:

1. The singular proposition is a specific case belonging in the general category of particular propositions. Since it is a single case, it cannot be the whole or universal. Rather it belongs with the kind of proposition in which the subject is taken in less than its full extent, i.e., with the particular proposition.

2. The indefinite proposition is either universal or particular depending on the context in which it is used.

Since the four types of propositions utilize only the universal and particular divisions of the proposition, the following guidelines for the logical exercises should be observed:

1. The singular propositions should be classified as either particular affirmative or negative.

2. In many cases the indefinite propositions are general statements on a given topic. The following statement is a case in point: *Pets are good company*. Such propositions, reflecting a general opinion, should be classed as universal. This guideline can be followed in the logical exercises, unless a clearly particular statement is given.

4. SUMMARY

Important points concerning the qualitative and quantitative divisions of the proposition, as well as the four types flowing from such division, are summarized as follows:

1. The Quality of the Proposition
It is determined by the main verb, not by a negative subject, predicate, or clause.

2. <u>The Quantity of the Proposition</u>
   a. universal proposition: formed only by *every* and *no*
   b. particular proposition:
      (affirmative) *Some............... are*
      (negative) *Some............... are not*
      Not every......... is
      Not all............. are
      Every............... is not
      All.................... are not
   c. singular proposition: placed under the particular
   d. indefinite proposition: determined from context; general opinions, taken as universal

3. <u>Four Types of Propositions</u>
   A------- universal affirmative
   I-------- particular affirmative
   E------- universal negative
   O------- particular negative

STUDY QUESTIONS   **CHAPTER 8**

1. Define judgment.
2. List the basic elements of the proposition. What is the purpose of the subject? What is the work of the predicate?
3. List a distinction found in predicates in relation to the verbal element.
4. What is the purpose of the copula? What is another meaning of *to be*?
5. Define the proposition. What are three of its characteristics?
6. What grammatical expression is an actual affirmation or denial? List the kinds of complex expressions with no affirmation or denial. Show that these expressions do not affirm or deny.
7. Why must the categorical proposition be simple? If the proposition is one thing said of one thing, to what does this limitation refer?
8. Define truth. What essential knowledge must the mind possess when it knows the truth?
9. State the sequence of truths which explains why the mind knows truth in its act of judgment, rather than in its act of apprehension.
10. Simple apprehension is naturally conformed to reality. Nevertheless, list two ways in which this act is accidentally deceived.
11. According to quality, what are the two kinds of propositions?
12. According to quantity, list the four kinds of propositions. Explain why each of these propositions is so classified.
13. What are the four types of propositions? From what combination are they derived? What is the origin of their names?
14. How do singular and indefinite propositions fit under these four types of propositions?

CHAPTER 9

CONVERSION AND OBVERSION OF PROPOSITIONS

A. Conversion
   1. The extension of the terms
   2. The rules for conversion
B. Obversion
C. Summary

In the preceding chapter the student learned that the judging intellect combines or divides the concepts of simple realities through an act of affirmation or denial. Thus the intellect judges that the weather is or is not fine. The result of this judgmental process is the categorical proposition with its property of truth or falsity. Such propositions, through a combination of their quality and quantity, can be classified as follows:

1. *Every sparrow is hungry.*	*universal affirmative*	*(A)*
2. *Some sparrows are hungry.*	*particular affirmative*	*(I)*
3. *No sparrow is hungry.*	*universal negative*	*(E)*
4. *Some sparrows are not hungry.*	*particular negative*	*(O)*

Now it is possible to take these four types of propositions and change them in certain ways without losing their basic truth or falsity. Two of the processes used for this end are conversion and obversion. These two operations are defined as follows:

1. <u>Conversion</u>
   the process of reversing the subject and predicate, while retaining the same quality, in order to have the appropriate derived truth
   e.g.: No soldiers are vaccinated.
   No vaccinated ones are soldiers.

2. <u>Obversion</u>
   the process of reversing the quality of the proposition, while retaining the same subject and predicate, in order to have the equivalent truth
   e.g.: No soldiers are vaccinated.
   Every soldier is non-vaccinated.

Why does the student of logic need to know these processes? The most obvious reason is that the average human being is constantly using conversion and often needs obversion. The following dialogue illustrates the frequent use of conversion:

A. *Do you see how quiet he is? He must be thinking again.*	*(Every quiet person is a thinker.)*
B. *What do you mean? You cannot say that every quiet person is a thinker just because every thinker is a quiet person. Haven't you learned the rules of conversion?*	*(Every thinker is a quiet person.)*

The purpose of this chapter is to explain the rules of conversion and obversion, not primarily because of the mechanical steps involved, but because of the advance in truth that these processes facilitate.

A. CONVERSION

As noted above, conversion is the process of reversing the subject and predicate, while retaining the same quality, in order to have the appropriate derived truth. Before the rules for conversion can be given, it is necessary to treat the extension of the proposition's terms. The reason is simple. Since the subject and predicate are reversed, it is necessary to understand these elements carefully before changing them in any way.

1. THE EXTENSION OF THE TERMS

The extension of the subject of the proposition was treated in the last chapter. As noted there, the extension of the subject was one basis for the classification of the proposition. These propositions, taken from the appropriate extension of the subject, were classified as follows:

1. *Every eagle is powerful.*   *(universal)*
   No eagle is weak.   *(universal)*
2. *Some children are tired.*   *(particular)*
   Some children are not tired.   *(particular)*
3. *Mary is tall.*   *(singular)*
   This man is not coming.   *(singular)*
4. *Women are fickle.*   *(indefinite)*
   Politicians cannot be trusted.   *(indefinite)*

Whenever the extension of just the subject or predicate of the proposition is considered, the logician speaks of such extension as distributed or undistributed. These terms are distributed if they stand for every individual under them. Thus *every eagle* is a distributed subject. These terms are undistributed if they stand for only some of the individuals under them. Thus *some children* is an undistributed subject.

Granted the above meaning of *distributed* and *undistributed*, the logician classifies the subjects of the various kinds of propositions, quantitatively speaking, as follows:

1. the subject of a universal proposition   (distributed)
2. the subject of a particular proposition   (undistributed)
3. the subject of a singular proposition
   (which falls under the particular proposition)   (undistributed)
4. the subject of an indefinite proposition
   (when taken in a universal sense)   (distributed)

In summary, the rules for the extension of the subjects of propositions are as follows:

1. Every universal proposition has a distributed subject.
2. Every particular proposition has an undistributed subject.

What is the extension or distribution of the predicate in the four types of propositions? This distribution is summarized in the following rules:

1. Every negative proposition has a distributed predicate.
   e.g.: No apples are sweet.
           Some apples are not sweet.

2. Every affirmative proposition has an undistributed predicate.
   e.g.: Every apple is sweet.
          Some apples are sweet.

In order to understand the above rules, one needs an explanation. The general guideline throughout the explanation will be the predicate's meaning intended by the proposition. When the predicate is separated from the subject in a negative proposition, what meaning is intended? Plainly it is that the subject (whether taken in its full extent or not) is separated from the predicate in the latter's full extent. This meaning can be seen in the following examples:

1. *Some men are not handsome.*
   (Some men are none of the handsome things.)
2. *Some horses are not swift.*
   (Some horses are none of the swift things.)
3. *No beaver is dangerous.*
   (No one of the beavers is any of the dangerous things.)

As the above propositions illustrate, the meaning of the predicate in a negative proposition is that it is separated totally from the subject, whether the latter is taken in its full extent or not. Therefore the following rule holds: Every negative proposition has a distributed predicate.

When the predicate is combined with the subject is an affirmative proposition, what meaning is intended? As one will note from the following examples, the meaning or intent is that the predicate is not taken in its full extent or scope. In other words, it is not taken in its full universality or distribution. This meaning of the predicate can be seen from the following propositions:

1. *Every swan is white.*
   (All the swans are some of the white things.)
2. *Every potato is a plant.*
   (All the potatoes are some of the plants.)
3. *Some snakes are large.*
   (Some of the snakes are some of the large things.)

As the propositions illustrate, the meaning of the predicate in an affirmative proposition is that it is not taken in its full extent. Therefore the following rule holds: Every affirmative proposition has an undistributed predicate. (A word of caution: This latter rule often goes unobserved or is forgotten.)

The following chart combines the four types of propositions with the distribution of their subjects and predicates:

Type of Proposition		Distribution of S	Distribution of P
universal affirmative	(A)	D	U
particular affirmative	(I)	U	U
universal negative	(E)	D	D
particular negative	(O)	U	D

2. THE RULES FOR CONVERSION

Again, conversion is the process of reversing the subject and predicate, while retaining the same quality, in order to have the appropriate derived truth. As the definition designates, the reversal of the subject and predicate cannot be done haphazardly. If this reversal is to be performed validly, the following general guidelines must always be followed:

1. The same quality must be retained.
2. The terms must never be overextended.

The first guideline simply means that an affirmative proposition must be kept affirmative and that a negative one stays negative. The second guideline is not so simple. As the above chart on distribution reveals, both the subjects and predicates of the four types of propositions admit of variation in their distribution. Given a certain distribution, one must never overextend it in the process of conversion. One may, however, underextend a given term if it is necessary. Because of this second guideline, the following conversion is invalid.

1. Some children are not happy.	*U*	*D*
2. No happy ones are children.	*D*	*D*

As one can easily surmise, the reason for no overextension of a term is that the logician must stay within the confines of the truth given to him. He cannot arrive at a proposition with greater extension than the original one. If he does try to perform this feat, he resembles the person who overdraws on his bank account. Both are relying on what is not in the original amount.

Granted the above general guidelines, the rules for the conversion of the four types of propositions are charted as follows:

1. <u>Propositions with Simple Conversion</u> (with no change in quantity)

E to E	No eggs are broken.	D	D
	No broken things are eggs.	D	D
I to I	Some balloons are blue.	U	U
	Some blue things are balloons.	U	U

2. <u>Proposition with Accidental Conversion</u> (with change in quantity)

A to I	Every tree is a plant.	D	U
	Some plants are trees	U	U

3. <u>Proposition with No Valid Conversion</u>

O	Some dogs are not cats.	U	D
	No cats are dogs.	D	D
	(overextension in converse)		

As the above chart indicates, the E and I propositions can be converted simply. Because the remaining two propositions do not fall in this category, the student must note carefully the rules about conversion of the A and O propositions. In spite of the fact that the A proposition permits only accidental conversion, people frequently attempt to convert it simply. The following examples illustrate this common error:

1. *Every wealthy person rides a Cadillac.*
   Every person riding a Cadillac is wealthy.
2. *Every explosive is dangerous.*
   Every dangerous thing is an explosive.

In addition, individuals tend to convert simply the O proposition even though it has no valid conversion. Examples of this error follow:

1. *Some Europeans are not Italians.*
   Some Italians are not Europeans.
2. *Some plants are not turnips.*
   Some turnips are not plants.

A knowledge of the rules of conversion is very necessary for every student. Only if he knows the above restrictions in this process will the student be able to evaluate the frequent conversions that he will meet in his studies. He might, for example, read the following implications:

1. *We know that everything true is useful.*
   Therefore everything useful is true.   (invalid)
2. *Everything that I see and touch is real.*
   Therefore everything real is what I see and touch.   (invalid)
3. *Everyone wearing the Arrow shirt is handsome.*
   Therefore everyone handsome wears the Arrow shirt.   (invalid)

As the above conversions point out very clearly, the careful thinker must know and practice the proper rules for this process.

B. OBVERSION

As stated at the beginning of this chapter, obversion is the process of reversing the quality of the proposition, while retaining the same subject and predicate, in order to have the equivalent truth. In contrast to the process just treated, obversion seeks the counterpart of a given proposition, rather than its converse. The rules for the process of obversion, together with several examples, are as follows:

1. Retain the same subject.	1. A to E Every apple is edible.
2. Contradict the linking/nonlinking verb.	No apple is non-edible.
	2. I to O Some cars are Plymouths.
3. Contradict the predicate.	Some cars are not non-Plymouths.
	3. E to A No rabbits are brave.
	Every rabbit is non-brave.
	4. O to I Some trees are not tall.
	Some trees are non-tall.

The process of obversion, which is the reversal of the proposition's quality, is based on the principle that, if something is true, the denial of its contradictory is also true. Thus, if it is true that the sky is blue, it is also true that this same sky is not non-blue. Another application of this same principle is the grammatical rule that two negatives equal a positive. Thus, if the student is not non-worthy, then he is worthy.

As can be noted, the contradictory of anything is formed by placing a *not* or *non-* before that thing. This contradictory means everything which is not the given thing. Thus the contradictory of *tree* is *non-tree*. *Non-tree*, meaning everything which is not tree, signifies all but tree; i.e., a dog, a tulip, a stone, and even nothing.

In obtaining the obverse of various propositions, the student should observe the following procedures:

1. One should use *non-*, rather than *un-* or *in-*, because these latter prefixes sometimes do not signify the required contradictory opposition.
2. One should always recall that the proper form of the E proposition is *No S is P*, rather than *Every S is not P*.

In order to show clearly the process of obversion applied to the four types of propositions, the following summary is given:

1. A to E   Every S is P.
               No S is non-P.
2. I to O   Some S is P.
               Some S is not non-P.
3. E to A   No S is P.
               Every S is non-P.
4. O to I   Some S is not P.
               Some S is non-P.

Of what value is the process of obversion for the typical student? One of its chief contributions is the light it can shed on obscure and confusing propositions. As many politicians know, the clever use of negatives can easily obscure an issue. Obversion, with its procedures for shifting from the negative to the positive, can clarify such obscurity and confusion. The following examples illustrate this fact:

1. *The governor is not a non-atheist.*
The governor is an atheist.
2. *Death is not non-threatening.*
Death is threatening.
3. *Every book is not non-boring.*
Some books are boring.

C. SUMMARY

Important points concerning conversion and obversion are summarized in the following outline:

1. <u>Conversion</u>
   a. extension of terms (distributed or undistributed)

Type of Proposition	Distribution of S	Distribution of P
A	D	U
I	U	U
E	D	D
O	U	D

   b. rules for conversion
      1) Retain the same quality.
      2) Do not overextend the terms.
      3) Convert as follows: simple conversion   (E to E; I to I)
                                    accidental conversion   (A to I)
                                    no conversion   (O)

2. <u>Obversion</u>
   — rules for obversion
     1) Retain the same subject.
     2) Contradict the linking/ nonlinking verb.
     3) Contradict the predicate.

STUDY QUESTIONS   **CHAPTER 9**

1. Define conversion and obversion.
2. Give the rules for the distribution of the subjects of propositions. How do the singular and indefinite propositions fit under these rules?
3. State the rules for the distribution of the predicates of propositions. On what guideline does the soundness of these rules rest?
4. What are two general guidelines for conversion? List the kinds of conversion possible for the four types of propositions.
5. Of what value to the student is the process of conversion?
6. List the rules for obversion. On what principle is the process of obversion based? What does the contradictory of a given thing mean?
7. Of what value to the student is the process of obversion?

CHAPTER 10

OPPOSITION OF PROPOSITIONS

A. The square of opposition
B. Rules for truth and falsity

The preceding chapter treated the conversion and obversion of categorical propositions. By means of conversion the student is able to reverse accurately the subject and predicate of a given proposition. Thus he knows that the valid converse of *Every vulture is a scavenger* is *Some scavengers are vultures.* Utilizing the rules of obversion, the student can obtain the logical counterpart of any categorical proposition. Thus he is able to obvert the negative proposition *Some politicians are not non-ambitious* to its plainer affirmative form *Some politicians are ambitious.*

In both of the above procedures the student is performing a logical operation on one given proposition. In this chapter he will learn how to oppose one proposition to another one. Instead of working with one proposition, he will be learning the possible ways in which two propositions can be opposed to each other. Actually many individuals are familiar with the most straightforward form of opposition, which is quite properly called contradiction. The following dialogue indicates the commonplaceness of contradictory opposition:

A. *I have good news. Mary is first in her class.*
B. *She is not. I distinctly heard that Jane is first.*
A. *Well, you may be right. I do know, though, that the top person is eligible for a free day.*
B. *Where did you hear that? That's not true.*
A. *Oh! I guess I have no more news.*
A. *(when alone) It's no fun talking to her. She always contradicts me.*

In this chapter the student will learn that there are various ways in which one proposition can be opposed to another one. He will also discover how truth and falsity are related to these different kinds of opposition.

A. THE SQUARE OF OPPOSITION

Following the treatment of the categories in chapter four, an explanation of both contradictory and contrary opposition was given. The latter was defined as the opposition existing between the positive extremes of the same subject, each of which excludes the other from that subject. Thus the positive extremes in the subject, water, are hot and cold, which cannot both be present at the same time in that given water. Since contrary opposition is between the positive extremes within a given subject, there may be an intermediate or middle position which is neither of these extremes. Thus lukewarm is a middle state between hot and cold, while mediocre is a middle between good and bad. Because a middle may exist between contraries, it is true to say that neither contrary may be present in a subject. Thus a given human being, being mediocre, is neither good nor bad.

Contradictory opposition, differing from contrariety, was defined as the absolute opposition between an affirmation and a negation, an opposition which has no intermediate or middle. Thus the affirmation *Henry is sick* is opposed absolutely by the negation *Henry is not sick*. In this example there is an either-or situation. Thus Henry is either sick or not sick. There is no other alternative. In other words, contradictory opposition, consisting of an affirmation and its denial, does not have the possibility of any intermediate or middle position. There are only two choices: either the thing is or is not.

Contradictory and contrary opposition are the two chief ways in which categorical propositions are opposed. Opposition in general, considered in relation to the proposition, is defined as the affirmation and denial of the same predicate in respect to the same subject. Such affirmation and denial can be noted easily in the following pairs of propositions:

1. *Every tiger is hungry.*
   No tiger is hungry.
2. *Some tigers are hungry.*
   Some tigers are not hungry.

In each of the above pairs, one proposition, through affirmation or denial, is opposed to the other one. Now there are several gradations of opposition. When the four types of propositions are opposed, the following kinds of opposition are possible:

1. contradictory opposition
2. contrary opposition
3. subcontrary opposition

Contradiction, the most basic kind of opposition, is the simple or absolute denial of the original proposition. In order to contradict or simply deny a universal proposition, whether affirmative or negative, it is sufficient to state one exception. This method of accurately contradicting a universal proposition can be noted in the following examples:

1. *Every European is coming.*
   That's not true. Hans, Fritz, and Carl are not coming.
2. *No pies are baked.*
   You are wrong. That pie in the corner is baked.

Just as the universal proposition is directly opposed by a single contradictory exception, so conversely the singular or particular proposition demands a whole universal in order to shake its validity. The need for the entire universal to oppose a particular or singular proposition is evident from the following examples:

1. *Some of the students are finished.*
   You cannot say that. As you can see, no student is finished.
   (The teacher had to look at every single student to contradict the first proposition.)
2. *Some of the dogs are not fed.*
   Wrong again. Every single dog is fed.
   (The kennel keeper had to check all of his dogs to contradict the first proposition.)

In summary, contradictory opposition, which is the simple denial of the original proposition, is achieved as follows:

1. The universal proposition is contradicted by an opposing particular or singular proposition.
2. The singular or particular proposition is contradicted by an opposing universal proposition.

Beyond the simple denial or contradiction of propositions, it is possible to oppose one proposition by its contrary. Contrariety is that form of opposition in which one universal proposition is set against its other extreme, which is the opposing universal proposition. In propositions, which vary from the universal to the singular, the two extremes would be the universals in opposing camps, i.e., the affirmative and negative universals. This opposition by extremes is illustrated by the following propositions:

1. *Every highway is open.* *(A)*
   No highway is open. *(E)*
2. *Every person is smiling.* *(A)*
   No person is smiling. *(E)*

As the above examples indicate, contrary opposition is accomplished by setting one extreme against the other; i.e., by opposing the universal affirmative with the universal negative.

In addition to the definite kinds of opposition just explained, a rather subdued form is subcontrary opposition. This type is defined as the opposition between particular propositions. Because subcontrariety is between particulars, no direct or head-on opposition is possible. This lack of direct opposition can be noted in the following examples:

1. *Some tomatoes (in this box) are ripe.* *(I)*
   Some tomatoes (in that box) are not ripe. *(O)*
2. *Some secretaries (in this office) are excellent.* *(I)*
   Some secretaries (in that office) are not excellent. *(O)*

As the above pairs illustrate, the subjects in the opposed particular propositions may be different parts within the universal subject. Thus the tomatoes in this box are different from the tomatoes in that box. Since these subjects may or may not be identical, no direct opposition is possible. Nevertheless the given propositions do at least point in an opposite direction or present a different perspective. Therefore subcontrariety, which is the opposition between particulars, is at best an opposition of reduced value.

When the above three types of opposition are treated, one further relationship between propositions is explained. It is subalternation, which is defined as the relation between a given universal and the particulars contained under it. The following pairs are examples of the relationship of subalternation:

1. *Every package is wrapped.* *(A)*
   Some packages are wrapped. *(I)*
2. *No truck is loaded.* *(E)*
   Some trucks are not loaded. *(O)*

As the above examples indicate, subalternation is the relation between a universal and the particulars under it. As can also be noted, the subalterns can be both affirmative or both negative. They are never a combination of one affirmative and one negative. Thus the proposition *Some packages are not wrapped* is not subalternated to the proposition *Every package is wrapped*. Since the subalterns are not opposed to each other, they are not one of the kinds of opposition found in propositions. Rather subalternation is a relation between a universal and the particulars of the same quality directly under it.

In this treatment of the opposition between propositions, it must be emphasized that the most direct and easily seen opposition is that between a singular proposition and its contradictory. This clear-cut opposition is illustrated by the following pairs:

1. *Susan is sleeping.*
   Susan is not sleeping.
2. *Brian is sick.*
   Brian is not sick.

In summary, the above explanation treated the following kinds of opposition, as well as the relationship of subalternation:

1.	contradiction:	the simple denial of the original proposition	A and O; E and I
2.	contrariety:	the opposition between extremes	A and E
3.	subcontrariety:	the opposition between particulars	I and O
4.	subalternation:	the relation between a universal and its particulars	A and I; E and O

The above four forms are charted very clearly in a traditional diagram which is known as the Square of Opposition. This square, together with illustrative propositions, follows:

Every tulip is red. 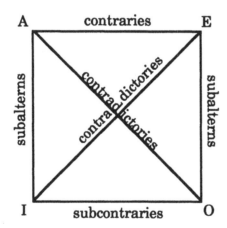 No tulip is red.

Some tulips are red. Some tulips are not red.

B. RULES FOR TRUTH AND FALSITY

Not only does the logician need to know ways in which categorical propositions can be opposed to each other but also he must know the rules for truth and falsity concerning these opposed propositions. Thus, faced with such opposed statements, he needs the answers to questions such as the following:

1. If one opposed proposition is true, is the other one false?
2. If one opposed proposition is false, is the other one automatically true?

As the following explanation will reveal, the rules for truth and falsity will vary according to the type of opposition.

1. CONTRADICTORY OPPOSITION

Of two contradictories, one must be true and the other must be false.

1. *Every peach is peeled.*	*(A)*	*If true,*
Some peaches are not peeled.	*(O)*	*then false.*
2. *No banana is ripe.*	*(E)*	*If false,*
Some bananas are ripe.	*(I)*	*then true.*

As the simple denial of the original proposition, contradiction presents an either-or situation. In other words, contradictory opposition states simply that the thing either is or is not so. As such, there is no middle ground between the two positions. Thus the contradictory of *Thomas is coming* is *Thomas is not coming.* As this example indicates, there is no middle in contradictory opposition. Since contradiction presents only two alternatives (it is or it is not), then its rule for truth and falsity follows automatically:

Of two contradictories, one must be true and the other must be false.

2. CONTRARY OPPOSITION

Of two contraries, whereas they both cannot be true, they both may be false.

1. *Every bluebird is singing.*	*(A)*	*If true,*
No bluebird is singing.	*(E)*	*then false.*
2. *Every blackbird is gone.*	*(A)*	*If false,*
No blackbird is gone.	*(E)*	*then unknown.*

Since contrariety is the opposition between extremes, it deals only with the two poles or remote terms of the subject. Therefore contrary opposition is not an either-or situation. It always has the possibility of a third or middle position. Thus the middle between black and white is gray.

Because of the kind of opposition it is, contrariety cannot have the forthright rule for truth or falsity found in contradiction. At most, only the following fact is known: If one extreme is present, the other one cannot be present. Thus if one's hair is white, it cannot be black. On the other hand, if one extreme is not present, one cannot assert any definite alternative. The reason is that the alternative might be either the other extreme or some middle ground. Thus the absence of white hair does not automatically indicate the presence of black hair. It might be red. Because of the nature of contrary opposition, the following rules for truth and falsity hold:

Of two contraries, if one is true, the other is false;
if one is false, the other is unknown.

3. SUBCONTRARY OPPOSITION

Of two subcontraries, whereas they both cannot be false, they both may be true.

1. *Some baskets are full.*	*(I)*	*If true,*
Some baskets are not full.	*(O)*	*then unknown.*
2. *Some pictures are hung.*	*(I)*	*If false,*
Some pictures are not hung.	*(O)*	*then true.*

Since subcontrary opposition is between particular propositions, it is always possible that the subjects may be two different parts of the universal subject. Thus some baskets (in the kitchen) are different from some baskets (in the basement). Since the two propositions do not necessarily have the same subject, they are not necessarily opposed. Therefore they may both be true. Thus one might say in truth both of the following:

Some chickens are fed.	*(I)*	*true*
Some chickens are not fed.	*(O)*	*true*

On the other hand, it can be proved through the use of both contradictory and contrary opposition that the falsity of one particular proposition leads to the truth of the other one. The steps of this proof are as follows:

1.	If some S is P, then no S is P.	If false, then true.	(contradictory)
2.	Granted no S is P, then every S is P.	If true, then false.	(contrary)
3.	Granted every S is P, then some S is not P.	If false, then true.	(second subcontrary)

In summary, the rules of truth and falsity for subcontrary opposition are as follows:

Of two subcontraries, if one is true, the other is unknown;
if one is false, the other is true.

4. SUBALTERNATION

Of two subalterns, both are true when moving from the universal to the particular;
both are false when moving from the particular to the universal.
(Otherwise their truth or falsity remains unknown.)

1.	*Every thunderstorm is violent.*	*(A)*	*If true,*
	Some thunderstorms are violent.	*(I)*	*then true.*
2.	*Some ships are not wrecked.*	*(O)*	*If false,*
	No ships are wrecked.	*(E)*	*then false.*

Since the relation of subalternation is between a universal and the particulars under it, only the above rules for truth and falsity can be obtained. Thus it is evident that, if all of a thing is true, then some of it is also true. In addition, it follows that, if even some of a thing cannot be held, then certainly none of it can be held. These rules for subalternation can be summarized as follows:

Of two subalterns, descend with truth;
rise with falsity.
(The opposites are unknown.

In summary, the rules of truth and falsity for the above four forms can be aligned with the Square of Opposition as follows:

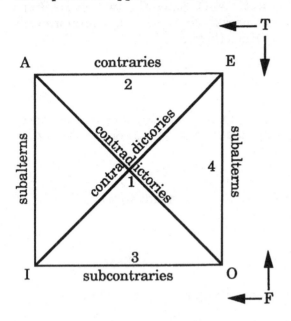

(1) One, true; the other, false.

(2) Both cannot be true.

(3) Both cannot be false.

(4) Descend with truth; rise with falsity.

As the arrows outside the Square indicate, the logician moves with surety both when he has truth at the outside universal position and when he has falsity at the outside particular one. The reasons for such surety are as follows:

1. truth in the outside universal position
   a. If one contrary is true, the other one is false.
   b. From a true universal subaltern, one moves to a true particular one.
2. falsity in the outside particular position
   a. If one subcontrary is false, the other one is true.
   b. From a false particular subaltern, one moves to a false universal one.

These two positions show the interplay among three of the four forms found in the Square of Opposition and thus streamline the use of its rules. (See appendix one for a discussion of the existential nature of universal propositions.)

Of what value is a knowledge of the opposition of propositions? If one both knows and practices the rules of truth and falsity for opposing statements, he will attend to the following:

1. He will be careful of any sweeping or universal statement that he may make, knowing that it can be contradicted by a single exception.
2. Knowing that particular statements are hard to challenge, he will restrict his comments to this level in many situations.
3. If he is forced to argue against some particular statement, he will be aware of the following problems:
   a. A particular cannot be proved false by another particular.
   b. A particular can be contradicted only by its opposing universal.
4. Remembering that contraries present extreme positions, he will use this form of opposition only if he is on sure ground.

5. SUMMARY

In the opposition of propositions, the rules concerning their truth and falsity may be made more understandable by the following chart:

RULES	IF--------THEN	REASON FOR RULE
CD: One, true; the other, false.	T------------- F F------------- T	Simple denial; no middle ground.
CT: Both cannot be true.	++T------------- F F------------- ?	Extremes have middle ground.
SC: Both cannot be false.	T------------- ? **F------------- T	Indirect proof.
SA: In universal position, descend with truth only.	++T------------- T F------------- ?	All-------------to some.
SA: In particular position, rise with falsity only.	T------------- ? **F------------- F	If some not held, then all not held either.

SUMMARY FOR OUTSIDE OPPOSITION
1. At universal position: knowledge with *truth* only.   ++
2. At particular position: knowledge with *falsity* only.   **

STUDY QUESTIONS   CHAPTER 10

1. Define contrary opposition. Why is a middle possible in this opposition?
2. Define contradictory opposition. Why is no middle possible in this opposition?
3. Define opposition in general as related to the proposition. List the three gradations of opposition.
4. In relation to the proposition, define contradiction. State the way to contradict both a particular and a universal proposition.
5. In relation to the proposition, define contrariety.
6. In relation to the proposition, define subcontrariety. Why is no direct opposition possible in subcontrariety?
7. Define subalternation.
8. In relation to the proposition, what is the most direct and easily seen form of opposition?
9. What is the rule for truth and falsity in relation to contradiction, contrariety, subcontrariety, and subalternation? Give the rationale for each of these rules.
10. Of what value is a knowledge of the rules of opposition?

THIRD ACT OF THE MIND: REASONING

CHAPTER 11

THE CATEGORICAL SYLLOGISM

A. Act of reasoning
B. Structure of the syllogism
C. Rules for the syllogism
D. Procedure for a valid syllogism

As noted in chapter eight, the human mind has three operations: simple apprehension, judgment, and reasoning. By means of simple apprehension, the intellect grasps the nature or whatness of every simple material reality. Thus it apprehends the whatness of such simple realities as sun, water, ice, rock, freezing, and expanding. Then it combines or divides the concepts of these simple realities through its act of judgment. Thus it makes the following judgments:

1. *The water is freezing.*
2. *Ice is not a rock.*
3. *The rock is not expanding.*
4. *The sun is not ice.*

Finally the intellect climaxes its work by reasoning to a conclusion which can be obtained only through its previous apprehensions and judgments. In other words, the intellect in its third operation reasons to an unknown from what it already knows. Thus it may reason as follows:

1. *I wonder why freezing water can force rocks apart.*
2. *I do know that freezing water expands and creates pressure.*
3. *I also know that such expansion and pressure can force rocks apart.*
4. *Therefore I now see why freezing water can force rocks apart.*

As the above example indicates, reasoning is a much more complicated operation than apprehension or judgment. In these latter two operations there is a kind of direct understanding. Thus the intellect, abstracting from sufficient sense data, has a direct perception of what water, ice, or rocks are like. It also combines or divides the concepts of these realities in a straightforward or direct fashion. Thus it asserts, without any additional intermediary, that ice is not a rock. On the other hand, reasoning does not proceed in such a direct manner. Rather it obtains its answers only by utilizing some intermediate information. The need for this mediating knowledge may be diagrammed as follows:

Freezing water ⟵————— *because it expands and* ⟵————— *can force*
　　　　　　　　　　　　　　creates pressure　　　　　　　　*rocks apart.*

This complex process of reasoning, as well as the categorical syllogism which results from it, will be treated in this chapter.

A. ACT OF REASONING

Reasoning is defined as the human process of going from one thing to another, i.e., of moving from the known to the unknown. This process is illustrated as follows:

Why is peat a poor fuel?   *unknown*
I know that peat has a high water content.   *known*
I also know that anything with high water content is a poor fuel.   *known*
Therefore I now see why peat is a poor fuel.   *unknown solved*

As the above example illustrates, reasoning is the process of moving from one thing to another, i.e., of moving from the known to the unknown. Utilizing what he knows, the human being is able to move to what he doesn't see directly. In other words, the rational person, by means of what he already knows, is able to go beyond his immediate perception and solve very obscure problems. This is the nature of the reasoning process: to go from the known to the unknown. Since reasoning is a movement from one thing to another, it is often called discursive thought. This name is well taken, for the literal meaning of *discourse* is to run through something or to go from one thing to another. In addition, reasoning may be called argumentation, inference, or deduction. As can be easily noted, each of these terms also denotes a movement from one thing to another.

Is there any attribute which particularly marks out this movement from one thing to another? A basic characteristic of the reasoning process is that it states a cause-effect relationship. This relationship is quite evident in the following examples:

1. *Peat is an inefficient fuel because it has a high water content.*
2. *Freezing water can force rocks apart because it expands and creates pressure.*
3. *Sue was late because she overslept.*
4. *The house is cold because the furnace is broken.*

As these examples point out, the reasoning process basically involves a cause-effect relationship. It can be spotted easily in spoken or written material by such words as the following: *because, since, for,* and *therefore.* Its grammatical counterpart is the discursive statement. This statement, which must present the movement from the known to the unknown, may be limited to a single complex sentence or it may include a whole paragraph. In each of the above examples, the reasoning process requires only a complex sentence. In other cases, one or several paragraphs may be needed. Whether the process is concise or extensive, it is expressed by a discursive statement which gives the movement from the known to the unknown.

The reasoning process is the distinctly human way of obtaining knowledge. The lower animals are unable to connect cause and effect, while the angelic intellects see both cause and effect in a single glance. Thus a dog might wait for his master for many days, but he could never figure out why he has been deserted. In marked contrast, an angel, hearing a knock on a door, would know instantly who was on the other side. The human being, placed on a middle between these two extremes, is able to discover the causes of things, but he must do it in a step-by-step process. The human way is to discover the answer by moving from one thing to another. The specific difference of the human being is his ability to reason.

Of what value is the reasoning process to the human being? It is of supreme importance, for the ultimate questions in any human life cannot be solved by simple, direct observation. Thus the individual, wishing to know if God exists, cannot solve his problem by simply looking up at the sky. He must move carefully through many, many proofs. In like manner, the scientist, analyzing the nature of the atom, must utilize every known fact that he possesses in order to reach any new breakthrough. Providing the procedure for unraveling the remote and obscure, the reasoning process is of unparalleled importance in the natural order for the human being.

B. STRUCTURE OF THE SYLLOGISM

The reasoning process, moving from the known to the unknown, always begins with some problem and reaches its solution through some intermediate information. Without this intermediary or middle term, no solution is possible. These elements of reasoning may be exemplified as follows:

Bundled newspapers ←——— *because they have little air* ←——— *burn slowly.*		
subject of problem	*middle term*	*predicate of problem*
(S)	*(M)*	*(P)*

As the above example illustrates, the problem solver is able to affirm the predicate *burn slowly* of the subject *bundled newspapers* only through the middle term *have little* air. This is the nature of the reasoning process. First it inquires whether or not some predicate may be connected with some subject. Then it concludes in the affirmative or negative through the help of some mediating or middle term. Pondering some unknown, the thinker is able to solve it through an intermediate known. (These elements of the problem-solving process were illustrated at the beginning of chapter one.)

It is this reasoning process which is formalized in the categorical syllogism. In fact, this syllogism may be defined as the linking (or separating) of the conclusion's subject and predicate through the middle term. The steps leading to this syllogistic structure may be illustrated with the same example:

problem	*Why do bundled newspapers*	*(S)*	*burn slowly?*	*(P)*
subject defined	*Bundled newspapers*	*(S)*	*have little air.*	*(M)*
known general principle	*Whatever has little air*	*(M)*	*burns slowly.*	*(P)*
conclusion	*∴ Bundled newspapers*	*(S)*	*burn slowly.*	*(P)*

As the above syllogism exemplified, the problem is solved through a mediating or middle term (M). This middle term is the subject's definition which falls under the background of general principles. Thus bundled newspapers are defined as having little air. This definition, placed under the appropriate general principle, is the means of solving the problem. Truly this definition stands as a middle term between the subject and the predicate of the problem.

In the above example, the categorical syllogism is stated in the informal, natural pattern of thinking about a given subject. When this syllogism is formalized into the strict, logical order, the general principle is given first. Thus the same example, stated in the formal syllogistic pattern, is as follows:

known general principle	*Whatever has little air*	*(M)*	*burns slowly.*	*(P)*
subject defined	*Bundled newspapers*	*(S)*	*have little air.*	*(M)*
conclusion	*∴ Bundled newspapers*	*(S)*	*burn slowly.*	*(P)*

To clarify the categorical syllogism, the text will now treat the components, definition and validity, and three figures of this logical form.

1. ITS COMPONENTS

Resulting from the reasoning process, the categorical syllogism consists of two categorical propositions, now called premises, and a conclusion. These two premises and conclusion contain only three terms, each of which is used twice. These three terms are aptly named as follows:

1. the *major term* because it is the predicate of the conclusion and therefore of greater extension (P) (See extension of terms under conversion.)
2. the *minor term* because it is the subject of the conclusion and therefore of lesser extension (S)
3. the *middle term* because it links the major and minor terms together (M)

An example of the formal syllogism, with the three terms labeled P, S, and M, follows:

major premise	Every mammal	(M)	nurses its young.	(P)
minor premise	Every fox	(S)	is a mammal.	(M)
conclusion	∴ Every fox	(S)	nurses its young.	(P)

Utilizing the above example, one can note the following characteristics of the syllogism's components:

1. Both the major (P) and minor (S) terms appear once in a premise and once again in the conclusion.
2. The middle (M) term appears once in each premise and never in the conclusion. It serves to link the major and minor terms. Said in another way, the middle term is the reason or cause for what is asserted in the conclusion.
3. The premise in which the major (P) term appears is called the major premise. This premise contains the general principle.
4. The premise in which the minor (S) term appears is called the minor premise. This premise contains the definition of the subject.

As stated above, the major and minor premises contain respectively the predicate and subject of the conclusion. These premises are never designated simply by the order in which they appear in an argument. Thus a given premise is not the major premise because it is first. Rather it is the major premise because it contains the predicate. In like manner, the minor premise is so designated because it contains the subject, not because it is second. In fact, the minor premise is often stated first because it contains the subject, which is the given topic of conversation. This informal order, in contrast to the above logical order, is exemplified as follows:

conclusion as problem	Why does every fox	(S)	nurse its young?	(P)
minor premise	Every fox	(S)	is a mammal.	(M)
major premise	Every mammal	(M)	nurses its young.	(P)
conclusion as solution	∴ Every fox	(S)	nurses its young.	(P)

The way to discover the major and minor premises seemingly creates a problem. Since the premises are labeled from the elements in the conclusion and the conclusion follows the premises, how can they be labeled from something appearing after them? The answer lies in the fact that the conclusion is stated first as a question to be solved. Then the premises are utilized. Finally the conclusion as the solution to the problem appears. This twofold appearance of the conclusion, which the logician must always remember, can be noted in the above informal syllogism.

2. ITS DEFINITION AND VALIDITY

In the previous section the components of the categorical syllogism were given. As already stated, this syllogism may be defined as the linking (or separating) of the conclusion's subject and predicate through the middle term. This definition is easily charted by using the symbols for the syllogism's three terms:

Why	S	is	P?
	S	is	M.
Also	M	is	P.
∴	S	is	P.

As the above chart shows, the categorical syllogism is the linking of the conclusion's subject and predicate through the middle term.

This syllogistic process, which connects or separates two things by means of a third, rests on the following general principles:

1. Whatever is affirmed of all a thing is affirmed of whatever falls under that thing.
   e.g.:   If _tired_ (P) is affirmed of _all the swimmers_ (M), then it is affirmed of _Mary_ (S), who is one of the swimmers.

Syllogistic Form

Every swimmer	_(M)_	_is tired._	_(P)_
Mary	_(S)_	_is a swimmer._	_(M)_
∴Mary	_(S)_	_is tired._	_(P)_

Euler's Circle

2. Whatever is denied of all a thing is denied of whatever falls under that thing.
   e.g.:   If _blooming_ (P) is denied of _all the flowers_ (M), then it is denied of the _roses_ (S), which are one kind of flower.

Syllogistic Form

No flower	_(M)_	_is blooming._	_(P)_
Every rose	_(S)_	_is a flower._	_(M)_
∴No rose	_(S)_	_is blooming._	_(P)_

Euler's Circle

The above general principles, illustrated and charted for better understanding, state the foundations on which the syllogistic process is laid. These principles assert clearly how two things can be connected or separated by means of a third thing.

Focusing on just the above affirmative principle, one can see that a subject can be connected with a given predicate if the subject is contained under a middle term, which in turn is contained under the predicate. Thus Mary can be said to be tired because Mary is one of the swimmers, who are all contained under the predicate, tired. As one can easily note, it is necessary for all the swimmers (middle term) to be tired before one can state with assurance that Mary, one of the swimmers, is tired. If the syllogistic process is to function, the middle term must span completely the gap between the subject and predicate. In other words, this term must be taken in its full extension. Only in this way can the middle term be a strong, viable link between the subject and predicate. It also goes without saying that there can be only one link or middle term.

In summary, if there is to be a real link between the subject and predicate in the basic affirmative syllogism, the middle term must be only one term and must be taken at least once in its full extension. Then, and then only, can the subject and predicate be connected. To illustrate the complete linkage needed among these three terms, one might utilize the following case of levels of containment:

1. *How shall I prove that every prairie dog is in the ground?*
2. *I see that every prairie dog is in its burrow.*
3. *I also know that every burrow is in the ground.*
4. *Therefore I can conclude that every prairie dog is in the ground.*

Because of the nature of the syllogistic process described above, Aristotle defined the syllogism in the *Prior Analytics* as follows: "A syllogism is discourse in which, certain things being stated, something other than what is stated follows of necessity from their being so" (Richard McKeon, ed., *The Basic Works of Aristotle* [New York: Random House, 1941], 1. 1. 24^{b}15–20). Within this classic definition, Aristotle points out the following qualities of the syllogism:

1. The syllogism is discourse, which moves from certain things to other things.
2. The syllogism requires that certain kinds of things must be stated; i.e., premises that give a proper connection or separation between the subject and predicate.
3. Granted the premises, the syllogism leads to a conclusion which follows necessarily from the premises.

In reference to the third point given above, it must be explained that *follows necessarily* does not mean that the conclusion is necessarily true. Rather this phrase means that, granted the premises, the conclusion necessarily follows or is valid. Said in another way, it means that, since all the syllogistic rules have been obeyed, the very form of the syllogism leads to a third proposition or conclusion. This phrase addresses itself only to the form of the syllogism, not its content. It guarantees only that a conclusion follows from the format of the syllogism, not the truth of what follows. This limited guarantee can be noted in the following example:

All breathing indicates that one is alive.
This teddy bear is breathing.
∴ This teddy bear indicates that he is alive.

Since all the syllogistic rules were obeyed in the above syllogism, the conclusion is valid or follows from the premises. These rules give no assurance, however, that the given conclusion is true. Indeed, one's common sense points out the error in its content. Its form, however, is impeccable. Perfect form, as already stated, is all that is guaranteed by the introductory rules of the syllogism. This first study of logic does not lay down the rules for the content or truth of the topic under discussion. That is the concern of material logic and of the various sciences.

3. ITS THREE FIGURES

What are the three figures of the categorical syllogism? These figures are constituted from the different ways of arranging the basic components of the premises. Since these components are the major, minor, and middle terms, the figures of the syllogism result from the different possible combinations of these three terms. Examples of these three figures follow:

First Figure (I)

M ------------P	*Every mammal*	*(M)*	*nurses its young.*	*(P)*
S -------------M	*Every fox*	*(S)*	*is a mammal.*	*(M)*
∴ S--------- P	*∴ Every fox*	*(S)*	*nurses its young.*	*(P)*

Second Figure (II)

P -------------M	*No porcupine*	*(P)*	*is a carnivore.*	*(M)*
S -------------M	*Every bear*	*(S)*	*is a carnivore.*	*(M)*
∴ S----------P	*∴ No bear*	*(S)*	*is a porcupine.*	*(P)*

Third Figure (III)

M -----------P	*Every porcupine*	*(M)*	*is vegetarian.*	*(P)*
M -----------S	*Every porcupine*	*(M)*	*is spiny.*	*(S)*
∴ S----------P	*∴ Some spiny things*	*(S)*	*are vegetarian.*	*(P)*

The three figures of the categorical syllogism given above are the only possible combinations of the terms in the premises. The reason is that the terms are set according to the way that the middle term is related to the subject and predicate. Now it is possible for the middle term to be between (I), above (II), or below (III) the subject and predicate. (These situations for the middle term are exemplified in the above three figures.) Since there are no other possibilities for the middle term, the above three figures exhaust the combinations for the terms of the premises. (See appendix two for a discussion of the fourth figure.)

The first figure produces the perfect syllogism, for here the middle term is actually in the middle. In other words, it is between the subject and predicate. Since here the middle term is situated in a perfect linking position, the logician can see clearly the syllogizing which is occurring. Thus, utilizing the basic affirmative syllogism, the logician can see that the subject is contained in the middle term, all of which is contained in the predicate. Therefore, because of the position of the middle term, the first figure produces the perfect syllogism.

In contrast, the second and third figures produce imperfect syllogisms, for here the middle term either planes above or falls below the subject and predicate. Since the middle term does not have the perfect linking position in these two cases, the second and third figures produce syllogisms which are imperfect or which may need further clarification. In such an event, they can be reduced to the perfect first figure by the process of conversion or of indirect proof.

C. RULES FOR THE SYLLOGISM

1. GENERAL RULES

There are five general rules, each of which is derived from the basic meaning of the syllogism given above. These rules are only a specification of what is required in order to have a valid syllogistic procedure. Knowing the nature of the syllogism, one could proceed without them. Nevertheless they streamline the process and make it more efficient. In a word, these rules help the thinker to be an artist.

Rule 1: The syllogism may have only three terms.

This rule is evident from the fact that the subject and predicate of the conclusion are related to each other because of their connection to a third term. If they were related to two different terms, nothing could be said about their connection to each other. This rule is easily violated if the middle term, though one term, has two meanings. Then one would actually have four terms in the syllogism. This violation can be seen in the following example:

Every democracy (one meaning)		*is a government of, by, and for the people.*	*(P)*
Russia	*(S)*	*is a democracy.*	*(another meaning)*
∴ Russia	*(S)*	*is a government of, by, and for the people*	*(P).*

Rule 2: The middle term must be distributed (universal) at least once.

If the middle term is not universal at least once, the subject and predicate may be connected to two different parts of the middle and therefore not related to each other. This problem is illustrated by the following example:

1. *All dogs are some of the animals. (one part)*
2. *All men are some of the animals. (another part)*
3. *Since the subject and predicate are related to two different things, they are not related to each other. Therefore no conclusion can be drawn.*

To avoid connecting the subject and predicate to two different parts of the middle, one must use this term in its full extension with either the subject or predicate. Then, since the middle is connected (or excluded) totally with one of the two terms, it serves as an adequate bridge between them. To continue the analogy, one might say that the middle, taken in its full extension once, spans the entire gap between the subject and predicate. Then, and then only, can the latter two terms be connected. This need for a distributed middle can be seen in the following example:

Why does every bear	*(S)*	*have canine teeth?*	*(P)*
Every bear	*(S)*	*is a carnivore.*	*(undistributed M)*
Every carnivore	*(distributed M)*	*has canine teeth.*	*(P)*
∴ Every bear	*(S)*	*has canine teeth.*	*(P)*

(since every kind of carnivore has canine teeth)

This rule about the distributed middle can be easily violated in the second figure. The reason is that this figure places both middle terms in the predicate position. In this situation, a beginning logician, forgetting that affirmative propositions have undistributed predicates, might argue with two undistributed middles. This common error, called the fallacy of consequent, is illustrated as follows:

Every bear is a carnivore.	*(undistributed M)*
Every wolf is a carnivore.	*(undistributed M)*
∴ Every wolf is a bear.	*(invalid conclusion)*

One final word: In order to observe rule 2, the student must always watch the predicates of affirmative propositions.

Rule 3: Two negative premises yield no conclusion.

If the two premises are negative, both the subject and predicate are thereby separated from the middle term. In such an event, one has no way of deducing if these two terms can be related to each other. Thus, if no rock is green and if no grass is a rock, one cannot conclude from just such negative information that all grass is green.

Rule 4: Two particular premises yield no conclusion.

This rule is clear from the following possibilities in particular premises:

1. If one has two particular affirmative premises, then all the terms would be particular. (The predicates of affirmative propositions are particular.) In such an event, the middle term would not be distributed at least once.
2. Two particular negative premises are excluded by rule 3.
3. If one has one particular affirmative and one particular negative premise, then one has a format requiring not only a distributed middle but also a distributed predicate. This format is plain from the following example:

Some cats (undistributed P)		are sick.	(M)
Some dogs	(S)	are not sick.	(distributed M)
∴ Some dogs	(S)	are not cats.	(distributed P)

    If the above example is to be valid, the major premise must be universal.

Therefore two particular premises cannot lead to a valid conclusion.

Rule 5: The conclusion always follows the weaker part.

What is meant by the weaker part? In relation to the four attributes found in the premises, negative is weaker than affirmative and particular is weaker than universal. Therefore the following rules hold:

1. If one of the premises is negative, the conclusion is negative.
2. If one of the premises is particular, the conclusion is particular. In other words, the conclusion cannot have greater extension than the premises.

The soundness of rule 5 may be seen by laying down the appropriate premises and then observing the only valid conclusions which follow.

The above general rules for the syllogism are listed in the following summary. In this listing, note that four of the five rules refer to the premises.

1. Three terms only.
2. Middle universal at least once.
3. Two negatives do not conclude.
4. Two particulars do not conclude.
5. Conclusion follows weaker part.

2. PARTICULAR RULES FOR EACH FIGURE

When the above general rules for the syllogism are applied to each of the three figures, certain particular rules arise. As will be seen, there are two special rules for each of the three figures. This twofold restriction of the general rules in each syllogistic figure limits the combinations of premises which can validly be used.

Both the special rules and the resulting, valid combinations of premises will now be presented. Preceding this explanation will be listed an exhaustive combination of the four types of premises, so that the resulting limitations for each figure will be more evident. This exhaustive combination of the four types of premises is as follows:

1	2	3	4	5	6	7	8	9	10	11	12	13	14	15	16
A	A	A	A	I	I	I	I	E	E	E	E	O	O	O	O
A	I	E	O	A	I	E	O	A	I	E	O	A	I	E	O
					x		x			x	x		x	x	x

As already indicated (x) in the above list, some of the combinations are automatically eliminated because of the rules concerning two negatives and two particulars. The structure of each figure will make further eliminations necessary. The resulting combinations of premises will be the valid moods for each figure.

Figure I: M ------ P
             S ------- M
             ‾‾‾‾‾‾‾‾‾‾‾
             S ------- P

When the general rules are applied to the first figure, the following restrictions occur:

1. <u>Middle Universal at Least Once</u>
   This middle must be universal in the major premise.
   Otherwise it will be universal in the minor premise.
   Then the minor will have to be negative.
   Then the conclusion will be negative and its predicate universal.
   Then the major premise (with the predicate) will have to be negative.
   Then the syllogism will have two negative premises. (invalid)
   Therefore the middle must be universal in the major premise.
2. <u>Two Negatives Do Not Conclude</u>
   The minor premise must be affirmative.
   If the minor premise is negative,
   then the conclusion will be negative and the predicate universal.
   Then the major premise will have to be negative to distribute the predicate.
   Then the syllogism will have two negative premises. (invalid)
   Therefore the minor premise must be affirmative.

Therefore the rules for figure I are as follows:

1. The major premise must be universal.
2. The minor premise must be affirmative.

These restrictive rules allow only the following combinations of premises for figure I: 1, 2, 9, 10.

109

Figure II: P------- M
              S------- M
              _____
              S------- P

When the general rules are applied to the second figure, the following restrictions occur:

    <u>Middle Universal at Least Once</u>
    Therefore one of the premises must always be negative.
    Then the conclusion will always be negative and the predicate universal.
    Therefore the major premise (with the predicate) must be universal.

Therefore the rules for figure II are as follows:

1. The major premise must be universal.
2. One premise must be negative.

These restrictive rules allow only the following combinations of premises for figure II: 3, 4, 9, 10.

Figure III: M ------ P
               M ------ S
               _____
               S ------- P

When the general rules are applied to the third figure, the following restrictions occur:

1. <u>Two Negatives Do Not Conclude</u>
    The minor premise must be affirmative.
    If the minor premise is negative,
    then the conclusion will be negative and the predicate universal.
    Then the major premise will have to be negative to distribute the predicate.
    Then the syllogism will have two negative premises. (invalid)
    Therefore the minor premise must be affirmative.
2. <u>Conclusion Follows Weaker Part</u>
    The conclusion must be particular.
    Since the minor premise is always affirmative,
    then the subject (in the predicate position of that premise) is always particular.
    Therefore the conclusion (with that given subject) is always particular.

Therefore the rules for figure III are as follows:

1. The minor premise must be affirmative.
2. The conclusion must be particular.

These restrictive rules allow only the following combinations of premises for figure III: 1, 2, 5, 9, 10, 13.

3. VALID MOODS FOR THE THREE FIGURES

The moods of the syllogism are the possible combinations of its premises, which vary according to quality and quantity. Thus the valid moods for figure I are as follows:

```
A  A  E  E
A  I  A  I
```

In contrast, the figures of the syllogism are the possible combinations of the terms of its premises. As already noted, these possible combinations result in three figures.

In the preceding section, the valid moods for each figure were given. When one applies to them the general rule that the conclusion follows the weaker part, then one sees that the conclusions will be negative if one premise is negative (always in figure II). Also the conclusions will be particular if one premise or the subject is particular (always in figure III).

During the Middle Ages, a series of words was devised to codify the vowels designating the premises and conclusions for the three figures' valid moods. (These nonsense words also codify the means to reduce the imperfect figures to the perfect figure, but that is not of concern in this introductory course.) These mood words are as follows:

Figure   I: *Barbara, Celarent, Darii, Ferio*
Figure   II: *Cesare, Camestres, Festino, Baroco*
Figure   III: *Darapti, Datisi, Disamis, Felapton, Ferison, Bocardo*

As can be noted, the vowels designating the premises and conclusions are the only ones given in the above mood words. Also the sequence of vowels is in the following order: major premise, minor premise, and conclusion. In addition, only four different initial consonants are used. Finally, the same initial consonant indicates that the moods so designated are related. Thus Darapti, Datisi, and Disamis are all related to Darii. This is evident from their use of the A and I premises. These fourteen mood words, aiding the human being's reliance upon his memory, have great value.

D. PROCEDURE FOR A VALID SYLLOGISM

The following steps give the procedure for constructing a valid syllogism or for evaluating one already constructed:

1. First find the conclusion/problem.
   Then note the subject and predicate.
   Then note the major and minor premises.

2. Then note the middle term/definition of subject.
   Then note the figure. (The first figure is the perfect one.)

3. Remember the format of the O proposition.
   Remember that affirmative propositions have undistributed predicates.
   Remember that negative propositions have distributed predicates.

4. Then apply the general and special rules.
   (The mood words codify these rules.)

111

5. <u>General Rules</u>
   a. Three terms only.   (for one middle)
   b. Middle universal at least once.   (for complete link)
   c. Two negatives do not conclude.   (no link)
   d. Two particulars do not conclude.   (no link)
   e. Conclusion follows weaker part.   (for given limits)

6. <u>Special Rules</u>

   <u>I</u>
   M -------- P   a. Major premise universal.   (for distributed middle)
   S --------- M   b. Minor premise affirmative.   (to avoid two negatives)

   ∴ S ------ P   A   E   A   E
                       A   A   I   I
                       A   E   I   O
                  Barbara, Celarent, Darii, Ferio

   <u>II</u>
   P --------- M   a. Major premise universal.   (for distributed predicate)
   S --------- M   b. One premise negative.   (for distributed middle)

   ∴ S ------ P   E   A   E   A
                       A   E   I   O
                       E   E   O   O
                  Cesare, Camestres, Festino, Baroco

   <u>III</u>
   M -------- P   a. Minor premise affirmative.   (to avoid two negatives)
   M -------- S   b. Conclusion particular.   (for undistributed subject)

   ∴ S ------ P   A   A   I   E   E   O
                       A   I   A   A   I   A
                       I   I   I   O   O   O
                  Darapti, Datisi, Disamis, Felapton, Ferison, Bocardo

112

1. Why is reasoning a more complicated operation than simple apprehension or judgment?
2. Define the act of reasoning. State four other names for this operation.
3. What type of relationship is expressed in the reasoning process? List some words indicating this relationship. What is the grammatical counterpart of the act of reasoning?
4. Why is the act of reasoning a distinctly human operation? Why is the reasoning process of value to the human being?
5. Define the major, the minor, and the middle terms. State where and how many times each of these terms appears in the syllogism.
6. Define the major and the minor premises. Explain how it is possible to discover the two kinds of premises from the conclusion.
7. Define the syllogism. On what two general principles does the syllogism rely?
8. What are two necessary characteristics for the middle term?
9. State Aristotle's definition of the syllogism. Clarify the three parts of this definition. (Explain carefully the meaning of *follows necessarily*.)
10. How are the three figures of the syllogism constituted? State these three figures. Why are there only three figures for the categorical syllogism?
11. Why is the first figure the perfect one? Why are the second and third figures imperfect ones?
12. State the five general rules for the categorical syllogism. Explain why each one is required for a valid syllogism. Why is rule two easily violated in the second figure?
13. State the particular rules for each figure and give the rationale for each rule.
14. Distinguish the moods from the figures of the categorical syllogism. State the mood words for the valid moods in each figure.
15. State the four procedural steps for constructing a valid syllogism.

CHAPTER 12

VARIATIONS IN THE SYLLOGISM

A. Preliminary types
    1. Hypothetical syllogism
    2. Disjunctive syllogism
B. Truncated type: enthymeme

In the preceding chapter the structure and rules of the categorical syllogism were explained. When validly constructed from categorical propositions containing a common element or middle term, this syllogism leads to a categorical conclusion which follows of necessity from such premises. This conclusion, like all categorical propositions, affirms or denies some predicate of some subject. This affirmation or denial is illustrated by the concluding affirmation in the following syllogism:

Every crustacean has a hard outer shell.

Every lobster is a crustacean.

∴ *Every lobster has a hard outer shell.*

In addition to the categorical syllogism, there are several variations related in different ways to this basic syllogism. Of these possible variations, this chapter will treat two preliminary types, i.e., the hypothetical and disjunctive syllogisms. Also it will explain the enthymeme, which is the truncated or abbreviated syllogism found in ordinary conversations.

A. PRELIMINARY TYPES

1. HYPOTHETICAL SYLLOGISM

a. ITS DEFINITION AND RULES

The hypothetical syllogism is defined as that preliminary syllogism in which the major premise is cast in a conditional form, rather than in a categorical one. This preliminary syllogism, very common in everyday conversation, can be illustrated as follows:

(condition: called the antecedent)   *(consequence: called the consequent)*

If a person has very low blood pressure, he will be dizzy.   *major premise*

This person has very low blood pressure.   *minor premise*

∴ *He will be dizzy.*   *conclusion*

As the above example indicates, the hypothetical syllogism is one in which the major premise is cast in a conditional form. Utilizing the same example, one can also observe the following points about this preliminary syllogism:

    1. The major premise contains both the antecedent and the consequent.
    2. The minor premise affirms the antecedent.   (or denies the consequent)
    3. The conclusion affirms the consequent.   (or denies the antecedent)

As already noted, the hypothetical syllogism is frequently found in everyday conversation. Thus the following conditional major premises might be a part of one's daily interchange with another person:

1. If you finish work early, you can ride home with me.
2. If you eat all of your vegetables first, you may have a piece of cake.
3. If we save a little money each week, we can take a vacation.

This if-then form of the hypothetical or conditional syllogism is also very much a part of modern scientific thinking. Thus the material implications of symbolic or mathematical logic are stated in this conditional form. This is easily exemplified by the subject's basic implication, which can be stated as follows: If p, then q. In addition, scientific theories are commonly phrased in a hypothetical format. Thus the atomic theory might be stated as follows: If the atomic theory is valid, then scientists have an explanation for the structure of chemical compounds.

Revealed by the conditional format, the crucial ingredient in the hypothetical major premise is the necessary connection between the antecedent and the consequent. The arguer is not concerned about the verification of its individual parts, i.e., the antecedent and the consequent. Rather he places his whole argument upon the necessary connection between these parts. This essential ingredient in the hypothetical premise is illustrated in the following dialogue:

A. If we eat an early dinner, we can attend the movie.
B. That's not true.
A. What do you mean? Are you referring to eating early or to attending the movie?
B. You know very well what I mean. I don't care about either one of those things. I am referring to the condition that you laid down. You said that, if we ate early, we could attend the movie. I don't agree with your thinking. I just don't see any connection between those two things.
A. Well, you may be right. Perhaps we should stay home tonight.

Not only must the logician know how to locate and define the hypothetical syllogism but also he must know its valid procedures or rules. These rules, as well as its invalid procedures, are as follows:

Valid Rules	Invalid Procedures
1. Affirm the antecedent and the consequent.	(no denial in this sequence)
2. Deny the consequent and the antecedent.	(no affirmation in this sequence)

Why are only two of the above procedures valid? The basic reason is that the extension of the consequent is ordinarily greater than the extension of the antecedent. This differing extension can be noted in the following example, as well as the limitation in valid rules flowing from this difference:

If the snake is a copperhead, it is poisonous.

But the snake is a copperhead.	*(less extension)*	*Affirm antecedent.*
∴ It is poisonous.	*(greater extension)*	*Affirm consequent.*

It is perfectly legitimate to move from the affirmation of the antecedent to the affirmation of the consequent. The reason is that this procedure rests on the necessary connection laid down between these two parts of the major premise.

It is not valid, however, to move from the denial of the antecedent to the denial of the consequent. The reason, as given above, is that the extension of the consequent is ordinarily greater than that of the antecedent. Thus it is plain that *poisonous* has greater extension than *copperhead snakes*. Because of this differing extension, the following procedure is invalid:

If the snake is a copperhead, it is poisonous.
But the snake is not a copperhead.   *Deny antecedent.*
∴ *It is not poisonous.*   *Deny consequent.*
(This procedure is not valid. The snake may be a cobra
  and therefore poisonous.)

The above example illustrates the only valid procedure if the antecedent is placed in the minor premise. The following syllogism exemplifies the proper use of the consequent in the minor premise:

If it is a bat, it is able to fly.
But it is not able to fly.   *(greater extension)*   *Deny consequent.*
∴ *It is not a bat.*   *(less extension)*   *Deny antecedent.*

It is a valid procedure to move from the denial of the consequent to the denial of the antecedent. The reason is that this procedure rests on the necessary connection laid down between these two parts of the major premise.

It is not valid, however, to move from the affirmation of the consequent to the affirmation of the antecedent. The reason, as given above, is that the extension of the consequent is ordinarily greater than that of the antecedent. Thus it is plain that *able to fly* has greater extension than *bat*. Because of this differing extension, the following procedure is invalid:

If it is a bat, it is able to fly.
But it is able to fly.   *Affirm consequent.*
∴ *It is a bat.*   *Affirm antecedent.*
(This procedure is not valid. The flying thing may
  be a robin.)

Is there any situation in which the above invalid procedures may be validly used? In other words, is it ever possible to deny the antecedent and to affirm the consequent? These two procedures are valid only if the antecedent and the consequent have the same extension or are coterminous with each other. This situation arises whenever the consequent is related to the antecedent as its specific difference, definition, or property. This coterminous situation may be illustrated as follows:

1. *If it is a man, it is a rational animal.*
2. *If it is a triangle, it has three sides.*

Whenever the antecedent and consequent are coterminous, they can be reversed. Then an invalid denial of the antecedent becomes a valid denial of the consequent. Also an invalid affirmation of the consequent becomes a valid affirmation of the antecedent.

Granted an understanding of the special situation arising from a coterminous antecedent and consequent, one may summarize the valid rules of the hypothetical syllogism as follows:

Valid Rules
1. Affirm the antecedent and then the consequent.   (no denial here)
2. Deny the consequent and then the antecedent.   (no affirmation here)

b. ITS RELATION TO THE CATEGORICAL SYLLOGISM

Although the hypothetical syllogism may appear to be very different from the categorical one, it is only a variation of this latter basic type. More specifically, the hypothetical syllogism corresponds to a categorical syllogism with a necessary major premise. Because of this relationship, the following examples may be expressed in either syllogistic pattern:

Hypothetical Syllogism (It affirms the antecedent.)
If a snake is a copperhead, it is a poisonous pit viper.
These snakes are copperheads.
∴ These snakes are poisonous pit vipers.

Categorical Syllogism (This first figure requires an affirmative minor.)
Every copperhead snake is a poisonous pit viper.
These snakes are copperhead snakes.
∴ These snakes are poisonous pit vipers.

Hypothetical Syllogism (It denies the consequent.)
If a bird is a pelican, it has a distensible pouch.
These birds do not have a distensible pouch.
∴ These birds are not pelicans.

Categorical Syllogism (This second figure requires a negative premise.)
Every pelican has a distensible pouch.
These birds do not have a distensible pouch.
∴ These birds are not pelicans.

As stated above, the hypothetical syllogism corresponds to a categorical syllogism with a necessary major premise. Such a premise has the predicate related to the subject as its genus, species (definition), specific difference, or property. In other words, the predicate states an element which necessarily belongs or cannot be parted from the subject. As a result, the proposition or premise is classified as a necessary one. The following are examples of necessary major premises:

1. *Every porcupine is a rodent with long, stiff, sharp spines.*
2. *Every bat is a mouselike flying mammal.*
3. *Every muskrat is a rodent with a scaly tail flattened on the sides.*

Since the corresponding categorical syllogism has a necessary major premise, it will always have its major stated as a universal proposition. The reason is that whatever predicate belongs necessarily to a subject also belongs to any and every part of that subject. In other words, a necessary predicate also belongs universally to that subject. Thus any and every porcupine is a rodent.

Why is the above correspondence restricted to categorical syllogisms with necessary major premises? The reason lies in the necessary condition laid down in the hypothetical syllogism. Since such necessity is proper to the hypothetical form, it must also be proper to the corresponding one.

Returning again to the original pairs in this section, one can see that the sole mechanical difference between the two types is the following: The categorical syllogism states as a universal fact the same thing that is given as a condition in the hypothetical syllogism.

More briefly, the former syllogism is categorical, while the latter one is conditional. Now the human being's search for truth rests, not in conditions, but in factual and real answers. Therefore it is in this sense that the hypothetical syllogism, framed in a conditional mode, is only a preliminary to the categorical conclusions of the basic syllogism.

Finally, one should note that the antecedent and consequent of the hypothetical syllogism correspond to the subject and predicate of the categorical major premise. This correspondence is quite evident in the two pairs given at the beginning of this section.

c. ITS TWOFOLD OPERATION

As noted in the first section, the hypothetical syllogism has two valid procedures. It is possible to affirm the antecedent or to deny the consequent. In the first of these operations, the logician is proceeding from cause to effect. When he proceeds in this fashion, he is making a deductive application. Again, he then moves as the producer does in the practical order. This movement from cause to effect may be illustrated as follows:

cause--------------------------- effect
1. *If a person is rational, he has the right to private property.*   *(deductive application)*
2. *If the cook had some chocolate, she could make dessert.*   *(production of dessert)*

In this first movement one naturally wants to be sure that the effect will follow from the given cause. If no such assurance were possible, one could not lay down any given conditions. Such a requirement can be fulfilled only if there is a necessary connection between the cause and effect, between the antecedent and consequent. Now, as one knows well, one cannot have such a connection just by wishing that it were so. Rather such a necessary connection must be based on reality. Said from a logical viewpoint, the antecedent must be followed by a consequent giving the genus, specific difference, species, or property. Such consequents, giving inseparable elements of the antecedent, are necessarily connected to the antecedent. Thus it necessarily follows that, if a person is rational, he has a right to private property. Such a necessary connection, based on the nature of things, is well named natural necessity.

Natural necessity is crucial when one is producing something in the practical order. Thus the contractor for an elevator must be certain that, if he provides cables of a given tensile strength, they will support a given load. This person would not be long in business if the connection between his antecedent cables and the consequent loads was a matter of guesswork.

As noted above, natural necessity is paramount for the producer in the practical order. If one is not actually producing something, however, one may introduce a conventional or suppositional necessity. This second type of necessity is one based, not on the nature of things, but on man-made agreements (sensible or otherwise). Utilized daily, this man-made necessity is easily illustrated as follows:

1. *If a student will take an honors course, he must have a B average.*
2. *If a person is a Polish citizen, he is subject to the party's demands.*
3. *If you want a vacation, you must work overtime.*
4. *If p, then q.*
5. *If you want to play this game, you must believe that you are a dragon.*

As the above examples indicate, there is a suppositional, as well as a natural, necessity. Granted these two possibilities, the logician must realize that the necessary connection required in the hypothetical syllogism may be either natural or suppositional. Thus the premise *If p, then q* in no sense stems from the nature of things; at best it is based on man-made supposition. Also the logician, having weighed the type of necessity present in the premises, must weigh his conclusion accordingly.

The logician must also understand the distinction between natural and suppositional necessity because of the position of the latter in symbolic logic. This subject places the primary emphasis upon suppositional inference, which it calls material implication. Quite familiar to many individuals, its basic implication is the following: If p, then q. As one might expect, this subject then considers the inferences based on natural necessity as only a part of its broader suppositional implication. In a word, man-made necessity achieves greater importance than the necessity based on the nature of things. Such a position is justified only if human decision carries more weight than the laws of nature.

In the hypothetical syllogism, the second valid operation is to deny the consequent. In this procedure the logician is moving from effect to cause. Said in another way, he is moving inductively in the speculative order. From a given effect, the thinker or speculator is searching for a single, unifying cause. Thus the early astronomers, amazed by the eclipse of the sun, worked from this startling effect to its proper cause. The second valid operation of the hypothetical syllogism is a movement from effect to cause.

This speculative movement from effect to cause is a common procedure leading to scientific theories. Faced with many mysterious phenomena, the scientist naturally theorizes about the reasons for them. Thus a budding scientist, struck by the following effects, wonders and theorizes about their causes:

cause-------------------------- *effect*
1. *Why?*   *Ice floats on water.*
2. *Why?*   *Silver is the best conductor of electricity.*
3. *Why?*   *Plants manufacture their own food.*

In like manner, the ordinary layman moves from the daily circumstances about him to their causes. Thus, if a person is late for work, his companions construct a hypothesis to explain his tardiness. Also, if a friend neglects to write a letter, the other person worriedly concludes to the worst of possible reasons. And what is often the outcome? The given hypothesis, although workable, is not the right one.

In this movement from effect to cause, what characteristic of the hypothetical syllogism must both the scientist and layman remember? It is that the extension of the consequent and antecedent may not be coterminous. This means that a given consequent or effect might have come from one of several antecedents or causes. Thus the absence of a letter might be the result of several reasons, such as a new job, a new baby, or a new house. Therefore the scientist or layman, working from the effect, must not immediately select the first plausible cause. If he does, he errs by first affirming the consequent (effect) and then affirming the antecedent (cause). In other words, seeing the consequent before him, he could then identify the incorrect one of several possible antecedents. This error is rightly called the fallacy of consequence.

d. ITS USE IN SYMBOLIC LOGIC

The educated person today is quite familiar with the basic implication (if p, then q) used by symbolic or mathematical logic. The use of this implication, together with a possible conclusion, is illustrated in the following example:

If   p   , then   q.
If the sun comes out, it will be warm.
But   p.
The sun is out.
∴   q.
∴   It is warm.

As the above example illustrates, symbolic logic employs the hypothetical form for its reasoning process. Rather than the categorical format, this subject utilizes the conditional structure in drawing its conclusions. In addition, symbolic logic does not emphasize the necessity based on the nature of things. Rather it employs a conventional or suppositional necessity. In other words, symbolic logic uses a necessity derived entirely from the supposer. Not concerned primarily with natural necessity, this subject sets up a suppositional necessity between the antecedent and consequent which has no restrictions from reality.

What are the boundaries of this suppositional necessity laid down by the symbolic logician? Since there are no restrictions from reality, the supposer is allowed to have anything imply anything. Thus the following implications are completely legitimate:

1. *If p, then q.*   *If this year is 1995, then next year is 1996.*
2. *If non-p, then q.*   *If this year is not 1995, then next year is 1996.*
3. *If non-p, then non-q.*   *If this year is not 1995, then next year is not 1996.*

Granted no restrictions from reality, the above implications are acceptable for the symbolic logician. This logician, however, does lay down the following obvious qualifications:

1. One cannot contradict oneself.

    Therefore one cannot have an antecedent imply a consequent contradicting the antecedent.

    Thus p cannot imply non-p. $p \supset \sim p$
2. One cannot contradict one's freely chosen implication.

    Granted: If p, then q. $p \supset q$

    One cannot grant: If p, then non-q. $p \supset \sim q$

    (As one can note, the negation of propositions is expressed by ~. Also the implication *If p, then q* is expressed by $p \supset q$.)

Granted the above minimal restrictions related to contradiction, the symbolic logician lays down his basic implication or inference. This implication, called material implication, is the following: If p, then q ($p \supset q$). Although this implication will not permit the contradictory of its consequent, it considers valid any other possible variety of this basic implication. As noted above, anything goes except the obvious contradictory. Both the restriction and the possibilities of the basic implication may be charted as follows:

invalid implication:	If p, then non-q.	$p \supset \sim q$
basic implication:	If p, then q.	$p \supset q$
valid implications:	If non-p, then q.	$\sim p \supset q$
	If non-p, then non-q.	$\sim p \supset \sim q$

One may also organize the above basic implication and its valid possibilities according to the following invalid procedures of traditional logic: (1) Deny the antecedent. (2) Affirm the consequent. Then the above valid implications for symbolic logic are listed as follows:

Given $p \supset q$:

1.	Deny antecedent:	$\sim p$ validly implies q or $\sim q$:	$\sim p \supset q$ or $\sim q$
2.	Affirm consequent:	q is validly implied by p or $\sim p$:	p or $\sim p \supset q$

Translated into the world of materiality, the above valid implications of symbolic logic may be exemplified as follows:

1. *~p validly implies q or ~q:*
   If Jane does not have a fever, she will go to bed.
   If Jane does not have a fever, she will not go to bed.
2. *q is validly implied by p or ~p:*
   Jane will go to bed if she does have a fever.
   Jane will go to bed if she does not have a fever.

As one can easily note, each of the above implications illustrates a valid form in symbolic logic.

Utilizing the above examples and lists, one can also observe the following: (1) From the denial of the antecedent, one can imply anything. (2) The consequent is implied by anything. These two conclusions follow from the basic implications laid down by symbolic logic. The thinking leading to them may be outlined as follows:

1. Given $\sim p$, one can imply either q or $\sim q$.
   As contradictories, q and $\sim q$ cover anything and everything.
   Thus Mary is sick or not sick. If she is not sick, she can be anything else—even an angel.
   ∴ From the denial of the antecedent, one can imply anything.
2. Given q, it can be implied by either p or $\sim p$.
   As contradictories, p and $\sim p$ cover anything and everything.
   ∴ The consequent is implied by anything.

As noted above, the symbolic logician has no restrictions in relation to the denial of the antecedent and to the affirmation of the consequent. In contrast, the traditional logician considers both of these procedures invalid. Aware of this difference, the symbolic logician presents material implication as a welcome expansion of the restrictive procedures of traditional inference. For him, the denial of the antecedent leads to either the affirmation or denial of the consequent. In addition, given the consequent, he considers it to be implied by either the affirmation or denial of the antecedent. This expansion provided by material implication is summarized as follows:

$\sim p$ validly implies q or $\sim q$.
q is validly implied by p or $\sim p$.

Is the expansion proffered by the symbolic logician a realistic one? Using this very expansion, one can see that it is not. In actuality, the symbolic logician can make no valid inference either from the denial of the antecedent or from the affirmation of the consequent. The reasoning leading to this conclusion is as follows:

1. From the denial of the antecedent, the symbolic logician can infer nothing.
   The reason is that, from the denial of the antecedent, he can either affirm or deny the consequent.
   Granted these conditions, whatever he affirms can be immediately denied.
   If such is the case,
   from the denial of the antecedent, he can infer nothing.
   (This is one of the traditional invalid procedures.)
2. Given a consequent, nothing specific can be inferred about its antecedent.
   The reason is that, according to the symbolic logician, a given consequent can be implied by either the affirmation or denial of its antecedent.
   Granted these conditions, whatever he affirms can be immediately denied.
   If such is the case,
   from the affirmation of the consequent, nothing specific can be inferred.
   (This is the second traditional invalid procedure.)

Granted the above argumentation, one can see that in reality the valid procedures for the symbolic logician are the same as those for the traditional one. For hypothetical reasoning, both logicians can only affirm the antecedent and deny the consequent. (This restriction for the symbolic logician is confirmed by the valid forms of the truth tables.)

As noted above, both the traditional and the symbolic logician employ the same valid procedures in hypothetical reasoning. In addition, the modern artist has worked out a helpful system for analyzing complex arguments. These symbolic procedures provide a fast and effective method for unlocking the complexities of human thought. Therefore every advantage of such a system should be utilized by the student learning how to reason well. (See appendix three for a condensed version of symbolic logic.)

2. DISJUNCTIVE SYLLOGISM

The second preliminary type of syllogism is the disjunctive one. It may be defined as a syllogism in which the major premise contains two alternatives. This type of syllogism may be illustrated as follows:

A given subject must be either X or not-X.
But it is not not-X.
∴ It must be X.

As the above example indicates, the disjunctive syllogism is one in which the major premise contains two alternatives. Utilizing the same example, one can also observe the following points about this preliminary syllogism:

1. The major premise contains two alternatives.
2. The minor premise denies or affirms the one alternative.
3. The conclusion contains the other alternative.

This preliminary syllogism is simply an application of the truth that one of two contradictories must be true. It is a useful schema in that an individual, unable to prove one side of a position, may be able to prove the impossibility of its contradictory. Thus an arguer might utilize a disjunctive syllogism as follows:

That student was either here or not-here.

But he was not not-here.

∴ He was here.

As this example illustrates, the arguer lays down that he can prove his point by proving the impossibility of its contradictory.

In setting down alternatives, the arguer must be careful that they are contradictories, not contraries. As noted in chapter four, contradictories have an either-or position. Contraries, on the other hand, may or may not contain a middle. Thus the contraries, hot and cold, have a third or middle position, which is lukewarm. This is not true of the contradictories, hot and non-hot. As these examples indicate, the arguer, wanting true alternatives, must be careful to lay down contradictories.

Having set down his alternatives, the arguer must still remember that the disjunctive syllogism is not a syllogistic proof. It is simply a preliminary structure enabling the arguer to know which side of his argument he intends to prove. Having established his position through the disjunctive syllogism, he must still prove the chosen side of his dichotomy. Thus, to be sure that the student was here, the arguer must proceed by a proper syllogism to prove how he knows that the student was not not-here.

B. TRUNCATED TYPE: ENTHYMEME

The enthymeme is a truncated categorical syllogism. It may be defined as a categorical syllogism in which one of the premises or the conclusion is not expressed but implied. This meaning is indicated by the name *enthymeme*. This word, taken from the Greek *en* and *thymos*, means in the mind—and therefore not expressed. Two examples of the enthymeme follow:

1. *Tom will be late because he has to work overtime.*
2. *The baseball players are happy because they won the game.*

When these enthymemes are expanded to the regular categorical form, they read as follows:

1. *Whoever has to work overtime*	*(M)*	*will be late.*	*(P)*
Tom	*(S)*	*has to work overtime.*	*(M)*
∴ Tom	*(S)*	*will be late.*	*(P)*

2. *Whoever wins the game*	*(M)*	*will be happy.*	*(P)*
The baseball players	*(S)*	*won the game.*	*(M)*
∴ The baseball players	*(S)*	*are happy.*	*(P)*

Aware of the nature of the abbreviated syllogism, one can readily note that such argumentation is a common practice, not only in rhetorical or dialectical reasoning, but also in ordinary speech. There are two reasons for such a shortened form of the syllogism. The most basic one is that the omitted proposition is generally accepted and therefore too obvious to be stated. Thus everyone should know that those working overtime will be late. A more subtle reason is that the omitted proposition, of a rather doubtful nature, cannot afford to be stated. Thus one may not be too sure that everyone winning the game will be happy.

Among the three propositions of the categorical syllogism, the major premise is the one most commonly omitted. This practice can be noted in the above examples. Since the arguer is focusing on his subject (found in the minor premise), it is quite natural for him to omit the major premise.

The omission of one of the propositions of the categorical syllogism is not only a common but also a legitimate procedure. Since any two of the three propositions contain all three of the needed terms of the syllogism, the meaning of the argumentation is present in this reduced form. In brief, the enthymeme contains the essential ingredients of the full-blown argumentation. Because of this fact, it is easily possible to expand the enthymeme to the complete categorical syllogism.

What are the procedures to follow when one expands the common enthymeme? Utilizing both the thought and words of this reduced syllogism, one should proceed as follows:

1. Find the conclusion first.
   a. Look for the basic fact for which a reason (the middle term) has been given. Watch that this fact is related to the other information as the conclusion following from such information.
   b. Utilize key words which commonly introduce a conclusion, such as *therefore*, *hence*, and *consequently*.
2. Then find the premises.
   a. Remember that the conclusion presents plainly the subject and predicate of the argument.
   b. Look for the reason (the middle term) linking such a subject and predicate. Use key words, such as *because*, *for*, and *since*.
   c. Note that one now has the three terms of the argument: the subject, predicate, and middle term.
   d. Remember that the premise containing the subject will be the minor premise. Also the premise containing the predicate will be the major premise.
   e. Utilizing the knowledge of figure and mood, expand the enthymeme into its categorical form.

An example utilizing the above rules follows:

The beaver is a water conservationist because it builds dams.

1. *conclusion:*	*The beaver*	*(S)*	*is a water conservationist.*	*(P)*
2. *middle term:*			*builds dams*	*(M)*
3. *minor:*	*The beaver*	*(S)*	*builds dams.*	*(M)*
4. *major:*	*Whatever builds dams*	*(M)*	*is a water conservationist.*	*(P)*

<u>*Logical Form*</u>

1. *major:*	*Whatever builds dams*	*(M)*	*is a water conservationist.*	*(P)*
2. *minor:*	*The beaver*	*(S)*	*builds dams.*	*(M)*
3. *conclusion:*	*∴ The beaver*	*(S)*	*is a water conservationist.*	*(P)*

The above explanation of the enthymeme concludes this chapter's presentation of some of the variations related to the categorical syllogism. The treatment of one additional variation, the sorites, can be found in appendix four.

1. Define the hypothetical syllogism and state its components. List three current areas for this syllogism. What is the crucial element in the hypothetical major premise?
2. State both the valid rules and the invalid procedures for the hypothetical syllogism. Why are there only two valid rules? In what special circumstances are the invalid procedures valid? How are these circumstances placed under the valid rules?
3. How does the hypothetical syllogism correspond to the categorical one? What constitutes the necessary major premise? Why is this major premise always universal? What is the sole mechanical difference between the hypothetical and categorical syllogism? Why is the former one a preliminary to the latter one?
4. When the logician affirms the antecedent, what logical sequence does he follow?
5. In this movement from cause to effect, distinguish between natural and suppositional necessity. In what area is natural necessity crucial? What is the position of these two kinds of necessity in symbolic logic?
6. When the logician denies the consequent, what logical sequence does he follow? In what two areas is this movement commonly found? In this sequence, what guideline must be carefully followed?
7. What type of necessity does symbolic logic utilize? What are the only restrictions laid down for this necessity?
8. What is the basic material implication of symbolic logic? List the valid and invalid implications which follow from it. State the valid possibilities according to the invalid procedures of traditional logic.
9. Show how the symbolic logician can imply anything from the denial of the antecedent. Show how the consequent is implied by anything.
10. Show that the expansion in procedures offered by the symbolic logician is not realistic.
11. What is a helpful contribution of the symbolic logician?
12. Define the disjunctive syllogism and state its components. Of what truth is this preliminary syllogism an application? What is its value?
13. Why does the disjunctive syllogism demand contradictory alternatives? Show that this syllogism is only a preliminary one.
14. Define the enthymeme. List two reasons for this shortened form of the syllogism. Why is the major premise most commonly omitted? Why is this shortened form legitimate?
15. State the basic procedure for the expansion of the enthymeme.

CHAPTER 13

APPARENT REASONING: FALLACIES

A. The fallacy in general
B. Fallacies dependent on language
C. Fallacies independent of language
D. Summary of the fallacies

In chapter eleven the structure and rules for the basic, categorical syllogism were explained. In the succeeding chapter three variations of this basic product of reasoning were treated; i.e., the hypothetical and disjunctive syllogisms and the enthymeme. As this latter chapter revealed, it is possible for human reason to proceed not only in a categorical, straightforward way but also in a conditional, disjunctive, or truncated mode. These possibilities in the reasoning process may be illustrated as follows:

Categorical Syllogism

Whatever expands	*(M)*	*can force rocks apart.*	*(P)*
Freezing water	*(S)*	*expands.*	*(M)*
∴ Freezing water	*(S)*	*can force rocks apart.*	*(P)*

Hypothetical Syllogism
If freezing water expands, it can force rocks apart.
This freezing water is expanding.
∴ It can force rocks apart.

Disjunctive Syllogism
Freezing water either forces rocks apart or it does not force them apart.
Freezing water does not not-force rocks apart.
∴ Freezing water does force rocks apart.

Truncated Syllogism
Freezing water forces rocks apart because it expands.

As the above examples indicate, human reason produces not only a basic syllogism but also many variations in this structure. As one can easily surmise, these variations can extend to a syllogism which actually works against the truth, which is unsound. This syllogism, well described as apparent reasoning or the fallacy, will be treated in this chapter.

A. THE FALLACY IN GENERAL

The fallacy or apparent syllogism is defined as reasoning which appears to conclude but does not. It is easily exemplified by the common rash judgment to which everyone is prone. This process of jumping too quickly to a conclusion, of reaching a conclusion with no sound basis, can be noted in the following examples:

1.	*problem:*	*The whole pie is eaten.*	*cause:*	*my younger brother* *(It might have been father.)*
2.	*problem:*	*The phone is ringing.*	*cause:*	*my wordy neighbor* *(It may be your employer.)*

In each of the above examples, no sound conclusion is reached because of the human propensity to jump too quickly to the wrong cause. Whenever the arguer reasons in such a rash fashion or neglects any of the other rules for a sound proof, he produces an apparent syllogism or fallacy.

In the above definition of fallacy, the emphasis is on the phrase *appears to conclude*. Fallacies are found wherever there is the appearance or likeness of the truth or of the reasoning process. Given that it is only a likeness, the fallacy by its very nature leads to deception, which may be intentional or unintentional. Since this apparent syllogism must present a likeness of truth or sound reasoning, the following are not cases of the true fallacy:

1. obvious and blatant errors in the reasoning process
   (not a good likeness or appearance of sound reasoning)
2. reasoning from false assumptions in a particular science
   (not a deception, but an honest error)

If the above errors do not qualify as true fallacies, in what material or process is the fallacy found? The most fertile ground for apparent reasoning lies in the following deviations:

1. reasoning starting from opinions which seem to be generally accepted, but which are not
2. reasoning which seems to follow a valid reasoning process, but which does not

As the above list indicates, the fallacy occurs both in opinion seemingly accepted and in reasoning seemingly valid. Relying on the power of common opinion and on the human need to connect ideas, the arguer creates an apparent syllogism through only the likeness of these things. It is precisely in this likeness that the possibility of deception is found. This possibility is captured in the very name *fallacy*, which is taken from the Latin *fallere* ("to deceive").

Another name for the fallacy is sophism which is taken from the Greek *sophos* ("wise"). Since apparent reasoning often seems quite valid and wise, this second name emphasizes this fact. In ancient Greece, certain teachers were willing to teach law students how to win either side of a case. This willingness presupposed that one was ready to appear correct even at the cost of truth. Such teachers, training their students how to produce apparent wisdom for the sake of profit, called themselves *sophoi* ("wise men"). Both their title and their pragmatic teaching are reflected today in the term *sophist* for the purveyor of specious wisdom.

Since fallacious or sophistic reasoning may enter any discussion, it is essential for every person to become skilled in the art of reasoning. It is not enough for one to hope that human reason will just naturally arrive at the right conclusion. On the contrary, because of selfish motives or just plain laziness, specious reasoning can always destroy the possibility of a sound conclusion. Therefore every person needs to learn the art of how to reason. To master this art, each individual must both benefit from the wisdom of capable logicians and also practice their artistic rules extensively. Just as an apprentice needs both clear rules and careful practice in his trade, so each beginning logician needs not only sound theory but also constant exercise in the art of thinking. Then, armed with the art of the mind, the human being can guard against fallacious reasoning.

Fallacious or sophistic reasoning can originate from two sources: (1) the words used in reasoning, (2) the connections made between the things thought about. Since the human being not only connects his various thoughts but also expresses them in words, it is possible to have specious reasoning in both of these areas. The designations for these two kinds of fallacies are as follows:

1. fallacies dependent on language
   (from plausible errors through words or their arrangement)
2. fallacies independent of language
   (from plausible errors in the reasoning process)

These two kinds of fallacies will be treated in the subsequent sections of this chapter.

B. FALLACIES DEPENDENT ON LANGUAGE

Every fallacy dependent on language is the result of a plausible error because of the words used or of their arrangement. As artificial signs of the concepts of material things, words do not have any natural correspondence with the material things which they represent. In fact one word functions in many and different senses. Thus the word *rocky* has the following meanings:

Analogical Relationship		*Analogical Relationship*
1. *consisting of rock* ⟵	— *equivocal* ⟶	1. *unsteady, wobbly*
2. *hard, unfeeling*	*relationship*	2. *uncertain, shaky*
3. *full of obstacles*		3. *(slang) groggy*

As chapter three explained, any word can be used univocally, analogically, or equivocally. Because of the poverty of the human imagination, one artificial sign does duty for quite diverse things at times.

The equivocal usage of words does indeed set the stage for fallacious reasoning, since it opens the way for the presence of four, rather than the required three, terms. The sophist, however, relies on more than such equivocal usage. His craft utilizes at least the following:

1. Any word can have equivocal meanings.
2. The human being may tend to forget that he gives everything its name.
3. Then this same human being may begin to think that one given word always stands for the same thing.
4. Then this person may tend to miss the double meanings given to words by the sophist.

The above sequence enables the clever sophist to fool many human beings. The following is an example of such sophistry:

A. *I am finally convinced that the computer is able to think just as the human being does. I see now why some persons say that this machine will replace people.*
B. *What makes you say that?*
A. *That's easy to answer. We press the button, and the computer just thinks through all the steps of the problem. Now, don't you see? Mark my words, the computer will replace people.*
B. *I guess that you're right.*

The average human being may be easily fooled by the above reasoning. He need only forget that the word *think* can stand for a mechanical, as well as a rational, operation. Then he may find himself agreeing with the above fallacious conclusion. Needless to say, such confusion can be avoided by a constant reliance on the definition of terms.

Aristotle lists six kinds of fallacies dependent on language. As noted above, each of these fallacies results from the way that the meanings or the arrangements of words are misused. As these specific fallacies will reveal, it is possible to have specious reasoning because of the following:

1. double meanings of words or of the grammatical construction
2. a misleading combination or division of words
3. a misleading placement of accentuation
4. a misuse of the form or inflection of a word

Each fallacy dependent on language will now be defined and then illustrated by several obvious examples. The purpose of these elementary illustrations is to clarify each definition, not to exemplify the subtlety of the art of deception. This latter purpose is accomplished every time an individual is deceived by some plausible, but unsound, argument. Throughout this section, the student should note that it is always through the misuse of words that the sophist is able to set up his pattern of fallacious reasoning.

1. AMBIGUITY

Ambiguity is defined as a fallacy resulting from two diverse and intended meanings of a word or phrase. This misuse of a given word or phrase is easily found in the common pun and in advertisements. Composed from diverse meanings, ambiguity automatically has four terms and is thus apparent or specious reasoning.

1. *If a child is brought up in church, he is seldom brought up in court.*
2. *If that explorer is able to shoot the rapids, he can shoot that crazed elephant.*
3. *If you will only beat your rugs, you will beat every neighbor on the block.*
4. *Did you hear about that case of whiskey? It is the last case in court.*
5. *Since the janitor did not fire the furnace, I intend to fire him.*
6. *Please show me the foot of the grave. Otherwise I shall put my foot down.*

2. AMPHIBOLY

Amphiboly is defined as a fallacy resulting from two diverse and unintended meanings caused by grammatical construction. These diverse meanings easily arise as a result of dangling or misplaced modifiers and of pronouns with unclear antecedents. Because of its different meanings, amphiboly is only apparent or specious reasoning.

1. *Henry likes ice cream better than his wife.*
2. *Lost: one umbrella by an old man with a carved, ivory head.*
3. *James told Fred that he would become a great musician.*
4. *Mary saw a hat in a window which she liked.*
5. *Speaking of the silent is possible.*
6. *Warning all to be quiet, the troops were led by the captain.*
7. *I nearly swam twenty laps the last time I was in the pool.*

3. COMPOSITION

Composition is defined as a fallacy resulting from taking something in a combined sense which is true only in a separated sense. This fallacious combination misconstrues the fact that two opposing things may exist in combination, but only if one is potential and the other is actual. Thus the sophist may say that water is both hot and cold, simply because it is potentially hot and actually cold.

1. *My husband chats with me and reads the paper every evening. Therefore my husband is able to both talk and not-talk.*
2. *All of our employees get eight hours of sleep, as well as work for eight hours. Therefore we are proud of the fact that our employees can sleep and work at the same time.*
3. *The flowers reach full bloom and die off. Therefore these flowers are both blooming and dying.*
4. *Today the waitress served the customers and washed the dishes. Therefore she can wait on table and keep the kitchen clean at the same time.*
5. *The school schedule permits the students to have periods of study and of recreation. Therefore they can both study and not-study at the same time.*

4. DIVISION

Division is defined as a fallacy resulting from taking something in a divided sense which is meant to be taken as a unit. When the sophist argues in this way, he ignores the whole which is composed of various parts. Instead he emphasizes the parts within this given whole. Thus, since 5 is composed of 3 and 2, the sophist may say that 5 is really both odd and even.

1. *The number 7 is not different from the number 5, for it is 5 with a little more.*
2. *The greater is equal, for it is that amount and more besides.*
3. *The union of husband and wife is both odd and even, for their union makes them two in one flesh.*
4. *Water is one of the lightest substances, for it is composed of the lightest substance, hydrogen, which is combined with oxygen.*
5. *Life is only a type of opposition, for it is filled with good and bad times.*

5. ACCENT

Accent is defined as a fallacy resulting from the use of accentuation in order to change the meaning of a word or sentence. The meaning of this definition will be quite evident from the following examples.

1. *Send me a man who reads.*
   Send me a man. Who reads?
2. *The invalid case was brought up in court.*
3. *Brush regularly with Crest to reduce. New cavities stop bad breath too.*
4. *That kid, napping again.*
5. *Tylenol is the one. More pediatricians give their own children.*
6. *Don't. Let your family be a victim of the epidemic.*

6. FORM OF EXPRESSION

Form of expression is defined as a fallacy resulting from the expression of two different things in the same word-form. The sophist is able to deceive by means of the word-form because different categories of things (substance, quality, action, and so forth) are frequently expressed by the same word-form. The following sentence illustrates this possibility:

The cook smells (action) the soup, and the soup smells (quality) good.

This shift easily occurs because of the different contexts in which the given word is used. Aware of this fact, the sophist hopes that the average person may not note or may forget about such shifts in meaning.

1. *Advertisement: Lion tamer (relation) wants tamer (quality) lion.*
2. *The man's goodness shines out, even when he shines shoes.*
3. *The gardener is flourishing his hoe at the flourishing rose.*
4. *Time is passing swiftly every day, while the student is not passing his courses.*
5. *At the time the wind was blowing hard, the policeman was blowing his whistle.*
6. *As the years begin to decline, a man begins to decline everything.*

The definitions of the above six fallacies, each of which is dependent on the misuse of language, may be summarized as follows:

1. ambiguity: from two intended meanings of word or phrase
2. amphiboly: from two unintended meanings of grammatical construction
3. composition: from combining what is true only as separated
4. division: from dividing what is meant to be taken as a unit
5. accent: from the use of accent to change meaning
6. form of expression: from two different things expressed in same word-form

C. FALLACIES INDEPENDENT OF LANGUAGE

The second type of fallacies is concerned, not with the words used in reasoning, but with the reasoning process itself. These fallacies, designated as those independent of language, arise from an ignorance of the requirements for a valid proof. What are the requirements for a valid reasoning procedure? As chapter eleven stated, reasoning is the process of moving from the known to the unknown. In addition, the syllogism was described as the connecting of one thing to another by means of a middle term. The following is an example of a syllogism which proves its point by a valid reasoning process:

Whatever heavenly body is near	*(M)*	*does not twinkle.*	*(P)*
The planets	*(S)*	*are heavenly bodies that are near.*	*(M)*
∴ The planets	*(S)*	*do not twinkle.*	*(P)*

As can be noted from the above example, the arguer, to know and use a valid reasoning process, must observe at least the following:

1. He must know the exact point that he is trying to prove.
   (why the planets do not twinkle)
2. He must have a real or proper reason which will prove this point.
   (that the planets are heavenly bodies which are near)

3. He must observe the syllogistic rules so that his conclusion will follow with necessity from the granted premises.
4. He must watch that all of his terms have univocal meanings.

Since reasoning has such exact requirements, it is relatively easy to be ignorant of, or to deliberately ignore, these rules for a valid proof. Such ignorance can lead to the following plausible errors or fallacies in the reasoning process:

1. the use of only an accidental or a general reason
2. the use of only a partial reason or a sequential connection
3. the use of reasons which totally ignore the point to be proved
4. the use of the very point to be proved as the needed reason
5. stating the point to be proved in a misleading way

As the sophist knows well, it is not hard to be ignorant of a valid reasoning process. Making good use of such ignorance, he is able to create syllogisms which only seem to conclude because of the above erroneous procedures. Then the individuals listening to him may think that a valid conclusion has been reached, when actually nothing has been proved. This is the art of sophistry: to give only the appearance of reasoning, an appearance which leads to deception.

Aristotle lists seven kinds of fallacies independent of language. Each of them results from an ignorance of the valid reasoning process. These different kinds of specious reasoning utilize any of the plausible errors noted in the above listing.

Each fallacy independent of language will now be defined and then illustrated by several obvious examples. The purpose of these elementary illustrations is to clarify each definition, not to exemplify the subtlety of the art of deception. This latter purpose is accomplished every time an individual is deceived by some plausible, but unsound, argument. Throughout this section, the student should note that it is always through an ignorance of proof that the sophist is able to set up his pattern of fallacious reasoning.

1. ACCIDENT

Accident is defined as a fallacy resulting from treating what is true of the individual as though it were true of the species. Such reasoning is fallacious, for the individual is only accidental to the species. Thus the species, dog, can exist with or without the individual dog, Prince. Nevertheless the sophist, ignoring this accidental connection, creates a plausible argument by reasoning that whatever is true of the individual member must also be true of the species under which it falls. The following examples illustrate such specious reasoning:

1. *Every oak is covered with carvings, for that giant tree is covered with carvings and it is an oak.*
2. *Every lake is almost dried up, for the Western Reservoir, which is a lake, is almost dried up.*
3. *No secretary will work, for Miss Jones will not work and she is a secretary.*
4. *Every painter is a failure, for Mr. Baines, who is a painter, is a failure.*
5. *All human laughter is unnecessary, for that laughter was unnecessary and it was human laughter.*
6. *Every shepherd dog is too old to work, for Vigilant is too old to work and he is a shepherd dog.*

2. CONSEQUENT

Consequent is defined as a fallacy resulting from treating what is true of a genus as though it were peculiar to a species under the given genus. The following is a simple example of this fallacy:

If it rains, the ground will be wet.
The ground is wet.   *(general condition)*
∴ It has rained.   *(special cause)*

alternate form: It has rained because the ground is wet. (invalid)

As the student can easily surmise, the presence of this fallacy was already noted in the explanation of conversion and of the hypothetical syllogism. (See appendix five for a discussion of the connection between the theories of modern science and the fallacy of consequence.)

1. *There is a revolution in the country because the people are dissatisfied.*
2. *That man is a politician because he is a good talker.*
3. *A person is charitable because he is approachable.*
4. *My secretary has a responsible position because she is tense.*
5. *You took the advice of Bank America because you made a wise investment.*
6. *That novel is good literature because the general public appreciate it.*

3. ABSOLUTE AND QUALIFIED STATEMENT

Absolute and qualified statement is defined as a fallacy resulting from treating what is true in a certain respect as though it were true without qualification. Whenever the sophist produces this fallacy, he acts as though something which is true under certain circumstances is always true.

1. *That punishment was very good for her. Therefore I know that punishment is a good thing.*
2. *I couldn't give up smoking. Therefore I gave up giving up.*
3. *The depression taught the people many good lessons. Therefore depressions are good for the nation.*
4. *John kept the secret I told him. Therefore you can trust him with any secret.*
5. *I know that the public school teachers are excellent, for I went to a public school, and my teachers were well-prepared.*
6. *The Joneses always neglect their property. Therefore they must neglect all of their obligations.*

4. NON-CAUSE AS CAUSE

Non-cause as cause is defined as a fallacy resulting from treating what precedes or accompanies a thing as though it were the cause of the thing. This fallacy arises from taking a sequential relationship as though it were a causal one. Such a situation is caused by the illusion that, since an effect follows a cause, any preceding thing is the cause of the following thing. Instead there may be only a temporal connection.

1. *You caught a cold because you went out without your boots.*
2. *My wife is a good housekeeper because she always gets eight hours of sleep.*
3. *That man is the champion bridge player because he began playing at the age of six.*

4. *That writer is creative because he always begins his day with a quiet period.*
5. *My neighbor reduced because her friend lost thirty pounds.*
6. *Our vacation was pleasant because the farm work was finished.*

5. IGNORANCE OF PROOF

Ignorance of proof is defined as the comprehensive fallacy resulting from ignoring the requirements of proof, which are as follows:

1. to use words univocally.
2. to proceed from propositions granted, and not from the point to be proved.
3. to conclude with necessity, i.e., according to the rules of the syllogism.
4. to prove the point at hand according to the respect in which it is treated.
   This point can be ignored by the following:
   a. argument against the man   (irrelevant attack on personal character)
   b. argument of the stick   (use of force to prove a point)
   c. argument from reverence   (use of authority and esteem to prove a point)
   d. appeal to the crowd   (arousal of emotions to prove a point)

As the student can surmise, the explanation of this fallacy formed the introduction to this section. The reason for this choice is that ignorance of proof is the comprehensive fallacy which embraces any proof which seems to conclude, because of ignorance of arguers, but does not. It does not conclude because one of the above requirements has been violated. As the following examples indicate, this fallacy is commonly illustrated by arguments which ignore the point to be proved.

1. *You should not elect my opponent to the school board, for he never graduated from college.*
2. *Every up-to-date theologian agrees with this position.*
3. *If you vote for Samuel Brown, it may be necessary to turn off your gas.*
4. *Dental authorities have approved of this sugar-free drink.*
5. *How can you vote for a man who ignores your freedom as black people?*
6. *Glamour girls love Carl's hair styling.*

6. BEGGING THE QUESTION

Begging the question is defined as a fallacy resulting from taking for granted as a premise the very thing which has to be proved. The one trying to refute such a fallacy does not dispute the validity of the reasoning. Rather he questions whether such a premise should be accepted. On the other hand, the sophist acts as though only the validity of the reasoning need be established. In brief, that which is questioned, and needs to be proved, is begged.

Under this fallacy, one may try to justify a premise from a conclusion that has just been derived from such a premise. Then one has the vicious circle or circular demonstration. An obvious example of such circular reasoning follows:

conclusion	*Why was Mary ------- chosen to lead the debate team?*
premise	*Because Mary --------- is the most qualified.*
	Why is Mary ---------- the most qualified?
conclusion	*Because Mary --------- was chosen.*

1. *Mary is absolutely right, for she said that she was right.*
2. *Taxes will destroy our society because it is evident that they are ruining the people.*
3. *Capital punishment for murder is justified, because it is right (just) for society to do such a thing.*
4. *The state is absolutely supreme, for it is the end of man and, as such, is above all other societies (supreme).*
5. *Man is material, for he is only a bundle of tissue and nerves, which are material in nature.*
6. *God does not exist, for only the things which can be sensed exist, and God cannot be sensed.*

7. TWO QUESTIONS AS ONE

Two questions as one is defined as a fallacy resulting from forming a question in such a way that the answer to one part of the question appears to answer the other part also. This fallacy arises when one is deceived into thinking that a two-pronged question is really only one. Then, in answering one of these parts, the person unwittingly appears to answer the other part. Such an interrogation is called a leading question.

1. *Have you stopped beating your wife?*
2. *Are you still getting drunk every weekend?*
3. *Why have you stopped visiting your relatives?*
4. *Do you advocate the overthrow of the government by subversion or violence?*
5. *Do you feel shy and insecure because you fumble for names in a conversation?*
6. *Did you study hard after hours last night?*

The definitions of the above seven fallacies, each of which arises from an ignorance of the requirements for a valid proof, may be summarized as follows:

1.	accident:	from taking attribute of individual as though true of its species
2.	consequent:	from taking attribute of genus as though peculiar to its species
3.	absolute and qualified statement:	from taking truth in certain respect as truth in all cases
4.	non-cause as cause:	from treating sequential connection as causal one
5.	ignorance of proof:	from ignoring any of the requirements of proof
6.	begging the question:	from using as premise the point to be proved
7.	two questions as one:	from taking a two-pronged question as one

D. SUMMARY OF THE FALLACIES

Following the above treatment, the definitions of the thirteen fallacies will now be listed:

Fallacies Dependent on Language

1.	ambiguity:	fallacy resulting from two diverse and intended meanings of a word or phrase.
2.	amphiboly:	fallacy resulting from two diverse and unintended meanings caused by grammatical construction.
3.	composition:	fallacy resulting from taking something in a combined sense which is true only in a separated sense.

4. division:	fallacy resulting from taking something in a divided sense which is meant to be taken as a unit.
5. accent:	fallacy resulting from the use of accentuation in order to change the meaning of a word or sentence.
6. form of expression:	fallacy resulting from the expression of two different things in the same word-form.

Fallacies Independent of Language

1. accident:	fallacy resulting from treating what is true of the individual as though it were true of the species.
2. consequent:	fallacy resulting from treating what is true of a genus as though it were peculiar to a species under the given genus.
3. absolute and qualified statement:	fallacy resulting from treating what is true in a certain respect as though it were true without qualification.
4. non-cause as cause:	fallacy resulting from treating what precedes or accompanies a thing as though it were the cause of the thing.
5. ignorance of proof:	comprehensive fallacy resulting from ignoring the requirements of proof: (a) univocal words, (b) granted premises, (c) use of syllogistic rules, (d) proof of point; i.e., no use of character, force, authority, or emotions.
6. begging the question:	fallacy resulting from taking for granted as a premise the very thing which has to be proved.
7. two questions as one:	fallacy resulting from forming a question in such a way that the answer to one part of the question appears to answer the other part also.

For purposes of clarification, the following chart will list both the materials of the thirteen fallacies and the way in which these materials are used fallaciously:

FALLACY	THE LANGUAGE	FALLACIOUS USAGE
ambiguity	word/phrase	with two intended meanings
amphiboly	grammatical construction	with two unintended meanings
composition	what is true as separated	as combined
division	what is to be taken as unit	as divided
accent	accent	for new meaning
word-form	one word-form	for two things

FALLACY	THE REASONING PROCESS	FALLACIOUS USAGE
accident	attribute of individual	as true of species
consequent	attribute of genus	as peculiar to species
absolute/qualified	truth in certain respect	as true in all cases
non-cause as cause	sequential connection	as causal connection
ignorance of proof	character, force, authority, emotions	as reason for proof
begging question	point to be proved	as premise
two questions	two-pronged question	as one question

STUDY QUESTIONS **CHAPTER 13**

1. Define the fallacy and state its essential characteristic. Why does it lead to deception?
2. List two types of errors which are not true fallacies. In what areas are fallacies commonly found?
3. In relation to the fallacy, what does the name *sophism* emphasize? Describe the origin of the term *sophist* for the teacher of specious wisdom.
4. What are two sources for fallacious reasoning? List the two types of fallacies.
5. What is the general cause for every fallacy dependent on language?
6. In relation to the meanings of words, on what mistaken ideas does the sophist rely?
7. How is all sophistry related to words eliminated?
8. List four possible ways in which words may be misused by the sophist.
9. Define each of the fallacies dependent on language. State the source for each of the following: amphiboly, composition, division, and form of expression.
10. What is the general cause for every fallacy independent of language?
11. What are the requirements for a valid reasoning process?
12. List five plausible errors in the reasoning process.
13. Define each of the fallacies independent of language. State the source for each of the following: accident, non-cause as cause, begging the question, two questions as one.
14. Explain circular demonstration.

THE CONCEPT AND THE PROPOSITION

A. The universal concept
B. The existential nature of universal propositions

In parts one and two of this text, definitions were given of both the universal concept and the proposition. First, in chapter three the concept was defined as a sign which retains the nature or whatness of the sensed thing. Thus, having seen even a single bat, one notices upon reflection that this produces in the mind, subsequent to its sensible image, a universal notion of bat. This will be clear as soon as the person perceives the next one. If one has given the first bat a name (such as *bat*) and then sees another one, the person will say, "Ah, another bat." This experience may be summed up in the following statement: Words represent, not individuals as such, but the universal concept which is derived from the individual and stands for its nature or whatness. Thus the words *rose, horse,* and *man*, while signifying real things, do not stand for a single isolated individual but for a nature or whatness perceivable in many. This may be seen by the fact that, in the case of several individuals of the same nature, the individual requires further indication by some sort of pointing out. Hence, if in a florist shop one wishes a particular rose among several and says, "I'll take that rose," the words are not enough. One must further point out in a sensible manner the individual rose desired.

Then, in chapter eight the proposition was defined as a composite statement which is judged true or false to the extent that its composition (in the case of an affirmative proposition) or division (in the case of a negative proposition) is seen to conform to a matching composition or division in reality. Thus the proposition *The porcupine is clumsy* will be adjudged true to the extent that the composition of its concepts corresponds to a similar composition in reality.

In addition to the above definitions, the universality of the concept was explained. Also the Square of Opposition, following from various relationships of the four types of propositions, was treated. Since modern, symbolic logic raises certain questions about the nature of the concept and the Boolean interpretation eliminates "existential import" from universal propositions, this appendix will give a more detailed treatment of these two topics.

A. THE UNIVERSAL CONCEPT

The material world is filled with a vast array of various kinds of simple realities. Divided into minerals, plants, and animals, these realities are easily exemplified by such common entities as oxygen, iron, potato, strawberry, chicken, and dog. Now every material simple reality is at once an individual and has also a specific nature or form. Thus the tulips growing in various gardens are perceived to be individual flowers and also to have a definite nature or form making them different from every other type of flower. This may be seen by the fact that the word *tulip* is applied to many flowers, but discriminatingly. As this example points out clearly, every material simple reality is at once an individual and has also a specific nature, essence, or whatness.

Appendix One was written expressly for this text by Pierre Conway, O.P.

Now the human being, empowered with his senses and intellect, is able to know both the sensible singular and the nature or whatness of every material simple reality. Thus a given person, through his sense of sight, is able to see this individual tulip in his garden. In addition, his intellect enables him to apprehend or grasp the type of flower before him. Presented with only a single tulip, the human being is able to sense its singularity and to grasp, at least in an obscure way, its type, nature, or whatness.

It is the intellect's idea or concept which holds the nature or whatness of every simple reality. Just as the sense image retains a singular picture of whatever is sensed, so the mental image or concept holds the universal whatness of the sensed thing. More specifically, it is the sense image which retains the singular, cameralike picture of a swan seen on a peaceful lake, while it is the mental image or concept which retains the whatness of this particular swan. In fact, this idea or concept is defined as that mental mechanism or sign which retains the whatness of a sensed thing. Every concept, holding the nature common to every member, has a universal extension. Thus the concept of swan is applicable to each individual swan; i.e., is universal in its extension.

As noted above, the concept is a mental sign retaining the nature, essence, or whatness of the sensed thing. Retaining the whatness of the individual member, the concept, once grasped, does not require the presence of any individual members for its continued understanding. The memory of the individual, or individuals, is sufficient. Thus the statement *Robins' eggs are blue* remains realistically conceivable even at a time of the year when there may be no robins' eggs.

It is imperative to emphasize both that the concept holds the whatness of the sensed thing and that its understanding does not rest on the continued presence of individual members. What is the reason for this need? The reason lies in the fact that some symbolic logicians define the concept as the collection, set, or class of all its members. Under this thinking the concept is simply the aggregate of its members. Thus the concept of robin is the class or collection of all the individual robins. If one defines the concept as the class of its members rather than as a sign of the whatness of the sensed thing, then the presence of members is required for a viable definition. The reason is that, according to this thinking, the concept is only the collection or set of its members. But the concept, originating indeed from a sensible individual, does not require the continuing presence of even one member for its understanding. The concept is a sign, not of a collection of members, but of the essence or nature of the sensed individual thing.

As noted, the universality of the concept, its ability to represent any number of individuals of the same sort, derives from the mind's power (subsequent to the sensible grasp of a single individual) to perceive, even without formulating or defining it, the nature or whatness of the individual. This is seen by the fact that once an individual has been perceived and named, this same name will be applied to other individuals perceived as having the same nature. That this is something both in the individual and transcending the individual may be exemplified by the fact that, having contemplated one robin, one will unerringly (given the occasion) call other individuals *robin*. Yet the new robin may not have exactly the same dimensions, color, or movements as the previous one. Obviously the mind grasps the whatness of robin in abstraction from specifically individual characteristics.

The universal concept is not an artificial creation as held by the nominalists, who state that one grasps realistically only single sensible individuals. Rather it corresponds to the fact that in each individual the mind perceives, over and above the individual sensible characteristics proper to a given one, a certain, singular real nature or whatness. It is then the mind's experience that such a type of nature is found in many. While each nature is individual, many individual natures are perceived as having the same whatness. Hence the concept of a nature is said to be universal in the sense that many other individuals are seen to possess the same type of nature independently of singular characteristics of size, shape, shade, and so forth. From a philosophical viewpoint, one would state that, while the sensible individual perishes, nevertheless the species remains to the extent that the same type of nature continues to exist in succeeding individuals. (Should all the individuals perish, then all the identical natures perish: the species becomes extinct. However, to the extent that a sense memory of any individual remains in a mind, then the concept of the species can be recalled from that memory.)

To recapitulate, one may state that the concept is defined, not as a collection of its members, but as a sign which retains the nature or whatness of the sensed thing.

B. THE EXISTENTIAL NATURE OF UNIVERSAL PROPOSITIONS

As noted in chapter eight, the human mind combines and divides its concepts of simple realities into affirmative and negative propositions. This work of the judging intellect can be illustrated as follows:

Roses are red.	*affirmative*	*(composition)*
Vinegar is not sweet.	*negative*	*(division)*

At the same time these propositions are also divided into universal and particular statements according to the extension of their subject. (The singular proposition, such as *This rose is red*, is considered a particular statement.) Examples of this additional quantitative division are as follows:

Every rose is a flower.	*universal affirmative*	*(A)*
Some roses are red.	*particular affirmative*	*(I)*
No vinegar is sweet.	*universal negative*	*(E)*
Some vinegar is not used.	*particular negative*	*(O)*

Such propositions are then constituted into the traditional Square of Opposition and related as contradictories, contraries, subcontraries, and subalterns. This Square, together with illustrative propositions, follows:

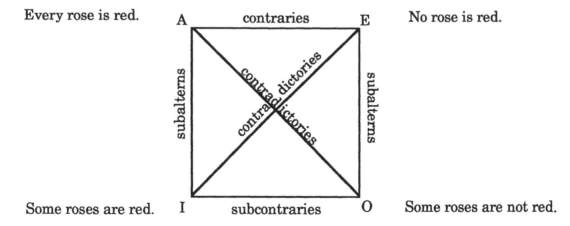

What are the implications of the universal propositions in the Square of Opposition?

Since all terms, including *rose* and *red*, represent universal concepts, their combination or division in universal propositions also has a universal connotation. Should one say, "Every rose is red," what would one be stating in connection with the universal concept of rose? One would be stating that wherever there was a rose, it would be accompanied by the color red. What could make such a statement valid? It would be the perception by experience that the nature of rose was accompanied by the property of being red. Just as the mind is seen to perceive the nature of a given thing, such as a robin, so too it comes to perceive certain properties as invariably associated with that nature, such as that a robin will have blue eggs. As experience attests, universal propositions are not mere artificial products of the mind, but represent real perceptions of reality.

1. UNIVERSAL PROPOSITIONS NECESSARY FOR ARTS AND SCIENCES

That universal propositions do represent real perceptions of reality may be seen by the fact that all the arts and sciences, all human learning, is postulated on the truth of such propositions arrived at experientially by the mind. Such a universal proposition is Galileo's law on the acceleration of falling bodies. This law holds that a body falls with a constant acceleration of so many feet per second per second, $v = gt$ (where g is 32 feet for bodies near the earth). It is expressed in the following universal proposition: *Every falling body accelerates at the rate, $v = gt$*. This having been experimentally established, one can now apply it to the case of any individual falling body, such as a space shuttle (whose trajectory is computed on the basis of a rectilinear horizontal motion combined with a vertical falling motion).

The above process also applies to the instructions on a packet of zinnia seeds. By experience one has discovered that the seeds grow best at a certain depth and should be spaced at a certain distance. All of this is expressed on the packet in implied universal propositions. One is instructed as follows: Plant seeds one-half inch deep. What universal proposition is implied? *Every zinnia seed grows best at one-half inch depth*. What is necessarily presupposed to all the successful universal propositions of the arts and sciences? It is the supposition verified by experience that there is in the material world an order and constancy that can be recognized by the human mind and put to use.

In order to be transmittable, such order and constancy must necessarily be in universal propositions. Thus it would not help in planning the trajectory of a space shuttle if all one could say about falling bodies was that *some* of them fall at the rate of 32 feet per second per second. One could then say nothing definite in advance about the case of the space shuttle. Likewise, what good would be instructions on a packet of zinnia seeds stating that only *some* zinnia seeds grow well at one-half inch depth? How then does one know whether this is true of the seeds in this packet?

2. SQUARE OF OPPOSITION RELATED TO NECESSITY AND CONTINGENCY

What is the significance of authentic universal propositions in the Square of Opposition? This significance may be summed up in the notes of necessity (that which cannot not be) and impossibility (that which cannot be) as referred to the relation of subject and predicate. An authentic A proposition is thus one in which the predicate is necessarily combined with the subject. An example of such is *Every human being is mortal*, standing for the fact that it necessarily belongs to the nature of the human being, a material thing, to be mortal, i.e., corruptible. In similar fashion an authentic E proposition states that it is impossible for the predicate to be combined with the subject, as in *No stone is living*.

Where such a note of necessity or impossibility producing authentic A and E propositions is not found, one has the notes of contingency or possibility expressed in I and O propositions. Thus, if a predicate is perceived as belonging to a subject in a given case but not necessarily, i.e., universally, one has a contingent proposition (expressing what is, but need not always be, and which would therefore not be expressed universally as applying to all). An example of such follows: *Some men have blue eyes.* If the predicate is not always true of the subject, but may be true in a given case, one has a proposition denoting possibility (what can be, but in the given case is not). Such possibility is exemplified as follows: *Some philosophers do not wear beards*; i.e., in this case it does not happen, but it is not impossible.

Granted the above necessity or contingency existing between a subject and its predicates, one can state the deeper meaning of the traditional Square of Opposition as follows:

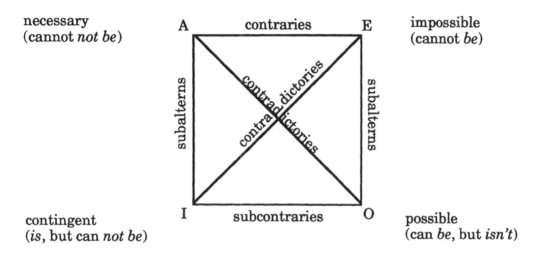

3. DISTINCTION BETWEEN FORMAL AND MATERIAL LOGIC

In addition to the above explanation about necessity and contingency, a further distinction must be made concerning the propositions in the Square of Opposition. This qualification is from that which exists between formal and material logic. In reference to formal logic, the terms used are not taken in an existential sense, but are simply symbols for diagramming purposes to exemplify relationships between propositions. Thus the following propositions can be legitimately used in formal logic to show the Square's various relationships:

1.	*an A proposition:*	*Every rose is red.*
2.	*its contrary:*	*No rose is red.*
3.	*its contradictory:*	*Some rose is not red.*
4.	*its subaltern:*	*Some rose is red.*

Subsequently the task of material logic is to discern experientially the existential relationship of *rose* and *red*, leading to *Some rose is red* and *Some rose is not red* as sole valid existential propositions.

4. "CLASS" NOT SUBSTITUTE FOR CONCEPT

With the above perceptions in mind, one can now address the following notions: (1) "class" as a substitute for concept, (2) "existential import" of Boolean interpretation. These notions are not purely logical in nature but represent philosophical tendencies, specifically the tenets of nominalism. In line with such tenets, the concept, perceived as the grasp by the mind in the individual material thing of a universal nature, is supplanted by "class," denoting the consciousness (upon experiencing one or several similar individuals) of a potential collection of individuals of similar nature. Hence the concept of robin as the grasp of a nature found in individuals but perceived as universal since not confined to a single individual, is supposedly better seen as the consciousness of a class, namely an (arithmetically countable) collection of entities having some common characteristic. These same tenets, denying the mind's perception of universal natures, attempt to reduce physics to mathematics. In this latter subject, geometry is then reduced to arithmetic, which itself is finally equated with logic.

What is to be said of the above proposal to supplant the concept by the notion of "class"? Simply that it does not correspond to reality. Take, for example, one's concept of a blue robin's egg. Supposedly it should take the form of a "class" seen as a "collection of entities having some common characteristic." Suppose it is winter and there are now no robins' eggs in existence, then one's consciousness should represent the "null class." Later it is spring and one's consciousness should now represent a class with a certain amount of members. But in effect this person's concept doesn't change. Why? Because it is obviously not predicated on any number of existing or nonexisting entities. Once one has seen a blue robin's egg he finds, for example, that he has a concept, not of an individual, unrepeatable egg, but of a certain nature or whatness which he recognizes, if the occasion arises, as being repeated in other individuals whether many or few. Even if all the individuals should perish, this person's concept, already present from an initial experience, remains unchanged as long as the sense memory thereof remains. The actual concept, therefore, is not a "class" as meaning a "collection," empty or having one or more members; since the concept, once had, clearly transcends the existence or nonexistence of the individual sensible entity causing the concept. In a word, the concept is universal.

Why does the concept not depend on the continued existence of the sensible individual causing it? It does not because material things are recognized as passing, corruptible. Thus a person has a concept produced by an apple. When that apple fades away, his concept of apple clearly does not fade with it. When there are millions and millions of apples in existence, must this person's concept be restricted to only *some* apples, the apples he knows? Clearly this person is conscious that his concept applies to all apples seen and unseen; is, in other words, in no way restricted to the amount of apples he has actually experienced.

All of this may be summed up in the recognition that counting—i.e., the number involved whether none, some, or all—has nothing to do with *what* things are. Thus, if one person were to tell another the *number* of things in his room, would the latter have any idea of *what* they were? Does one's concept of what a robin's egg is grow with a successive *number* of otherwise identical robins' eggs? What does a person know essentially with a second one that he did not already know with the first?

5. "EXISTENTIAL IMPORT" IN CONTINGENT THINGS

Next one can address the question of "existential import," which, in the Boolean interpretation, places universal propositions in a nonexistential state. Why? At least three reasons are listed. First, it is necessary initially to presuppose that such a universal class has members; for example, that *all* existing robins' eggs are blue even without seeing them all (an impossible task). Since one is presupposing, one is not affirming this as an actual fact. Therefore universal propositions do not have existential import. Second, such a pre-supposition is not in complete accord with actual usage since often the null set is inferred. Examples of this second situation follow: "Trespassers will be prosecuted." "Speeders will receive no warning." Third, a universal proposition may be presented *without* any supposition of existence. This happens when Newton's First Law of Motion is stated (incorrectly) as follows: "A body not acted upon by external forces perseveres in its state of rest or motion in a straight line." Scientists do not suppose any existing body to be *not* acted upon by external forces.

As to the first reason, one will note that, a universal proposition once established, its truth does *not* depend upon the actual existence of at least one member. Thus the truth of the proposition *Robins' eggs are blue*, in which a certain property (blue) is perceived as essentially connected with the nature and therefore true in all cases, does not depend upon the actual existence of at least one robin's egg. No one considers this proposition to be true in spring and false in winter. Rather its universality derives from the fact that a certain property, because it is a property, always accompanies the subject, abstracting from the actual existence of such a subject. Yet this proposition must be existential since, if one sees a robin sitting on a nest, one can predict, with no personal experience but solely by virtue of a universal statement in a bird book, that the eggs therein will be blue.

As to the second, there would be no need for signs saying "Trespassers will..." and "Speeders will...," if no such beings had ever existed. In anticipation of their possible, further future existence, law enforcement intends to affix to them a property, namely, prosecution. The truth of the propositions clearly does not depend upon the existence of trespassers and speeders, who at a given moment could be a "null class," but on whether the property affixed will be enforced, should they exist.

Finally in the third place, the First Law of Motion is not talking about what could well be a nonexistent category, a "necessarily null class," but affirms a certain property as antecedent to action by other bodies: "Every body perseveres in its state of rest or moving uniformly in a straight line except as it is compelled to change its state by forces impressed upon it" (translation of Latin text in Newton's *Principia*). Clearly such a universal proposition, the supposition of a body's basic tendency to move uniformly in a straight line, must have existential import; since all successful and verified calculations of motion, rectilinear or curved, presuppose its truth. The dialectical nature of such physical laws will be discussed below.

6. UNIVERSAL PROPOSITIONS NECESSARY FOR REASONING

Perhaps the most striking attestation to the existential import of universal propositions lies in the fact that no successful existential reasoning can take place *without* universal propositions. Why should this be so? It is caused by the fact that reasoning—whether valid or invalid, correct or incorrect—is nothing other than the application of already possessed universal knowledge to given circumstances, and is expressed in the following implied syllogistic rule: Every syllogism must contain at least one universal premise. The truth of this may be seen in any case of reasoning even quite particular in nature, such as when one says, "Boris must have been here because there are cigar ashes all over the place." The reasoning pattern of this example follows:

Whenever (a universal) there are cigar ashes all over, Boris must have been here.
But here and now there are cigar ashes.
Hence Boris must have been here.

Unless one holds that such a type of mess is invariably (i.e., universally and as a property) the work of Boris, the conclusion cannot follow.

Here one will note that the hypothetical proposition of a so-called "mixed" hypothetical syllogism as that above, is reducible, for purposes of testing validity, to a universal categorical proposition. When this has been done, one need not have recourse to a Venn diagram to test for validity but can simply compare the figure and mood attained to the traditional "Barbara, Celarent..." mood words.

Instead of the rule that at least one premise of a syllogism must be universal, the school of existential import has the rule that a valid particular conclusion may not be drawn from two universal premises ("no valid categorical syllogism with a particular conclusion can have two universal premises"). Why should this be so? Because a particular conclusion, whether affirmative or negative, expresses the *existence* of its subject, which cannot be derived from nonexistential universals.

But in *formal* logic, with which the laws of the syllogism are concerned, existence is not at stake. Rather the task is to see whether, from the supposition of certain premises (where the terms can be expressed by mere letters), a valid conclusion may be drawn. Then it is the task of *material* logic to ensure that the premises, in some valid form established in formal logic, contain true statements which will then lead to a true conclusion.

Thus, while "existential import" is taken as the particular affirmation in I and O propositions of at least one member in a class, the fact of the matter is that this is not at stake in formal logic; but rather if, given the premises, the conclusion (whether universal or particular) *follows*. Thus, in the second figure, from two universal premises, a universal conclusion follows. According to the rules of formal logic, the universal conclusion implies a particular conclusion if desired. In the outlook of existential import, however, while a nonexistential universal conclusion is valid in such a case, an existential particular is not. Thus, in the third figure, a valid syllogism of the form AAI would have to be declared invalid because its necessarily particular conclusion asserts the existence of the subject, *not* asserted in the premises.

The above problem confounds formal and material logic. In the former, existence is not at stake but rather the procedure is: "Supposing such-and-such, what follows?" In the latter, it is required that the premises be *true*, but not that the subject of the universal need actually *exist* at the moment, as in the true statement *Robins' eggs are blue* during an egg-less winter. Reasoning using this proposition follows:

Robins' eggs are not metallic.
Robins' eggs are blue.
∴ *Some blue things are not metallic.*

No one would say that the above proposition, as derived from the premises, would be true in spring and false in a robin-eggless winter. Rather even in material logic, insofar as material things are concerned, the presupposition, "if they exist at the time," is universally present, whether the propositions involved are universal or particular.

7. EXISTENCE OF SUBJECT NOT PROVED BY REASONING

The presence of the above presupposition stems from the fact that in reasoning one does not prove the existence of a subject but rather that, *given the subject*, something is proved about it. In proving by reasoning the conclusion *John Smith is guilty*, one does not prove John Smith's existence, but that guilt is rightly, or existentially, predicated of him. Hence, if one has established, from the perception of robins' eggs, that they are blue; then, given the experience of a subsequent robin egg, one will know in advance that it will be blue. Does this mean that reasoning is nonexistential? No. Rather it means, given the existence of a certain subject and that the existence or nonexistence of the predicate in the subject is not immediately self-evident, reasoning is able to *prove* the existence (or nonexistence) of a certain predicate *in* the subject.

In the case of universal propositions in which the predicate has been established as necessarily inhering in the subject of the universal (as in *Robins' eggs are blue*), then, given an existing example of the subject (this robin's egg unseen in a high nest), one knows in advance it will be existentially blue. Thus every proposition is existential which denotes an actually existing subject accompanied by a predicate which actually exists in it; or which, in the case of universal propositions, denotes a discerned, necessary relation between predicate and subject such that, given an existing case of the subject, the predicate will necessarily exist in it.

8. NECESSITY IN PREDICATION AND EXISTENCE

In the above treatment, one perceives two varieties of necessity (that which cannot not be). In the first usage, one refers to necessary propositions as those in which the predicate, because it is a property (or inseparable accident, or a part of the essence), necessarily inheres in the subject, as in *Robins' eggs are blue*. It is because one has perceived such an inseparable connection that one enunciates the universal proposition indispensable to reasoning. Should the predicate not be inseparable from the subject as in *Roses are red* (some roses being white); then one cannot deduce with certainty, from the fact that an object is a rose, that it will be red. Hence such propositions, even if universally true accidentally—at a given moment all roses might be red—are by nature, if true, only true as particulars (are contingent or possible) and cannot be used with certitude in deduction.

But even should one be dealing with properties which are necessary in this first sense of a predicate necessarily connected with a subject, no propositions about material things are necessary in the second sense of their subjects necessarily existing. Thus, even though robins' eggs are necessarily blue, robins' eggs do not necessarily exist. Rather, such a proposition implies that, if a robin egg exists, it will be blue. In other words, the existence of robins' eggs, as of all material things, is contingent. This is caused by the fact that all material things, the things of this world, are corruptible.

Because of the corruptibility of material things, then, even when one has a universally true proposition applied existentially, the predicate, in a lesser number of cases, may fail to be found in the existing subject. Thus the normal robin's egg will have a predictable thickness; but, because the robin's organism is not totally incorruptible, a contrary cause, such as DDT, could make the egg, in a lesser number of cases, not to have the proper thickness and be defective. Thus, even if dealing with an actual robin's egg, one cannot predict with absolute certainty that it will have the normal thickness. However, the fact that duly established physical laws are used confidently indicates that such defects occur only in the minor part.

All such qualifications are the task of material logic, while the actual form of a valid reasoning process is described in traditional formal logic, in which the indispensability of universal propositions for all reasoning is clearly evident. With the additional qualifications of material logic on the question of necessity, there is no visible need for the introduction of "existential import."

Finally, it is clear that, since all the arts and sciences—in fact all reasonings—are constituted on universal A and E propositions, and these latter are maintained precisely because they yield existential results, such propositions themselves must be existential.

9. DISTINCTION BETWEEN DIALECTICS AND DEMONSTRATION

But *how* are universal A and E propositions existential? Here a distinction must be made between what is demonstrably true (demonstrative reasoning) and what works, without needing to be wholly true (dialectical reasoning). The latter is true of the basic premises of modern science. A classic example is Galileo's law on the acceleration of falling bodies, v = gt, which allows one to predict that a falling body will accelerate at the rate of 32 feet per second (g) per second (t). Hence, if a body falls for 3 seconds, it will be predictably falling, at the end of that time, at the rate of 32 x 3, or 96 feet per second. Why is this dialectical? It is so because, while this calculation works for practical purposes, it incorporates a supposition that a falling body moves from point to point with a corresponding measurement of second by second. But it can be demonstrated that it is impossible for a point on a moving body to be at a point, basically because motion is necessarily extended while a point is unextended. Nevertheless such a mathematical conception does reflect the supposition of *uniform* acceleration, a supposition confirmed by the results. This supposition must therefore correspond to something existential, something existing in reality. Nevertheless, since its mathematical expression, however workable, does not correspond to reality, it is stated as dialectical.

The same must be said of the often-unnoticed basic reduction in science of all curves to a series of straight lines, starting with the computation of the circumference of a circle in terms of its diameter, the classical π, whose numerical value is commonly given as 3.1416.... Actually this is a computation derived by taking an inscribed, or circumscribed, rectilinear polygon instead of the circumference (since a *curved* circumference clearly cannot be computed as so many times its *rectilinear* diameter). Yet the fact that such a substitution works perfectly for practical purposes demonstrates that the supposition of a constant ratio between diameter and circumference must be existential, since it works when even an approximation of a circle is substituted. The further supposition, even in rectilinear terms, of a *numerical* constant, π (such as 3.1416...), is illusory; since the value arrived at necessarily varies every time the number of the sides of the polygon is doubled for closer approximation (and even then the decimal points indicate that there is no actual number attained but rather something incommensurable, i.e., mathematically unmeasurable). Hence all such suppositions which work, but which clearly are not perfect reflections of reality, while necessarily existential as producing results in harmony with reality, are at the same time *dialectical*, i.e., satisfying appearances while not proven true.

Such a perception of the dialectical nature of various workable suppositions is vitally necessary, since the failure to do so can lead to taking suppositions as truth, leading in turn in some cases to a disastrous denial of truth, as when the supposition of an actual infinity in natural numbers leads, via "Cantor's Theorem," to the denial of the first principles of reason.

THE FOURTH FIGURE OF THE CATEGORICAL SYLLOGISM

In chapter eleven this text stated that the figures of the categorical syllogism are constituted from the different ways of arranging the basic components of the premises. Since these components are the major, minor, and middle terms, the figures of this syllogism result from the different possible combinations of these three terms. This text then explained that the only possible combinations of these terms are those in which the middle is between (I), above (II), or below (III) the other two. Such combinations lead to the following three figures:

First Figure (I)	Second Figure (II)	Third Figure (III)
M ----------- P	P -------------- M	M ----------- P
S -----------M	S ------------- M	M -----------S
∴ S--------- P	∴ S----------- P	∴ S-------- P

As one examines the above figures, an immediate question presents itself. Is there not one other combination of the three terms which would lead to a fourth figure? Its structure would be as follows:

Fourth Figure (IV)
P------------M
M------------S
∴S---------- P

The above combination of terms leading to the fourth figure does not result in a sound syllogistic or reasoning pattern. The explanation lies in the definition of the categorical syllogism itself. As already defined, this syllogism is the linking (or separating) of the conclusion's subject and predicate through the middle term. Said in another way, this syllogism is a reasoning pattern in which the predicate is said or attributed of the subject by means of some middle term. This pattern rests on the general principle that whatever is affirmed (or denied) of all a thing is affirmed (or denied) of whatever falls under that thing. Thus, since the predicate *carnivore* is affirmed of every canine, it can be affirmed of every fox falling under the canine class. The logical form of this example is as follows:

First Figure (I)				
M ----------- P	*Every canine*	*(M)*	*is a carnivore.*	*(P)*
S ----------- M	*Every fox*	*(S)*	*is a canine.*	*(M)*
∴ S--------- P	∴ *Every fox*	*(S)*	*is a carnivore.*	*(P)*

As the above example illustrates, the range of the above terms varies. As the name of each one indicates, the terms have a major, middle, and minor extension. In other words, these components range from a greater through an intermediate to a lesser universality. It is precisely because of this difference in universality or extension that one has the possibility of general principles which can be applied to cases falling under them. In other words, it is because some things fall under other things that whatever is said of the latter can be said of the former. Therefore the logician must remember this fact as he lays down the relationships among the terms of the various figures. These terms cannot be aligned as a result of a merely mechanical shifting of the components involved. They must reveal, at least to some degree, the interlocking relationships existing among the three terms.

As the above patterns indicate, the attribution of some predicate to a given subject through an intermediate or middle term is structured most clearly in the first figure. Thus S is P because *S is M and M is P*. Therefore this figure is designated as perfect. The second and third figures are imperfect because their structures retain only part of this syllogistic relationship. This partial retention can be noted in the following patterns:

Second Figure: S is P because *S is M* and P is M.
Third Figure: S is P because M is S and *M is P*.

Because of the nature of the second and third figures, they do not reveal so easily as the first figure the relationships found in the reasoning pattern. Therefore, if they are questioned, these figures must be reduced to the first figure by the process of conversion or of indirect proof.

The fourth figure, however, retains none of the regular relationships existing among the terms of the categorical premises. As the following pattern indicates, the intermediate position of the middle term is found in neither premise:

Fourth Figure: S is P because M is S and P is M.

Therefore, because of its particular structure and because of the meaning of the syllogistic process, the fourth figure is not considered one of the possible figures for the categorical syllogism.

A CONDENSED VERSION OF SYMBOLIC LOGIC

A. Truth-functional connectives
B. Material implication
C. The use of truth tables
D. Material and logical equivalence
E, Analysis of arguments

As the name itself suggests, symbolic logic has a special language for the various propositions obtained by the mind and for the connections made between them. This language can be noted in the symbols used for the following hypothetical argument:

If p, then q.	*More briefly:*	$p \supset q$
If it rains, the ground will be wet.		
But p.		p
It is raining.		
∴ *q.*		∴ q
∴ The ground is wet.		

This use of symbols is not original to modern logic. Rather Aristotle himself, the inventor of the subject, employed various letters of the alphabet to represent the subjects and predicates of syllogisms. Instead the modern subject is distinguished by its efforts to carry symbolization as far as possible. In a word, symbolic logic hopes to reduce all arguments, simple or complex, to some easily handled symbols. As a result, the human eye can read the elements and connections of a complex argument in a facile or mechanical way. Then the mind is spared the trouble of solving the argumentation on the mental level.

A. TRUTH-FUNCTIONAL CONNECTIVES

As the above example indicated, the various propositions are represented by lower case letters from the middle part of the alphabet, such as *p, q, r, s,* and so forth. The connecting links between these propositions are symbolized by truth-functional connectives. Four of these connectives are as follows:

Name	Symbol	Meaning	Derivation or Connection
1. wedge	∨	or	It is derived from the first letter of the Latin *vel* ("or").
2. dot	·	and	—
3. curl (or tilde)	~	not; a negation	This same symbol is used as a diacritical mark in Spanish and Portuguese.
4. horseshoe	⊃	if—then	—

The above symbols, together with the lower case letters, are illustrated in the following examples:

1.   *p*   ∨   *q*
    Either John is late or he has decided not to come.

2.   *p*   ·   *q*
    Indira Ghandi was prime minister and she was assassinated.

3.   *~p*
    It is false that every rabbit has webbed feet.
    No rabbit has webbed feet.
    Some rabbits do not have webbed feet.
    [The curl (~) symbolizes the negation of any statement.]

4. *If he has cholera, he will die.* ‖ $p \supset q$
   He has cholera.   ‖ *p*
   ∴ *He will die.*   ‖ ∴ *q*

Two comments must be made about the above symbols. First, the wedge (∨) symbolizing *or* is given the widest possible application. In English, the word *or* can be taken in either an exclusive or inclusive sense. The following statements illustrate this distinction:

1. exclusive meaning of *or*:
   Every number is either odd or even.
   (These are exclusive alternatives; only one of them can be true.)
2. inclusive meaning of *or*:
   The guest of honor will receive either a plaque or flowers (and possibly both of them). (Since the above alternatives are nonopposed, they do not exclude each other. In other words, the above are complementary or inclusive alternatives. In this case the meaning is not that one alternative *alone* is true. Rather the meaning is that *at least* one, and possibly both, of the alternatives is true.)

It is the second, inclusive meaning which is symbolized by the wedge. Therefore this symbol means either-or or both, rather than either-or but not both. As such, only the above second statement is symbolized as follows: p ∨ q.

The second comment concerning the four truth-functional connectives is that the dot (·) may be used only if both statements to be connected are true. The following example illustrates this requirement:

    p   ·   *q*
John F. Kennedy was an American president and a victim of assassination.

B. MATERIAL IMPLICATION

In ordinary conversation one frequently meets conditional, hypothetical, or implicative statements such as the following: *If Tom comes home, we will have a party*. In symbolic logic, such hypothetical propositions are called material implications. What is the agreed-upon scope of such implications? The symbolic logician sets down the lowest common denominator, the widest degree of possibility, or the most elementary supposition for his material implications. The scope of this supposition may be described in the following ways:

1. It is presupposed that the antecedent, whether its consequent is seen to follow clearly or not, is at least not seen to be blatantly accompanied by the contradictory of the proposed consequent.
2. In other words, it is presupposed that the combination of the antecedent and the contradictory of the proposed consequent (expressed as p · ~q) is not true. This supposition is expressed as follows: ~(p · ~q).
3. Granted this elementary restriction, both the restriction and the valid possibilities for material implication may be charted as follows:

invalid implication:	If p, then non-q.	p ⊃ ~q
basic implication:	If p, then q.	p ⊃ q
valid implications:	If non-p, then q.	~p ⊃ q
	If non-p, then non-q.	~p ⊃ ~q

4. In summary, material implication holds between any value of p or q, whether true or false, except the following: p implies non-q or p ⊃ ~q.

This wide scope of material implication is spelled out or defined by a truth table, which is a device used to lay down all the valid or invalid possibilities of a given formula. To complete a truth table, one must first place the different parts of the formula across the top row. Then the basic components of the formula (placed at the beginning of the row) are marked true or false in descending order in sufficient variation to include all possible combinations. These initial columns are then the guides whereby the remaining columns are labeled true or false. The truth table for the scope of material implication is as follows:

	p	q	p ⊃ q	
	T	T	T	
(Columns 1	T	F	F	[Column 3 indicates the
and 2 are	F	T	T	valid (T) or invalid (F)
the guides.)	F	F	T	material implications.]

As one can see from inspecting the last column, every possible implication for p implies q is permitted except when p is true and q is false. This is equivalent to saying that one will allow all implications except one in which, from a true antecedent (p), a false consequent (q) is implied. Hence, in the second row above, where p is true and q is false, the implication p ⊃ q is likewise false.

As the above truth table reveals, the agreed-upon scope for material implication includes any value of p or q, whether true or false, except the following: p implies non-q or (p ⊃ ~q). This minimal restriction permits material implication to be expressed also in the following ways:

1. Since material implication does not permit p and ~q to be simultaneously true, it may also be expressed as ~(p · ~q).
2. Also the statement *It is not true that there is a conjunction of p and ~q* ~(p · ~q) is reducible to the statement *Either p is false or q is true* (~p ∨ q). The reason for this reduction is that whenever p is false or q is true, it guarantees the truth of ~(p · ~q).

Because of the wide latitude of material implication, one finds oneself with a paradoxical situation. This situation, charted in the above truth table and called the paradoxes of material implication, is as follows:

153

1. *~p legitimately implies both q and ~q.*
   example:
   If you are not good, I will give you a lollypop.
   If you are not good, I won't give you a lollypop.
2. *q is implied by both p and ~p.*
   example:
   You will get a lollypop if you are good.
   You will get a lollypop if you are not good.

The only restriction, given p ⊃ q, is that p may not imply ~q. This means, with the above example, that it is not possible that you should be good and *not* get a lollypop.

Is there any conversational expression which reveals the minimal restriction found in material implication? As noted above, this broad implication excludes only the following of a false consequent from a true antecedent. A conversationalist would indeed have an oblique example of such a restriction whenever, in order to show that a given antecedent cannot possibly be true, he posits a consequent which he is sure will never take place. Such expressions may be exemplified as follows:

1. *If the stars fall from the heavens, then I will turn into a tulip.*
2. *If water is no longer important, then people will walk upside down.*

C. THE USE OF TRUTH TABLES

The previous section explained the way in which a truth table is constructed. These tables are used to set down the valid and invalid possibilities of the various forms in symbolic logic. In other words, the truth table defines the given logical form by showing under what conditions it is valid or true. Thus p ∨ q is defined as follows:

p	q	p ∨ q
T	T	T
T	F	T
F	T	T
F	F	F

In the above table, the last column points out that p ∨ q is true if one or the other of its members is true.

The logical form, p · q, is defined in the same fashion by the following truth table:

p	q	p · q
T	T	T
T	F	F
F	T	F
F	F	F

In the above table, the last column points out that p · q is true only when both members are true.

Through the use of a truth table, the valid forms of hypothetical reasoning are also defined. The possibilities on such a table would include the following hypothetical arguments:

1. valid form of affirming the antecedent (*modus ponens* in symbolic logic)
2. valid form of denying the consequent (*modus tollens* in symbolic logic)
3. fallacy of denying the antecedent
4. fallacy of affirming the consequent
    (These numbers will be used in the truth table.)

What rule enables the symbolic logician to retain only the above valid forms and to exclude the above fallacies? This basic rule is as follows: If a *single* case of the given argument form on the truth table has true premises and a false conclusion (TTF), then the argument form is invalid. All possible instances of these hypothetical forms, including the invalid ones, are listed on the following table:

	p	q	p ⊃ q	~p	~q	
valid—no. 1	T⟶	T	T	F	F	
	T	F	F	F	T	
invalid—no. 4	F⟵	T	T	T⟶	F	no. 3—invalid
	F	F	T	T⟵	T	no. 2—valid
			(major)			

As the above table reveals, the argument denying the antecedent (no. 3) has two true premises followed by a false conclusion (TTF). Also the argument affirming the consequent (no. 4) has the same problem. These two arguments may be charted as follows:

no. 3	p ⊃ q	(T)		no. 4	p ⊃ q	(T)
	~p	(T)			q	(T)
	∴ ~q	(F)			∴ p	(F)

Therefore, following the minimal restriction of material implication and the rule concerning true premises and a false conclusion, the symbolic logician has only two valid forms for hypothetical reasoning. These forms are affirming the antecedent and denying the consequent.

As noted above, the valid forms of the hypothetical argument are called *modus ponens* and *modus tollens* by the symbolic logician. Also this logician uses the general term *hypothetical syllogism* only for hypothetical reasoning which has a series of conditions. This argument form is as follows: p ⊃ q, q ⊃ r, ∴ p ⊃ r. Finally, the argument form (p ∨ q, ~p, ∴q) is called a disjunctive syllogism.

D. MATERIAL AND LOGICAL EQUIVALENCE

Material equivalence has a special meaning for the symbolic logician. It is defined as that equivalence in which two statements are either both true or both false. Then these two statements are said to be materially equivalent or equivalent in truth value. This concept is represented by the symbol (≡). Such material equivalence is defined by the following truth table:

p	q	p ≡ q
T	T	T
T	F	F
F	T	F
F	F	T

155

As the above table reveals, p and q are materially equivalent in that they are either both true (T) or both false (T). As such, these two statements materially imply each other.

In addition, two statements are said to be logically equivalent if the statement of their material equivalence has only true substitution instances. Such a statement is a tautology. This latter term is defined as a statement form having only true substitution instances. The presence of such true instances can be noted in the last column of the following truth table:

p	q	p · q	~(p · q)	~p	~q	~p ∨ ~q	~(p · q) ≡ (~p ∨ ~q)
T	T	T	F	F	F	F	T
T	F	F	T	F	T	T	T
F	T	F	T	T	F	T	T
F	F	F	T	T	T	T	T

conjunction   disjunction   tautology

As the above table reveals, a conjunction and disjunction are equated by means of denials. It can also be noted that these two forms have material equivalence. Since such equivalence has only true substitution instances (last column), these two forms have logical equivalence or are tautological. This above tautology is one of De Morgan's Theorems. His two theorems are expressed as follows:

1. The denial of the conjunction of two statements is equivalent to the disjunction of their denials. $\sim(p \cdot q) \equiv (\sim p \lor \sim q)$

2. The denial of the disjunction of two statements is equivalent to the conjunction of their denials. $\sim(p \lor q) \equiv (\sim p \cdot \sim q)$

There are many other examples of logically equivalent expressions in symbolic logic. Two of these, called Distribution, express the basic fact that a given element may be related to a group of elements either in their separate or combined form. The two statements of Distribution are as follows:

$$[p \cdot (q \lor r)] \equiv [(p \cdot q) \lor (p \cdot r)]$$
$$[p \lor (q \cdot r)] \equiv [(p \lor q) \cdot (p \lor r)]$$

E. ANALYSIS OF ARGUMENTS

The whole purpose for the symbols and rules of modern logic is to solve easily both simple and complex arguments. To reach these solutions this subject uses the following procedures:

1. One lists in order the symbolic expression of the succeeding statements.
2. In the same column, one consolidates these statements by using the appropriate rules of inference.
3. Opposite these consolidations, one states the justifications for them.

These procedures will now be exemplified by both a simple and a complex argument:

Argument 1

Either Henry will golf tomorrow or he will rake the leaves.
If he goes golfing, he will have to pay a parking fee.
If he has a parking fee, he will spend his lunch money.
But Henry cannot afford to spend his lunch money.
Therefore Henry will rake the leaves. (G, R, P, L)

1.	$G \lor R$	
2.	$G \supset P$	
3.	$P \supset L$	
4.	$\sim L$	/ $\therefore R$
5.	$G \supset L$	*from 2, 3 by Hypothetical Syllogism*
6.	$\sim G$	*from 5, 4 by <u>modus tollens</u>*
7.	R	*from 1, 6 by Disjunctive Syllogism*

Argument 2

Either Adam is doing his laundry or had gone earlier to the bakery and either Adam is doing his laundry or was playing Chopin.
If he was doing his laundry, he was thinking of going to a disco.
If he was thinking of going to a disco, it was because he felt he needed exercise.
If he went earlier to the bakery and was playing Chopin, then, if he felt fat, he felt he needed exercise.
But he didn't feel he needed exercise.
Therefore he didn't feel fat. (A, B, C, D, E, F)

1.	$(A \lor B) \cdot (A \lor C)$	
2.	$A \supset D$	
3.	$D \supset E$	
4.	$(B \cdot C) \supset (F \supset E)$	
5.	$\sim E$	/ $\therefore \sim F$
6.	$A \supset E$	*from 2, 3 by a Hypothetical Syllogism*
7.	$\sim A$	*from 6, 5 by <u>modus tollens</u>*
8.	$A \lor (B \cdot C)$	*from 1 by Distribution*
9.	$B \cdot C$	*from 8, 7 by a Disjunctive Syllogism*
10.	$F \supset E$	*from 4, 9 by <u>modus ponens</u>*
11.	$\sim F$	*from 10, 5 by <u>modus tollens</u>*

ARISTOTELIAN SORITES

A. Its formation and rules
B. Its illustration by Lewis Carroll

This appendix has a twofold purpose. It will first explain the formation and rules for the Aristotelian sorites (piled-up syllogism) and then illustrate this logical form by means of examples from Lewis Carroll's *Symbolic Logic*. The value of such an appendix lies in the fact that the student, working with Carroll's sorites, is given excellent practice in the following logical operations: conversion and obversion; the rules and relationships of the categorical and hypothetical syllogisms. In addition, the same student is introduced to the acceleration in thinking provided by the symbolization of subjects and predicates. Such an introduction gives valuable background for the procedures utilized by symbolic logic in its analysis of arguments.

A. ITS FORMATION AND RULES

Briefly the sorites may be described as a piled-up or heaped-up syllogism. This logical form, named from the Greek *soreites* ("heaped-up"), is nothing other than a series of categorical syllogisms lumped together. More formally, the sorites may be defined as an interlocking series of categorical syllogisms in the first figure. The structure of this logical form may be exemplified as follows:

A ------------ *B*	——————*initial subject*————————→	*Every fox is an animal.*
B ------------ *C*		*Every animal is living.*
C ------------ *D*		*Every living thing is a body.*
D ------------ *E*	————*final predicate* —————————→	*Every body is a substance.*
∴ *A* --------- *E*		∴ *Every fox is a substance.*

As the above example illustrates, the form of the sorites is as follows:

1. The minor premise with the initial subject (A) is stated first.
2. The initial predicate (B) becomes the succeeding subject. This same progression continues through an indifferent number of premises. No matter what the number, the terms always exceed the premises by one. (This same ratio is true in the basic categorical syllogism.)
3. The major premise with the final predicate (E) is stated last.
4. Then the conclusion attributing the final predicate (E) to the initial subject (A) is drawn.

In the Aristotelian sorites, the minor premise is stated first, while the major is the last one in the indifferent number of premises. As it was already explained in the treatment of the categorical syllogism, either premise may begin the process of categorical reasoning. It was then stated that the major premise is placed first in the formal logical structure. Contrariwise, the minor premise begins the informal pattern of reasoning. This latter procedure is the one followed in the sorites.

The sorites is possible solely in the first figure, for its diagonal structure is the only one permitting the preceding predicate to be placed immediately as the next subject. Such a structure enables a continuous sequence of reasoning to occur. Also such a series of syllogistic reasoning is possible at all only because the predicate of an affirmative proposition has equal and usually greater extension than the subject. Such gradually rising extension permits the final predicate to be affirmed of the initial subject. This range of extension can be noted in the above example.

It is of interest to note that the sorites' pattern is found in one of the basic forms of symbolic logic. In this latter subject a sorites stated in hypothetical form (with the terms p, q, r) is called a hypothetical syllogism. Other terms are then used for the valid forms of hypothetical reasoning. They are as follows:

1. valid form of affirming the antecedent   (*modus ponens*)
2. valid form of denying the consequent   (*modus tollens*)

Since the sorites is always in the first figure, it follows the special rules of this categorical form. They are as follows:

1. The major premise must be universal.
2. The minor premise must be affirmative.

Since the sorites always needs a universal major premise, only its first or minor premise may be particular. This means that, if the student finds a premise with a particular subject, he knows automatically that such a proposition is the first or minor premise. In addition, since the minor must be affirmative, only the last or major premise may be negative. In other words, every premise of the sorites has to be affirmative except the last one. Therefore, if more than one negative is present in a given sorites, the student must utilize obversion to reduce the number of negative premises to a single one. Otherwise he neglects to follow the rule concerning the impossibility of two negatives in a syllogism. A summary list adapting the rules of the first figure to the sorites is as follows:

1. Only the first or minor premise may be particular.
2. Only the last or major premise may be negative.
3. Excluding the above exceptions, every premise must be universal affirmative.

B. ITS ILLUSTRATION BY LEWIS CARROLL

As stated in the introduction, the sorites by Lewis Carroll provide excellent practice in various logical operations and also familiarize the student with the use of symbolization. In line with Carroll's purpose of popularizing logic, his sorites are a mine of unusual, delightful, and interesting examples. Since they are written in casual and detailed language, they give the student ample opportunity to utilize his logical skill in ordinary and lengthy discourse.

As already defined, the sorites is a heaped-up categorical syllogism. Now it is possible under certain conditions to express the categorical syllogism in the hypothetical mode. Finally this latter mode may be stated in a completely symbolic form. Therefore, in order that the student may obtain maximum benefit from these exercises, the directions for Carroll's sorites include this threefold transition. These directions, together with several worked-out examples, are as follows:

1. After each example, Carroll states its universe and appropriate symbols. Using the technique of a universe, the logician is able to designate otherwise particular terms as universal. The reason is that such terms are taken as all the members in that restricted universe.
2. Utilizing Carroll's universe and symbols, the student should symbolize each subject and predicate. If Carroll refers to his universe in a given premise, the student does not need this reference in his symbolized premise. While making this transition, the student must note if a given premise presents a term with its opposing meaning. (See sorites 1, no. 1.) Finally, the student must be aware of the equivalency of the following phrases: *none but A*; *none except A*; *none unless A = no non*-A.
3. Using the restricted universe, the student must be certain that every premise except the first, minor one is universal.
4. To place the premises in logical sequence, the student must first find the two terms which are not repeated. These are the initial subject and the final predicate. If one is a substantive and the other an adjective, the former is the subject, the latter the predicate. If both terms are one grammatical type, the student may start with either one. Then the conclusion may be converted, if necessary.
5. Beginning with the subject and remembering the first figure's diagonal structure, the student must then align the succeeding premises. To effect this alignment, he must frequently use conversion and obversion.
6. After all the premises are arranged in logical order, the student should state the final predicate of the initial subject.
7. After the categorical sorites is symbolized and solved, the student should transfer the categorical premises to a hypothetical form. Now the hypothetical format lays down that there is a necessary and universal connection between the subject and predicate. Therefore, to transfer any contingent or particular premise, the logician must consider such a premise as necessary either at the moment or from man-made necessity and as universal in the given restricted universe.
8. Taking the subject as antecedent and the predicate as consequent, the student should shift the categorical sorites to a hypothetical form. Because of the if-then structure of this form, he must frequently use obversion to retain the correct positive or negative meaning.
9. In order to place the hypothetical premises in logical sequence, the student will frequently need to deny the consequent. Then he will be able to draw the conclusion.
10. Finally the student can transfer the solved hypothetical sorites to a completely symbolic form by means of the following symbols:

Name	Symbol	Meaning
curl (or tilde)	~	not; a negative
horseshoe	⊃	if-then

Sorites 1§
1. *Babies are illogical;*
2. *Nobody is despised who can manage a crocodile;*
3. *Illogical persons are despised.*

Universe: "persons"; a = *able to manage a crocodile;* b = *babies;*
                           c = *despised;* d = *logical.*

Categorical Form
1. *Every b is non-d.*
2. *No a is c.*
3. *Every non-d is c.*

Logical Sequence
1. *Every b is non-d.*
3. *Every non-d is c.*
2. *No c is a. (conv.)*
∴ *No b is a.*

Hypothetical Form
1. *If b, then non-d.*
2. *If a, then non-c. (obv.)*
3. *If non-d, then c.*

Logical Sequence
1. *If b, then non-d.*
3. *If non-d, then c.*
2. *If c, then non-a. (d.c.)*
∴ *If b, then non-a.*
   (No b is a.)

Symbolic Form
1. $b \supset \sim d$
2. $a \supset \sim c$
3. $\sim d \supset c$

Logical Sequence
1. $b \supset \sim d$
3. $\sim d \supset c$
2. $c \supset \sim a$ *(d.c.)*
∴ $b \supset \sim a$

Carroll's answer: Babies cannot manage crocodiles.

Sorites 35§
1. *No birds, except ostriches, are 9 feet high;*
2. *There are no birds in this aviary that belong to anyone but me;*
3. *No ostrich lives on mince-pies;*
4. *I have no birds less than 9 feet high.*

Universe: "birds"; a = *in this aviary;* b = *living on mince-pies;*
                         c = *my;* d = *9 feet high;* e = *ostriches.*

Categorical Form
1. *No non-e is d.*
2. *No non-c is a.*
3. *No e is b.*
4. *No c is non-d.*

Logical Sequence
2. *Every a is c. (conv., obv.)*
4. *Every c is d. (obv.)*
1. *Every d is e. (conv., obv.)*
3. *No e is b.*
∴ *No a is b.*

Hypothetical Form
1. *If non-e, then non-d. (obv.)*
2. *If non-c, then non-a. (obv.)*
3. *If e, then non-b. (obv.)*
4. *If c, then d. (obv.)*

Logical Sequence
2. *If a, then c. (d.c.)*
4. *If c, then d.*
1. *If d, then e. (d.c.)*
3. *If e, then non-b.*
∴ *If a, then non-b.*
   (No a is b.)

─────────

§Each sorites with a section mark (§) is taken from the following source: Lewis Carroll, *Symbolic Logic* (London: Macmillan & Company, Ltd., 1896), pp. 112–24.

Symbolic Form	Logical Sequence
1. ~e ⊃ ~d	2. a ⊃ c (d.c.)
2. ~c ⊃ ~a	4. c ⊃ d
3. e ⊃ ~b	1. d ⊃ e (d.c.)
4. c ⊃ d	3. e ⊃ ~b
	∴ a ⊃ ~b

Carroll's answer: No bird in this aviary lives on mince pies.

Sorites 50§

1. No one, who is going to a party, ever fails to brush his hair;
2. No one looks fascinating, if he is untidy.;
3. Opium-eaters have no self-command;
4. Every one, who has brushed his hair, looks fascinating;
5. No one wears white kid gloves, unless he is going to a party;
6. A man is always untidy, if he has no self-command.

Universe: "persons";   a = going to a party; b = having brushed one's hair;
c = having self-command; d = looking fascinating;
e = opium-eaters; h = tidy; k = wearing white kid gloves.

Categorical Form	Logical Sequence
1. No a is non-b.	3. Every e is non-c. (obv.)
2. No non-h is d.	6. Every non-c is non-h.
3. No e is c.	2. Every non-h is non-d. (obv.)
4. Every b is d.	4. Every non-d is non-b. (obv., conv., obv.)
5. No non-a is k.	1. Every non-b is non-a. (conv., obv.)
6. Every non-c is non-h.	5. No non-a is k.
	∴ No e is k.

Hypothetical Form	Logical Sequence
1. If a, then b. (obv.)	3. If e, then non-c.
2. If non-h, then non-d. (obv.)	6. If non-c, then non-h.
3. If e, then non-c. (obv.)	2. If non-h, then non-d.
4. If b, then d.	4. If non-d, then non-b. (d.c.)
5. If non-a, then non-k. (obv.)	1. If non-b, then non-a. (d.c.)
6. If non-c, then non-h.	5. If non-a, then non-k.
	∴ If e, then non-k.
	(No e is k.)

Symbolic Form	Logical Sequence
1. a ⊃ b	3. e ⊃ ~c
2. ~h ⊃ ~d	6. ~c ⊃ ~h
3. e ⊃ ~c	2. ~h ⊃ ~d
4. b ⊃ d	4. ~d ⊃ ~b (d.c.)
5. ~a ⊃ ~k	1. ~b ⊃ ~a (d.c.)
6. ~c ⊃ ~h	5. ~a ⊃ ~k
	∴ e ⊃ ~k

Carroll's answer: Opium eaters never wear white kid gloves.

The following examples, also taken from Carroll's sorites, should be solved according to the above directions:

Sorites 5[§]
1. No ducks waltz;
2. No officers ever decline to waltz;
3. All my poultry are ducks.

Universe: "creatures"; a = ducks; b = my poultry; c = officers; d = willing to waltz.

Sorites 23[§]
1. Nobody, who really appreciates Beethoven, fails to keep silence while the Moonlight-Sonata is being played;
2. Guinea-pigs are hopelessly ignorant of music;
3. No one, who is hopelessly ignorant of music, ever keeps silence while the Moonlight-Sonata is being played.

Universe: "creatures"; a = guinea-pigs; b = hopelessly ignorant of music;
c = keeping silence while the Moonlight-Sonata is being played;
d = really appreciating Beethoven.

Sorites 29[§]
1. All my sons are slim;
2. No child of mine is healthy who takes no exercise;
3. All gluttons, who are children of mine, are fat;
4. No daughter of mine takes any exercise.

Universe: "my children"; a = fat; b = gluttons; c = healthy; d = sons; e = taking exercise.

Sorites 33[§]
1. None of the unnoticed things, met with at sea, are mermaids;
2. Things entered in the log, as met with at sea, are sure to be worth remembering;
3. I have never met with anything worth remembering, when on a voyage;
4. Things met with at sea, that are noticed, are sure to be recorded in the log.

Universe: "things met with at sea";   a = entered in the log; b = mermaids;
c = met with by me; d = noticed;
e = worth remembering.

Sorites 37[§]
1. No interesting poems are unpopular among people of real taste;
2. No modern poetry is free from affectation;
3. All your poems are on the subject of soap-bubbles;
4. No affected poetry is popular among people of real taste;
5. No ancient poem is on the subject of soap-bubbles.

Universe: "poems"; a = affected; b = ancient; c = interesting;
d = on the subject of soap-bubbles;
e = popular among people of real taste; h = written by you.

<u>Sorites 44</u>[§]
1. All writers who understand human nature, are clever;
2. No one is a true poet unless he can stir the hearts of men;
3. Shakespeare wrote "Hamlet";
4. No writer, who does not understand human nature, can stir the hearts of men;
5. None but a true poet could have written "Hamlet."

Universe: "writers"; a = able to stir the hearts of men; b = clever; c = Shakespeare;
           d = true poets; e = understanding human nature;
           h = writer of "Hamlet."

<u>Sorites 49</u>[§]
1. Animals, that do not kick, are always unexcitable;
2. Donkeys have no horns;
3. A buffalo can always toss one over a gate;
4. No animals that kick are easy to swallow;
5. No hornless animal can toss one over a gate;
6. All animals are excitable, except buffalos.

Universe: "animals"; a = able to toss one over a gate; b = buffalos; c = donkeys;
           d = easy to swallow; e = excitable; h = horned; k = kicking.

<u>Sorites 54</u>[§]
1. No shark ever doubts that it is well fitted out;
2. A fish, that cannot dance a minuet, is contemptible;
3. No fish is quite certain that it is well fitted out, unless it has three rows of teeth;
4. All fishes, except sharks, are kind to children;
5. No heavy fish can dance a minuet;
6. A fish with three rows of teeth is not to be despised.

Universe: "fishes"; a = able to dance a minuet; b = certain that he is well fitted out;
           c = contemptible; d = having 3 rows of teeth; e = heavy;
           h = kind to children; k = sharks.

<u>Sorites 59</u>[§]
1. All the dated letters in this room are written on blue paper;
2. None of them are in black ink, except those that are written in the third person;
3. I have not filed any of them that I can read;
4. None of them that are written on one sheet, are undated;
5. All of them, that are not crossed, are in black ink;
6. All of them, written by Brown, begin with "Dear Sir";
7. All of them, written on blue paper, are filed;
8. None of them, written on more than one sheet, are crossed;
9. None of them, that begin with "Dear Sir," are written in the third person.

Universe: "letters in this room"; a = beginning with "Dear Sir"; b = crossed;
                         c = dated; d = filed; e = in black ink;
                         h = in the third person; k = letters that I can read;
                         l = on blue paper; m = on one sheet;
                         n = written by Brown.

Sorites 60[§]

1. The only animals in this house are cats;
2. Every animal is suitable for a pet, that loves to gaze at the moon;
3. When I detest an animal, I avoid it;
4. No animals are carnivorous, unless they prowl at night;
5. No cat fails to kill mice;
6. No animals ever take to me, except what are in this house;
7. Kangaroos are not suitable for pets;
8. None but carnivora kill mice;
9. I detest animals that do not take to me;
10. Animals, that prowl at night, always love to gaze at the moon.

Universe: "animals";   a = avoided by me; b = carnivora; c = cats; d = detested by me;
e = in this house; h = kangaroos; k = killing mice;
l = loving to gaze at the moon; m = prowling at night;
n = suitable for pets; r = taking to me.

AVOIDING THE FALLACY OF CONSEQUENCE

A. Rise of the arts and sciences
B. Scientific theories, as not factual
C. Fallacy of consequence
D. Fallacy of consequence avoided
E. Scientific theories, as only workable
F. Scientific theories, as imaginary

We naturally believe that the real world is really out there, that the sun, moon and stars, and cockroaches are not simply images on the retina, as David Hume would have us believe. We consider that we do indeed perceive through such images on the retina (the 'perceptions' of Hume); but that we are looking, not at the images, but *through* the images at reality. In the same vein, when, from a room, we look out through a closed window at a tree, we do not consider ourselves as looking at the window pane, but *through* the window pane *at* the tree.

In the midst of this real world, whose existence as we see it only the advancedly educated are successful in doubting (science textbooks are fond of quoting the Einsteinian statement, "Common sense is what we have until the age of eighteen"), we naturally tend to look for the causes of what we are seeing. When we water the marigolds in our flower garden, we do so because we believe that water, among other things, is a necessary cause of the marigolds' staying alive. We either have discovered this causality in the real world by ourselves, or take it on the word of someone else.

To know the causes of things is an intrinsic and essential element of the human being's existence, causes that are considered as operating regularly and constantly. Thus the man who wants tomatoes on his table and has gone out and bought a packet of tomato seeds, in reading the instructions on the packet, is reading what he considers rightly to be the causes of a successful tomato plant: planting at a certain depth, at a certain distance, with certain amounts of sunlight and water, and so forth.

A. RISE OF THE ARTS AND SCIENCES

Aristotle, in the beginning of his *Metaphysics*, describes how the arts and sciences arise; for example, the art of successful tomato planting, out of sense experience and memory. Someone who does not know the rules of tomato planting, the regular and constant causes of successful tomato plants, can learn them by himself from sense experience and memory. He will note, for example, that a tomato seed planted at a certain depth will sprout, while a seed planted at some other certain depth will not. He observes and remembers. As his memory of successful sprouting at one depth and unsuccessful sprouting at another becomes more extensive, he develops experience; that is, the remembrance of what depth, from the experience of many cases, is best. Suddenly he perceives that repetition of good growth at one certain depth must correspond to a constant order and regularity in nature, a law, whereby tomatoes of their very nature, and universally, are programmed to sprout from one certain depth already perceived.

Appendix Five was written expressly for this text by Pierre Conway, O.P.

One has gone from memory to experience to art and science, consisting of the perception and enunciation of the universal in nature, which can now be printed on tomato seed packets as a universal law: Plant at such-and-such a depth. The perception of such universal laws in nature is what we call art and science. The art (or science) of tomato-growing will be put together and printed on seed packets from the perception of the universal laws in nature which govern and cause the production of successful tomato plants.

Aristotle also traces the gradual ascent of these arts, starting with those concerned with the necessities of life and rising to the speculative sciences, for example, theoretical physics. The first may be called the mechanical arts, which are used in the production of the necessities of life. These derive from the perception in nature of the laws governing successful production; for example, planting, weaving, brick-making, ship-building, fishing, and so forth.

Once the arts for the necessities of life have been discovered and codified by noting and retaining certain universal and constant laws in nature, the next ones to be developed are the arts of leisure. Once one has the necessities of life, one can afford to relax. Hence there arise the fine arts: music (involving the making of musical instruments, dancing, and singing), painting, sculpture, architecture, literature, and poetry.

Then, when the arts for the procurement of life are functioning and the arts of leisure are in place, the theoretical sciences appear, deriving from the now existent possibility of seeking the causes of things for themselves and no longer for immediate practical need. Thus Aristotle writes in his *Metaphysics*: "When all such inventions were already established [i.e., the mechanical arts and the fine arts], the sciences which do not aim at giving pleasure or at the necessities of life were discovered, and first in the places where men first began to have leisure. This is why the mathematical arts were founded in Egypt; for there the priestly caste was allowed to be at leisure" (Richard McKeon, ed., *The Basic Works of Aristotle* [New York: Random House, 1941], 1. 1. 981^{b}13–24).

Needless to say, when Aristotle says that the mathematical arts were founded in Egypt because there the priests were allowed to be at leisure, he is not talking about practical mathematics, since such a thing as counting sheep already belongs to the arts concerned with procuring the necessities of life. He is speaking rather of speculative mathematics, and the speculative sciences in general, where one looks for ultimate causes and reasons after practical needs have already received attention.

B. SCIENTIFIC THEORIES, AS NOT FACTUAL

In the search for the ultimate causes of things, the human being may arrive at quite opposing theories, of which none or only one might be true. Thus, when Columbus in 1492 set out to establish a sea route to China by sailing westward, he assuredly used the sun, moon, and stars in his navigation—and did so successfully. However he did so under the prevailing Ptolemaic or geocentric theory (a quite natural one insofar as general appearances are concerned) that the sun, moon, and stars revolve daily around an immobile earth. These astronomical notions held by Columbus in his navigation, those of an immobile earth at the center of the universe, perfectly served all practical purposes then—and continue to do so today in celestial navigation. Nevertheless, in the succeeding century the Polish astronomer, Copernicus, raised the speculative or theoretical question of whether the appearances whereby Columbus navigated were not caused, rather, by the earth's rotating daily on its axis and revolving yearly about an immobile sun as the center of the universe. He gave his reasons in a book, *On the Revolutions of the Heavenly Spheres*, which was published in 1543 and given to him on his deathbed.

Although the Ptolemaic or geocentric theory continues to serve for practical purposes in celestial navigation at sea, it is the Copernican or heliocentric theory, placing the sun at the center with the earth revolving around it as a planet, that is now considered factual. This concept agrees with what is known about universal gravitation, whereby a smaller mass (the earth) will revolve around a greater mass (the sun) rather than vice versa. It is also verified by the recent, actual photographic data from *Voyager I* and *Voyager II* as these spacecraft moved among the various planets orbiting around the sun.

What emerges from the above explanation is the fact that, while one concept can be held as representing reality (such as the Copernican theory in which the earth rotates daily and moves yearly around the sun), another quite different concept (such as the Ptolemaic theory of an immobile earth at the center of the universe) can, without being taken for a fact, produce practical and predictable results in that reality. Navigating on the Ptolemaic theory, Columbus was astoundingly accurate as he sailed back and forth to the New World (see Samuel Eliot Morison's *Admiral of the Ocean Sea*).

The characteristic that, in order to produce predictable, practical results, a theory need not be true (as celestial navigation at sea continues to proceed under the Ptolemaic theory of an immobile earth at the center of a universe revolving around it, a supposition not held as true) turns out to be found in theoretical science in general, of which the basic science is mathematical physics. This evaluation of physical theory is easily noted for the first law of motion (or the law of inertia) which appears at the head of Newton's *Principia*, a law originally formulated by Galileo. All subsequent physics, including relativity and quantum theory, presupposes and utilizes this fundamental law. Yet science today recognizes that, while absolutely indispensable to all physics, it is neither true nor factual!

What is the conclusion to be drawn from this perception, which is science's own? It is the conclusion that the theories and laws of science, from which predictions and practical results derive, are not presented as factual statements of the reality of nature. How is this conclusion related to logic, and reasoning in general? It is related to logic in the area of the fallacy of consequence.

C. FALLACY OF CONSEQUENCE

The fallacy of consequence is the one involved in the following thought process: "If it rains, the grass will be wet; but the grass *is* wet; therefore it must have rained." We often make judgments of this nature which later turn out to be incorrect. In this case, possibly someone may have turned on a sprinkler, unbeknownst to us, and later turned it off. How does this apply in science, for example, in the case of the Ptolemaic theory? When Columbus navigated, it is legitimate to believe that he held the earth as the center of the universe. This concept he could support by the following reasoning: "If the earth is the center of the universe, then the sun and other heavenly bodies will be seen as revolving around it; but I *do* see the sun as doing this every day, rising and setting; therefore the earth must be at the center of the universe, which revolves daily around it."

Is there a fallacy of consequence involved here? There is such a logical error, unless an immobile earth with revolving sun, moon, planets, and stars is the only possible explanation of the daily rising and setting of the sun and other heavenly bodies. But there *was* another possible explanation: that of an immobile sun and immobile fixed stars with the earth rotating daily on its axis, with the earth and the planets revolving around the sun. This quite different explanation, the one of Copernicus in modern times, accounted equally well for the appearances of a rising and setting sun, moon, stars, and planets. By the supposition of the revolving of the planets (now including earth) around the sun, it accounted even better for the motion of the planets, such as Venus, which (in the Ptolemaic system) appeared to move sometimes forward, sometimes backward.

What is the origin of the fallacy of consequence which, one may say, is closely related to modern physical theory? Whenever one finds oneself to have been guilty of the fallacy of consequence (e.g., if one attributes wet grass to rain and it later turns out to be caused by a sprinkler), it is in keeping with the mind's innate and indispensable looking for causes—which is at the heart of the discovery of all the arts and sciences. It is because the human being wanted to know what made tomatoes grow best (i.e., what caused good growth) that through observation, experience, and universalization, he arrived at the art of growing tomatoes, now reliably codified on a seed packet.

How then can such an innate and indispensable procedure terminate in a fallacy—reasoning which *appears* to be true, but is not? Obviously it occurs where more than one explanation can "satisfy the appearances." One has the fallacy of consequence even should one happen to conceptualize the correct explanation among several alternatives—since, if there are several possible answers, one cannot say, at the end of one's induction, that the answer one supports is *the* answer. Thus, in the case of Columbus sailing the ocean blue and satisfactorily navigating on the assumption that the sun, moon, stars, and planets were revolving daily around an immobile earth, he would (if actually the same appearances are equally satisfied by the assumption of an immobile sun with the earth rotating daily on its axis) be guilty, however unknowingly, of the fallacy of consequence. While it is natural for him, in the innate seeking for the causes of things, to believe the sun is revolving around an immobile earth, since this is what convincingly appears; nevertheless he is guilty of the fallacy of consequence since those identical appearances can be equally well explained—and ultimately, even better explained—by the supposition of the earth's rotating on its axis.

D. FALLACY OF CONSEQUENCE AVOIDED

How can the fallacy of consequence be avoided? It should be noted first that this fallacy is very much a part of our daily life: we constantly and necessarily look for the causes of things, and how often do we discover that the cause we have assigned satisfying the appearances is not the true one! Our friend passes us without a glance. Automatically we look for a cause. "We must have done something he doesn't like," comes naturally. Subsequently, however, we may discover that he was simply lost in thought about $e = mc^2$.

1. BY SEEKING THE PROPER CAUSE

There are two alternatives for avoiding the fallacy of consequence: one is in keeping with our natural reasoning as untouched by higher education; the other depends upon a universal skepticism favored by today's theoretical science. As to the first, it consists in ascertaining a cause which alone can be the cause of the effect in question. Thus, if the wet grass of the front lawn could *alone* be caused by rain, then one could say convertibly: "If it rains, the grass will be wet; if the grass is wet, it will have rained."

To say that the fallacy of consequence, erroneous reasoning in the assignment of a cause, may be avoided by ascertaining what is the sole cause of a given effect, is equivalent to saying that one must find the proper cause, of which the effect will then be a property. (This requirement, necessary for a true demonstration, is discussed at length by Aristotle, the founder of logic, in his *Posterior Analytics*.) Thus, supposing that a certain plant, such as serpentina, has a sedative effect, one is inclined to say: "If one uses serpentina, one will have a sedative effect; this given capsule has that sedative effect; therefore it must be made from serpentina." This reasoning escapes the fallacy of consequence only if it is serpentina alone that produces the given effect. Actually it has been subsequently discovered that this sedating effect is *not* peculiar to serpentina, but is found in other plants also containing the same sedating ingredient. One will therefore now reason correctly: "This certain ingredient, common to certain species of plants, produces sedation; this capsule produces that sedation; therefore it is derived from one or the other of these species of plants (without one's being able to discern which)."

Since the mind of its very nature seeks for the knowledge of causes and of proper causes, one can understand our tendency to the fallacy of consequence: when one finds or supposes a cause that "satisfies the appearances," one tends to take it for the proper cause, since that is what one is ultimately seeking. How then should one proceed in order to avoid the fallacy to which rash judgments belong? One must realize that, when one has found a cause that "satisfies the appearances" (as the Ptolemaic theory of an immobile earth and daily revolving sun satisfies the appearances of the sun's daily rising and setting), one can only exclude the possibility of another explanation if one can ascertain that the cause arrived at is the *only* possible answer.

We tend not to seek such certainty if the first explanation found seems completely satisfactory, such as the concept of a sun rising and setting around a seemingly immobile earth. There is no reason to believe that Columbus had any doubts about this, since he navigated successfully under this concept. Furthermore it was viewed by many as proven that the earth had to be the geometrical center of the universe, since it was composed of the heaviest element (earth) with the other three elements (water, air, fire) stratified above it, with the heavenly bodies—starting with the moon—circling around this central core. It was only to the extent that this theory was not completely satisfying (it had only a contrived explanation, the epicycle, for why Venus, for example, appeared to have both a forward and a retrograde motion when viewed as revolving around the earth) that an alternative theory was sought and proposed by Copernicus. The difficulty vanished when Venus was seen as revolving around the sun. (But it still seems easier, for practical purposes of celestial navigation, to imagine the earth as the center.)

One possible way to arrive at the proper cause of an effect, thereby allowing convertibility and avoiding the fallacy of consequence, is by reducing the possible causes to two. Then, if one can be eliminated, the other is the necessary and proper cause. Thus, starting with the admitted order in the universe as an effect, one knows that this order must be caused either by design or by chance—there are no other possibilities. Since it is not reasonable, either on theoretical or experiential grounds, to attribute the universe's order to chance, one must therefore attribute it to design.

As stated above, two alternatives are available in avoiding the fallacy of consequence. The first of these, already described, is to secure the proper and necessary cause as the explanation of an effect. If one is not able to establish that the effect results from one particular cause alone, then one can hold one's explanation as only provisional—at least for the time being. Thus, if the scientist is not able to establish definitively that the earth is rotating daily on its axis, to the exclusion of the same appearance being caused by the sun's revolving daily around an immobile earth, then he must present his theory as not yet finally settled. With this position, one is automatically admitting at least one other possibility. One will thereby avoid the fallacy of consequence—and rash judgments!

2. BY DENYING ANY PROPER CAUSE

To avoid the fallacy of consequence, the second, drastic alternative is the one employed by modern science. This approach consists in negating the possibility of arriving at *any* definitive explanation, at *any* proper cause. This is lucidly expressed by Einstein in *The Evolution of Physics*. In this text (p. 31) he describes the scientific approach as comparable to that of a man looking at the outside of a watch and speculating as to what kind of interior mechanism is causing what appears; that is, the movement of the hands, the ticking. He may arrive at different explanations or hypotheses, but he will never be able to open up the watch to verify which, if any, of his hypotheses are true. All that he can do is to continue to improve his hypotheses in the sense of putting together explanations which satisfy the appearances with greater and greater simplicity, with greater and greater universality. Using this approach, one avoids the fallacy of consequence, since *no* explanation may be taken as definitive or objective.

This outlook is traceable to Immanuel Kant who decreed, once he had been "awakened from his dogmatic slumbers" by David Hume, that we know only the appearances of things, the phenomena, and cannot know their natures, what causes them to be what they appear. (In Einstein's terms, one sees the outside of the watch but one can never know what makes it go.)

Needless to say, one is not compelled to model one's thinking on that of Immanuel Kant, abetted by David Hume. One is free to consider that one *does* know reality, the reality that we perceive from infancy by common sense—the common sense which Einstein says we have until age eighteen, when we lose it presumably because of critical enlightenment from scientific speculation. The knowledge we consider ourselves to have of reality implies also the ability to know the causes of things, such as what makes tomatoes grow. In pursuing these causes we must avoid the fallacy of consequence by being aware that, just because an explanation or postulated cause satisfies the appearances (as the Ptolemaic theory of an immobile earth satisfies the appearances of the sun rising and setting daily), it need not thereby be the true explanation or cause. The true cause is known to have been obtained only if it is perceived to be the necessary and proper cause of the effect, of which the effect is a property. One will then have convertibility. Meanwhile the fact that an explanation, a postulated cause, satisfies the appearances, indicates that it is only a possibility. Other possibilities need to be considered; and, unless they can be excluded, the favored possibility is a possibility at best, not a definitive fact.

This realization does not prevent what can be considered only a possibility from producing practical results. Thus the Ptolemaic theory, considered only as a possibility, continues to produce practical results in celestial navigation. One can go further: even when considered as a here-and-now impossibility (if the Copernican theory should have been proven to be a fact), the Ptolemaic theory clearly continues to work whenever one uses it, such as in celestial navigation.

E. SCIENTIFIC THEORIES, AS ONLY WORKABLE

The workability of physical theories leads to a profound perception, one already seen by contemporary theoretical physics. This insight is that, in order for a physical theory to work or to produce predictable results, it need not be taken as true. To use the Ptolemaic theory for practical purposes, one does not need to think the sun is actually revolving daily around the earth. This insight is perceived as not peculiar to the Ptolemaic theory, but as characteristic of all physical theories, starting with the fundamental theory of today's physics, Newton's first law of motion or the law of inertia. In this law all motion, including curved motion such as the trajectory of a cannon ball, is considered and is so calculated as basically rectilinear. Thus the curved trajectory of the cannon ball is calculated as a simultaneous combination of horizontal rectilinear motion and vertical, downward rectilinear motion (this last type caused by gravity)—which no one thinks to be actually happening.

Because of the realization that a physical theory need not be true to work, that is, need not be directly perceptible in nature or proved by necessary induction to be a fact of nature, scientists today are guided solely by the criterion of whether a constructed hypothesis or theory works. Their standard is this question: Does it satisfy the appearances and produce predictable results? No fallacy of consequence results because *no* theory (or law, which is a theory that has worked for a long time) is taken as a real cause. No one thinks that the curved trajectory of the cannon ball is the product of two *real* rectilinear motions.

This perception, that nature has been so constructed that a true theory is not necessary to produce predictable results, is shared equally by those who believe with Kant and modern physics that no possibility exists for knowing the causes of things (or even that there are such things as causes), and by those who believe that we do perceive a real world and can know its causes. Because of this shared perception, one will find modern science's utilization as facts of theories with no claim to objective verification, quite normal and proper. One will simply not make the mistake of thinking that such theories are being presented as true statements, as facts about reality—even should they be mistakenly so presented by the media.

F. SCIENTIFIC THEORIES, AS IMAGINARY

If today's scientific theories, thanks to the Kantian outlook, make no claim to being *true* as that word is generally understood, namely, as concepts corresponding to what is actually present in nature, how should one consider them? They are to be considered as imaginary, as *that* word is generally understood, namely, as characterizing combinations in the mind of elements derived from sense knowledge in reality, but which are not perceived as so existing in reality. Thus, in the scientific conception for calculation purposes of a cannon ball's trajectory as a combination of rectilinear motions, the notion of rectilinear motion is derived from sense reality; while the concept of curved motion (also perceived in sense reality) as a combination of rectilinear motions (a combination not so perceived) is a product of the imagination. (Webster: *imagination*. mental synthesis of new ideas [such as a curve conceived as a combination of straight lines] from elements experienced separately [curves and straight lines experienced separately].)

Let us return to the example of the wet grass. If one starts from the wetness, endeavors to ascertain inductively its cause, and grants that there may be several possible answers (such as rain, a sprinkler), *can* one arrive at a proper cause? One can do so by restricting oneself to what is necessarily true. In this case it is that something capable of causing moisture is responsible for the grass's being wet. This might seem like a meager finding. Yet the person who is aware, starting from no more than the wetness of the grass, that only this finding can be absolutely held, will thereby avoid the fallacy of consequence that could be engendered. This fallacy occurs when one jumps to the conclusion or makes the rash judgment that, because the grass is wet, it must have rained—and later learns that a sprinkler is the cause.

Beyond this awareness of the restrictions for proper causality, one will wish to go a step further. Then one will realize with science that predictable results may be deduced even from theories which, while inspired or suggested by observation, make no claim to representing reality. To the extent that one considers that no knowledge of causes is possible, all theories explaining effects (or appearances) will be equally valid. One simply uses the theory one prefers for a given situation. Thus, while not long ago science held that Ptolemy was wrong and Copernicus was right in explaining the sun's rising and setting (the "Copernican Revolution"), science today, in keeping with skepticism about the possibility of knowing causes, allows that *either* theory is valid. One's decision about which theory to use is dictated simply by the one appearing to work best in a given case.

Even, when focusing on the appearances to be explained, the modern theorist chooses, as appearance, the one which suits. Thus, in relativity, what is actually in reality known to be a single identical motion, is considered as two different motions by the first postulate of relativity. Thus the *same* motion of a coin falling downward in a moving car, seen as *vertical* by the driver, is seen as *curved forward* by an external observer. To take what is necessarily one as two is imaginary. This imaginary quality is strikingly found in "time dilation," which is the supposed slowing down of time as velocity increases. Since this concept requires the supposition of one as two (in this case a single light beam, seen differently within a space vehicle and by an earth observer), "time dilation" is, as depending upon the imaginary, imaginary.

Once one has acquired the relativistic mind-set (thanks to the imagination) of looking at what cannot be proved to be other than a single motion, as two different, equally valid, motions, one is prepared to grasp "time dilation," the slowing down of time for high velocities. For this understanding, one moves from a car moving along the ground to a spaceship moving through space. Instead of a coin's being dropped in a moving car, a light beam is now emitted vertically upward from a light source in the spaceship's floor and reflected back down from the roof's mirror to the source. The spaceship occupant sees the light beam as emitted and reflected back vertically (comparable to the car occupant's seeing the coin fall vertically).

What now of the earth observer? He has an experience similar to that of the external observer watching the coin as it falls in a forward curve because of the motion of the car. Since the earth observer sees the spaceship as moving forward, he likewise perceives the reflected light beam in the spaceship, not simply as making a vertical rise and fall to the same point in space, but as moving forward diagonally with the motion of the spaceship (as the external observer of the moving car sees the coin moving forward in a curve). Instead of a vertical rise and fall, the earth observer, because of the spaceship's movement, sees these two vertical lines as slanted forward and backward to become the diagonal sides of a triangle with its apex in the roof's mirror. This new triangular reference frame covers a greater distance than the vertical up-and-back trajectory seen by the spaceship occupant.

With an awareness of both the vertical and triangular reference frames, the theorist can state that the time it takes for the light beam to travel up and back on a spaceship is longer for the earth observer than for the spaceship occupant. Why is the *time* longer? Because the *distance* traveled by the light beam as seen by the earth observer is longer (and time is measured by the speed of light traveling at c: a longer distance covered means a longer time elapsed). Hence the longer distance for the earth observer, implying longer time, leads to *shorter* time for the spaceship observer: for the latter, time moves more slowly—time dilation.

What is to be noted here? It is the *same* light beam, conceived of as traveling two different distances—something admittedly impossible in reality. Then why does one say this? Because it is possible to *imagine* the same beam traveling two different distances.

In the previous material one spoke of differing explanations of the *same* appearance, such as the same appearance of the rising and setting sun being explained by two different theories. In relativity, one does not start with even the *same* appearance, but with *two* different appearances of what is necessarily, in reality, the same event. Hence relativity *starts* with imagination (taking one event as two), whereas physical science starts with reality, real appearance, and uses imagination in explaining the real appearance; for example, an imaginary combination of straight lines in the first law of motion to give a realistic prediction of a real appearance, such as the curved trajectory of a projectile.

This drastic elimination of the fallacy of consequence, by postulating that one cannot know the causes of things, leads to the position that *any* workable explanation is valid and hence that one will never hold *any* explanation as definitive——because one simply goes on with "free creations of the human mind." Such a position concerning causality is compatible with the quantum theory that every event comes about by chance—there are no per se causes. This position is also related to the material implication of symbolic logic: p implies q, and non-p equally implies q. In this implication one does not hold for any definitive and exclusive cause for q.

GLOSSARY

1.	**ABILITY**.	A QUALIFICATION—of a thing which is its proximate source of operation
2.	**ABSOLUTE/ QUALIFIED**.	FALLACY—resulting from treating what is true in a certain respect as though it were true without qualification
3.	**ACCENT**.	FALLACY—resulting from the use of accentuation in order to change the meaning of a word or sentence
4.	**ACCIDENT**[1].	FALLACY—resulting from treating what is true of the individual as though it were true of the species
5.	**ACCIDENT**[2].	THAT WAY OF PREDICATING—which states characteristics of a thing which are not part of its essence nor peculiar to it
6.	**ACCIDENT**[3].	A THING—which cannot exist in its own right, but which does exist in another thing as in a subject
7.	**ACTION**.	AN ACCIDENT—which is the doing of something to something else
8.	**AGENT**.	THAT FACTOR—by which the thing is accomplished
9.	**AMBIGUITY**.	FALLACY—resulting from two diverse and intended meanings of a word or phrase
10.	**AMPHIBOLY**.	FALLACY—resulting from two diverse and unintended meanings caused by grammatical construction
11.	**ANALOGICAL WORD**.	A SIGN—which stands for a primary meaning and related, secondary meanings when applied to different things
12.	**ART**.	THE MIND'S GRASP—derived from nature of the rules and the intermediate steps for a given end
13.	**ARTIFICIAL SIGN**.	A SIGN—in which the connection between the thing and the meaning conveyed is made by human institutions
14.	**BEGGING QUESTION**.	FALLACY—resulting from taking for granted as a premise the very thing which has to be proved
15.	**CATEGORIES**.	TEN ULTIMATE CLASSIFICATIONS—into which all material things can be placed

16.	**CAUSE.**	THAT FACTOR—from which another thing follows with dependence
17.	**COMPOSITION.**	FALLACY—resulting from taking something in a combined sense which is true only in a separated sense
18.	**COMPREHENSION.**	THE NUMBER—of qualifications which determines the content of a concept
19.	**CONCEPT (IDEA).**	THE SIGN—which holds the whatness of a simple material thing
20.	**CONSEQUENT.**	FALLACY—resulting from treating what is true of a genus as though it were peculiar to a species under the given genus
21.	**CONTRADICTION.**	THE SIMPLE DENIAL—of the original proposition
22.	**CONTRADICTORY OPPOSITION.**	THE OPPOSITION—between an affirmation and a negation, an opposition which has no middle
23.	**CONTRARIETY.**	THE OPPOSITION—between the extremes of a given proposition
24.	**CONTRARY OPPOSITION.**	THE OPPOSITION—between the positive extremes of the same subject, each of which excludes the other from that subject
25.	**CONVERSION.**	THE PROCESS—of reversing the subject and predicate, while retaining the same quality, in order to have the appropriate derived truth
26.	**DEFINITION.**	THE MIND'S REFINEMENT—of the whatness of a simple material thing, giving its genus and specific difference
27.	**DISJUNCTIVE SYLLOGISM.**	THE PRELIMINARY SYLLOGISM—in which the major premise contains two alternatives
28.	**DIVISION.**	FALLACY—resulting from taking something in a divided sense which is meant to be taken as a unit
29.	**END.**	THAT FACTOR— for the sake of which a thing is accomplished
30.	**ENTHYMEME.**	THE CATEGORICAL SYLLOGISM—in which one of the premises or the conclusion is not expressed but implied
31.	**EQUIVOCAL WORD.**	A SIGN—which stands for different meanings as applied to different things

32.	**EXPERIENCE.**	UNIFIED SENSE KNOWLEDGE—built from many singular, similar memories
33.	**EXTENSION.**	THE NUMBER—of inferiors to which the concept is applicable
34.	**FALLACY.**	REASONING—which appears to conclude but does not
35.	**FALLACY DEPENDENT ON LANGUAGE.**	APPARENT REASONING—resulting from a plausible error because of the words used or their arrangement
36.	**FALLACY INDEPENDENT OF LANGUAGE.**	APPARENT REASONING—resulting from a plausible error in the reasoning process
37.	**FIGURES OF SYLLOGISM.**	THE POSSIBLE COMBINATIONS—of the terms of the syllogism's premises
38.	**FORM.**	THAT FACTOR—which makes the thing to be what it is
39.	**FORMAL SIGN.**	A THING—which only stands for something else
40.	**FORM/FIGURE.**	QUALIFICATIONS—of a thing which refer to its shape, whether natural or artificial
41.	**FORM OF EXPRESSION.**	FALLACY—resulting from the expression of two different things in the same word-form
42.	**GENUS.**	THAT WAY OF PREDICATING—which states the essence of the thing in a way common to several different species
43.	**HABIT.**	A QUALIFICATION—of a thing disposing it well or ill in a durable way
44.	**HYPOTHETICAL SYLLOGISM.**	THE PRELIMINARY SYLLOGISM—in which the major premise is cast in a conditional form
45.	**IGNORANCE OF PROOF.**	COMPREHENSIVE FALLACY—resulting from ignoring the requirements of proof: (a) univocal words, (b) granted premises, (c) use of syllogistic rules, (d) proof of point (no use of character, force, authority, or emotions)
46.	**IMAGE.**	THE SIGN—which holds the unique, one-time factors of an individual member of a certain kind or type
47.	**IMMANENT OPERATION.**	ACTION—which is the simple use of one's powers and therefore remains within the agent to change or perfect this agent

48.	**INDIVIDUALITY.**	THOSE FACTORS—which make the thing a unique member of a given kind or type
49.	**INDUCTION.**	THE PROCESS—of moving from singulars to universal concepts and principles by the abstractive power of the intellect
50.	**INSTRUMENTAL SIGN.**	A THING—in itself and also an indicator of something else
51.	**JUDGMENT.**	THAT ACT OF THE MIND—which obtains the proposition by combining or dividing the concepts of simple realities. This proposition is judged true or false if it conforms or does not conform to reality
52.	**LINKING VERB.**	TIME-BEARING LINK—between the subject and predicate for those propositions (sentences) requiring such a sign
53.	**LOGIC.**	THE ART—of moving from the known to the unknown
54.	**MAJOR PREMISE.**	THE PREMISE—in which the major term appears
55.	**MAJOR TERM.**	THE TERM—which is the predicate of the conclusion
56.	**MATTER.**	THAT FACTOR—from which the thing comes to be
57.	**MIDDLE TERM.**	THE TERM—which links or separates the major and minor terms
58.	**MINOR PREMISE.**	THE PREMISE—in which the minor term appears
59.	**MINOR TERM.**	THE TERM—which is the subject of the conclusion
60.	**MOODS OF SYLLOGISM.**	THE POSSIBLE COMBINATIONS—of the syllogism's premises, which vary according to quality and quantity
61.	**NATURAL SIGN.**	A SIGN—in which there is a real connection between the thing and the meaning conveyed
62.	**NON-CAUSE AS CAUSE.**	FALLACY—resulting from treating what precedes or accompanies a thing as though it were the cause of the thing
63.	**OBVERSION.**	THE PROCESS—of reversing the quality of the proposition, while retaining the same subject and predicate, in order to have the equivalent truth
64.	**OPPOSITION (proposition).**	THE AFFIRMATION AND DENIAL—of the same predicate in respect to the same subject

65.	**PASSION.**	AN ACCIDENT—which is the receiving of something from something else
66.	**POSITION.**	AN EXTRINSIC ACCIDENT—said of a thing which is the order of a thing's parts in a given place
67.	**POSSESSION.**	AN ACCIDENT—peculiar to the human being which includes all external equipment added to his natural body
68.	**PREDICABLES.**	WAYS—in which the predicate is related to the subject
69.	**PREDICAMENTS.**	TEN ULTIMATE KINDS OF PREDICATES—said about a subject
70.	**PREDICATE.**	ELEMENT IN THE SENTENCE—which is said about the subject
71.	**PROPERTY.**	THAT WAY OF PREDICATING—which states some characteristic that follows from and is peculiar to a given essence (It leads to identification.)
72.	**PROPOSITION.**	A COMPOSITE STATEMENT—which is judged true or false if it conforms or does not conform to reality
73.	**QUALITY.**	AN ACCIDENT—by which a thing is a certain sort or kind, or which is the external, qualifying form
74.	**QUANTITY.**	AN ACCIDENT—whereby material things are extended into space, measurable by some mathematical standard, and capable of being divided into separate parts
75.	**REASONING.**	THAT ACT OF THE MIND—which links or separates the conclusion's subject and predicate through the middle term
76.	**RELATION.**	AN ACCIDENT—in a thing which is the bearing or reference of that thing toward another thing
77.	**SENSE QUALITIES.**	QUALIFICATIONS—of a thing which affect the powers of sensation
78.	**SIGN.**	A THING—which, in addition to what it is in itself, also means something else
79.	**SIMPLE APPREHENSION.**	THAT ACT OF THE MIND—which grasps the whatness of simple material things
80.	**SIMPLE MATERIAL REALITY.**	ANY MATERIAL THING—which is one because it has one form or nature

81.	**SPECIES**.	THAT WAY OF PREDICATING—which states the complete essence of a thing, not just a note common to other things
82.	**SPECIFIC DIFFERENCE**.	THAT WAY OF PREDICATING—which states the identifying mark within a genus distinguishing one species from another
83.	**SUBALTERNATION**.	THE RELATION—between a universal proposition and its particulars
84.	**SUBCONTRARIETY**.	THE OPPOSITION—between the particulars of a given proposition
85.	**SUBJECT**.	ELEMENT IN THE SENTENCE—about which something is said
86.	**SUBSTANCE**.	A THING—which can exist in its own right, not just as a modification of something else
87.	**SYLLOGISM**.	A DISCURSIVE STATEMENT—which links or separates the conclusion's subject and predicate through the middle term
88.	**TRANSIENT OPERATION**.	ACTION—which goes out from the agent to something else in order to change this latter thing
89.	**TRUTH**.	THE CONFORMITY—between the intellect and the thing
90.	**TWO QUESTIONS AS ONE**.	FALLACY—resulting from forming a question in such a way that the answer to one part of the question appears to answer the other part also
91.	**UNIVERSALITY**.	AN ATTRIBUTE—of the concept by which it is applicable to many members
92.	**UNIVOCAL WORD**.	A SIGN—which stands for one meaning as applied to different things
93.	**WHATNESS**.	THAT FACTOR—which makes the thing a certain kind or type
94.	**WHEN**.	AN EXTRINSIC ACCIDENT—said of a thing which makes a reference to time
95.	**WHERE**.	AN EXTRINSIC ACCIDENT—said of a thing which makes a reference to place
96.	**WORD**.	A SIGN—of the concept or idea

BIBLIOGRAPHY

The following books are the primary sources for either the doctrine or the examples of this text:

DOCTRINE

Aquinas, Thomas. *Exposition of the Posterior Analytics of Aristotle*. Translated by Pierre Conway. Quebec: La Librairie Philosophique M. Doyon, 1956.

Aquinas, Thomas, and Cajetan. *Aristotle: On Interpretation*. Translated by Jean T. Oesterle. Milwaukee, Wisconsin: Marquette University Press, 1962.

Aristotle. *The Works of Aristotle*, vol. 1, *Categoriae and De Interpretatione, Analytica Priora, Analytica Posteriora, Topica and De Sophisticis Elenchis*. Edited by W.D. Ross. London: Oxford University Press, 1928.

Conway, Pierre. "Grammar-Logic-Rhetoric." 1st rev. ed. Mimeographed. Columbus, Ohio: Alum Creek Press, College of St. Mary of the Springs, 1964.

_____ . "Learning to Challenge." Mimeographed. Washington, D.C.: Dominican House of Studies, n.d.

_____ . "Philosophy of God Class Notes." Mimeographed. Washington, D.C.: Dominican House of Studies, n.d.

_____ . "Thomistic English-Logic." Mimeographed. Columbus, Ohio: College of St. Mary of the Springs, 1958.

EXAMPLES

Burton, Maurice. *Systematic Dictionary of Mammals of the World*. New York: Thomas Y. Crowell Co., 1962.

Guralnik, David B., ed. *Webster's New World Dictionary of the American Language*. Second College Edition. Englewood Cliffs, N.J.: Prentice-Hall, 1970.

Peterson, Roger Tory, ed. *The Peterson Field Guide Series*, vol. 5, *A Field Guide to the Mammals*, text by William H. Burt. 3d ed. Boston, Mass.: Houghton Mifflin Co., 1976.

Scott, John M. *Adventures in Science*. Chicago: Loyola University Press, 1963.

For the given problems, make a list of the following essential elements: (1) the problem; (2) the case and its definition; (3) the general principle used. Use the following example as a guide:

O. Snowshoes or skis enable a person to walk on snow because this footwear distributes the person's weight over a larger area and causes less pressure on a given point.
    1. problem: Why do snowshoes or skis enable a person to walk on snow?
    2. case defined: Snowshoes or skis distribute the person's weight...and so forth.
    3. principle used: Whatever distributes the person's weight (and so forth) enables a person to walk on snow.

1. Travelers to the tropics have often remarked that this climate is very hard on machinery. In fact, the person touring by car is amazed at the danger from rust. Then the natives only smile and wonder why the tourists do not notice the amount of moisture in the air.

2. Do you know why a stack of magazines tied in a bundle will be very difficult to burn up in a trash pile? If you understand about a fire's need of oxygen, you have the answer. As you can see, the magazines have very little air, except on the outer surface. That is the reason they are so difficult to burn.

3. Two fire fighters were talking the other day about using carbon dioxide to put out fires. They said that, since this gas is heavier than air, it can sink down over a fire and shut off the supply of oxygen. They were glad it is useful.

4. Those people who remember the *Hindenburg* know why helium is used today in dirigibles and blimps. As some individuals may recall, this airship, filled with hydrogen, exploded as it was landing in New Jersey. On the other hand, helium is both very light and also safe from explosion.

5. As you know, the people in Ireland use peat as a fuel. In order to do this, they must dry out the spongy brown substance. Peat, however, is not an economical form of fuel because it still has a very high water content.

6. Have you ever seen a farmer cover his plow with a thin coating of oil before he puts it away? Do you know why he does this? You need only to remember that the plow is usually made from pig iron, which rusts easily.

7. Why is the earth a suitable home for the higher forms of life? Let us first remember that the earth does house many living things, such as all kinds of exotic plants and the extraordinary variety of animals, which range from the tiniest insect to the enormous elephant. Above all, earth is the natural habitat of the human being. Why can mother earth shelter such a variety? One of the reasons is that this planet has a marvelous blanket of air surrounding it.

8. Scientists have proof that the area one hundred miles above the earth contains a thin sprinkling of air molecules. How do they know this? They have discovered that at this distance falling meteors burst into flame because of the friction against them.

9. I've often wondered why a bedroom with a large south window gets so hot. It cannot be from the glass itself, for it always feels cold. If it is not the glass, then it must be the room's opaque objects which absorb the sun's rays and the emit waves of radiant energy.

10. When the rainwater seeps into the earth, it dissolves small amounts of the minerals there. In turn, these minerals are carried into wells, rivers, lakes and finally the sea. It is for this reason that salt and other compounds are so plentiful in the seawater.

For the given cases of induction, identify the following:
  1. the universal_____
  2. the singulars supporting it_____

1. Since much damage can be wrought by a buildup of static electricity, great care must be taken to avoid such a condition. It is for this reason that gasoline trucks have a hanging, back chain which conducts the electrical charges into the ground. Also operating rooms are kept damp to prevent sparks generated by the friction of shoes on a dry floor. There are even tassels placed on the tips of airplane wings to drain off electrical charges picked up during storms.

2. While the sun is the most important source of heat, this useful form of energy can also be produced mechanically. One simple mechanical method is the use of friction. Have you ever noticed that rubbing your cold hands together makes them warmer? Also a Boy Scout will rub two pieces of wood together until they are hot enough to kindle a fire. Probably the most common case of friction is striking the tip of a match on a rough surface in order to light it.

3. Bacteria are the smallest of simple known plants. Many of them are some of the human being's best friends. It is their task to decompose dead plants and animals. Without the bacteria, forests would be one of the world's largest trash cans. Again, certain bacteria help to make butter and cheese from milk, vinegar from apple juice, and sauerkraut from cabbage. It should also be noted that the bacteria growing on pea and bean roots produce nitrogen needed by plants.

4. Changes in temperature cause materials to expand or contract. This fact cannot be ignored by those who wish to make or build something. Remembering this fact, highway engineers allow for gaps filled with tar along their concrete roads. There are even spaces left between the individual sections of a railroad. Bridges are frequently anchored securely only at one end, while the other side may slide back and forth on roller supports.

5. Although friction may harm many human artifacts, it is also essential for many human operations. Without some friction a person could not walk on the ground. Those individuals who fall on ice know this need for friction from sad experience. Every person brushing his teeth relies on friction to obtain a good polish. Even the drivers of cars attest to the need for friction when they have to buy new tires.

6. While metals are the best conductors of heat, porous materials with their many air pockets are good insulators of heat. It is for this reason that fiber glass is wrapped around hot-water pipes. Also a blanketlike insulation is placed in the attics of many homes. Even the sides of stoves have sheet insulation to prevent the loss of heat. Finally, down jackets wrap a secure coat around the hiker and explorer.

7. If you know that black, dull, rough surfaces absorb heat, you must not forget that white, silvered, and polished exteriors reflect heat. This fact is recognized whenever refrigerator manufacturers finish their products in shiny white. If long steel bridges are painted with aluminum, they absorb less heat and do not expand too much. Also people in tropical climates are advised to dress in light colors.

Label the following signs as natural (N) or artificial (A).

____	1.	smile as a sign of	friendliness
____	2.	buds	spring
____	3.	diploma	graduate
____	4.	handshake	greeting
____	5.	frown	annoyance
____	6.	gavel	presiding officer
____	7.	blush	embarrassment
____	8.	dove	peace
____	9.	fingerprints	human being
____	10.	rainbow	sunshine in the rain
____	11.	miter	bishop
____	12.	breathing	life
____	13.	Cadillac	wealth
____	14.	tears	sorrow
____	15.	decorated evergreen	Christmas
____	16.	sun directly overhead	noon
____	17.	blowing whistle	foul in a game
____	18.	green	hope
____	19.	Hercules	strength
____	20.	obesity	overeating
____	21.	shamrock	Ireland
____	22.	candy-striped pole	barber
____	23.	words	concepts
____	24.	quack	duck
____	25.	flag at half mast	mourning
____	26.	snoring	sleep
____	27.	scream	terror
____	28.	Roman collar	priest
____	29.	lilies	Easter
____	30.	yawn	boredom

Classify the following words as univocal (U), equivocal (E), or analogical (A).

____	1. pitcher as signifying	container of water, baseball player
____	2. money	quarter, dime
____	3. animal	puppy, kitten
____	4. cool	kind of weather, kind of temperament
____	5. nerve	living cordlike fiber, pluck
____	6. metal	iron, copper
____	7. pit	hole in ground, hard stone of fruit
____	8. walk	path, station in life
____	9. emotion	love, hatred
____	10. peck	part of a bushel, sharp stroke of beak
____	11. number	odd, even
____	12. story	tale, all the rooms on one floor
____	13. green	color of grass, color of a dress
____	14. flower	daisy, lilac
____	15. pen	place for animals, writing instrument
____	16. furniture	bed, table
____	17. bubble	a ball of air, anything ephemeral
____	18. bank	place for money, steep rise or slope
____	19. bow	bending of body, front part of ship
____	20. rose	flower, color
____	21. music	symphony, opera
____	22. mint	place for coining money, unlimited supply
____	23. mint	unlimited supply, aromatic plant
____	24. case	example, container
____	25. dance	rhythmic movement, party
____	26. right	direction, privilege
____	27. utensil	knife, fork
____	28. tree	maple, oak
____	29. ring	sound of bell, band of metal
____	30. stand	view or opinion, raised platform

Classify the following words as univocal (U), equivocal (E), or analogical (A).

____	1. colt	as signifying	young horse, young person
____	2. ferret		narrow ribbon of cotton, weasellike animal
____	3. jewel		diamond, pearl
____	4. shoes		oxfords, pumps
____	5. magpie		black and white bird with noisy chattering, person who chatters
____	6. parade		pompous display, public promenade
____	7. mail		letters delivered by post office, flexible body armor
____	8. mail		flexible body armor, hard covering of animals
____	9. pallet		wooden tool used by potters, an inferior bed
____	10. signal		in traffic, in armed forces
____	11. tale		narrative, falsehood
____	12. stud		buttonlike device on a shirt, horse for breeding
____	13. tram		twisted silk thread, open railway car
____	14. mud		wet, soft, sticky earth; defamatory remarks
____	15. lantern		gasoline, electric
____	16. last		a form on which shoes are made, a measure or weight
____	17. book		biology, chemistry
____	18. fence		picket, rail
____	19. lash		to strike with great force, to fasten with a rope
____	20. food		potatoes, peaches
____	21. forge		to move forward steadily, to shape with blows from hammer
____	22. government		democratic, oligarchic
____	23. train		something that drags behind, events following some happening
____	24. swim		to move through water, to be dizzy
____	25. box		for candy, for a dress
____	26. house		bungalow, mansion
____	27. poor		lacking material possessions, lacking mental qualities
____	28. leader		a person who directs, a beginning section of blank tape
____	29. dog		spaniel, beagle
____	30. spade		flat-bladed tool, black figure on playing cards

In reference to each of the ten categories, fill in possible answers for the human being. (One possibility is given for each one.)

1. category stating whatness------------------------------------ man _____
        SUBSTANCE   _____

2. categories stating accidents
    a. accidents inhering in essence
        1) from material principle-------------------------- six feet in height _____
                QUANTITY   _____

        2) from formal principle----------------------------- artistic _____ (habit) _____
                QUALITY   _____

                                                            sensitive _____ (ability) _____
                                                                        _____

                                                            blond hair _____ (sense quality) __
                                                                        _____

                                                            lanky _____ (form) _____
                                                                        _____

        3) from relation to another thing----------------- taller _____ (from quantity) __
                RELATION   _____

                                                            father _____ (from action) ___
                                                                        _____

    b. accidents from outside, but
        said of essence
        1) as mover or moved------------------------------- raking _____ (action) _____
                ACTION/PASSION   _____
                (to/from another)
                                                            is helped _____ (passion) _____
                                                                        _____

        2) as measured
            a) by place------------------------------------ in the country _____
                    WHERE   _____

            b) by position--------------------------------- erect _____
                    POSITION   _____

            c) by time------------------------------------- in autumn _____
                    WHEN   _____

        3) as having special possessions----------------- dressed in jeans _____
                POSSESSION   _____

In reference to each of the ten categories, fill in possible answers for the chimpanzee. (One possibility is given for each one.)

1. category stating whatness------------------------------ <u>chimpanzee</u>
        SUBSTANCE   _____
2. categories stating accidents
    a. accidents inhering in essence
        1) from material principle------------------------- <u>four feet in height</u>
            QUANTITY   _____

        2) from formal principle---------------------------- <u>healthy</u>   (habit)
            QUALITY   _____

                                                             <u>tree climber</u>   (ability)
                                                             _____

                                                             <u>black hair</u>   (sense quality)
                                                             _____

                                                             <u>long-armed</u>   (form)
                                                             _____

        3) from relation to another thing----------------<u>smaller</u>   (from quantity)
            RELATION   _____

                                                             <u>captive</u>   (from passion)
                                                             _____

    b. accidents from outside, but
        said of essence
        1) as mover or moved------------------------------ <u>stealing</u>   (action)
            ACTION/PASSION   _____
            (to/from another)
                                                             <u>is caught</u>   (passion)
                                                             _____

        2) as measured
            a) by place-- <u>in the tree</u>
                WHERE   _____

            b) by position ----------------------------------- <u>curled up</u>
                POSITION   _____

            c) by time-- <u>at night</u>
                WHEN   _____

        3) as having special possessions----------------- <u>does not apply</u>
            POSSESSION   _____

In reference to each of the ten categories, fill in possible answers for the mouse. (One possibility is given for each one.)

1. category stating whatness-------------------------------- house mouse
      SUBSTANCE   _____
2. categories stating accidents
    a. accidents inhering in essence
        1) from material principle-------------------------- three inches long
              QUANTITY   _____

        2) from formal principle-------------------------- cunning   (habit)
              QUALITY   _____

                                                          swift   (ability)
                                                          _____

                                                          albino   (sense quality)
                                                          _____

                                                          long-tailed   (form)
                                                          _____

        3) from relation to another thing----------------- tiny   (from quantity)
              RELATION   _____

                                                          prey of cat   (from passion)
                                                          _____

    b. accidents from outside, but
       said of essence
        1) as mover or moved------------------------------ gnawing   (action)
              ACTION/PASSION   _____
              (to/from another)
                                                          is poisoned   (passion)
                                                          _____

        2) as measured
            a) by place----------------------------------- in its hole
                  WHERE   _____

            b) by position-------------------------------- crouching down
                  POSITION   _____

            c) by time------------------------------------ during the day
                  WHEN   _____

        3) as having special possessions----------------- does not apply
              POSSESSION   _____

State in which category each of the following primarily belongs.

____ 1. animal	____ 41. daughter
____ 2. observant	____ 42. is washed
____ 3. seeing	____ 43. in the morning
____ 4. eagle	____ 44. oriole
____ 5. cousin	____ 45. oxygen
____ 6. seated	____ 46. tall
____ 7. was painted	____ 47. standing
____ 8. same	____ 48. upside down
____ 9. tree	____ 49. gallon
____ 10. fickle	____ 50. blind
____ 11. walking	____ 51. reading
____ 12. bravery	____ 52. tomorrow
____ 13. larger	____ 53. roses
____ 14. baking a cake	____ 54. bitter
____ 15. slouching	____ 55. is struck
____ 16. woman	____ 56. planting
____ 17. ten feet	____ 57. in the garden
____ 18. in the room	____ 58. gold
____ 19. was cut	____ 59. in the house
____ 20. yesterday	____ 60. temperate
____ 21. wearing boots	____ 61. mature
____ 22. on the floor	____ 62. grandmother
____ 23. slimy	____ 63. small
____ 24. courageous	____ 64. feverish
____ 25. angular	____ 65. dressed
____ 26. four pounds	____ 66. reclining
____ 27. friend	____ 67. early
____ 28. later	____ 68. two feet wide
____ 29. ladybug	____ 69. hitting
____ 30. little	____ 70. apple
____ 31. now	____ 71. short
____ 32. hard	____ 72. ten
____ 33. talking	____ 73. jumping
____ 34. healthy	____ 74. brother-in-law
____ 35. square	____ 75. is scolded
____ 36. flowers	____ 76. in costume
____ 37. lame	____ 77. at school
____ 38. swimmer	____ 78. sitting
____ 39. gowned	____ 79. knitting
____ 40. honey	____ 80. in formal attire

State in which category each of the following primarily belongs.

____ 1. locust	____ 41. in work clothes
____ 2. slippered	____ 42. washing dishes
____ 3. singer	____ 43. leaning
____ 4. awkward	____ 44. in the pool
____ 5. tulips	____ 45. uniformed
____ 6. curved	____ 46. is built
____ 7. beautiful	____ 47. treasurer
____ 8. thinking	____ 48. growing
____ 9. pungent	____ 49. twenty feet
____ 10. four o'clock	____ 50. equal
____ 11. huge	____ 51. eagle
____ 12. bluebird	____ 52. slamming the door
____ 13. after lunch	____ 53. eighty pounds
____ 14. captain	____ 54. twelve years ago
____ 15. three quarts	____ 55. slanted
____ 16. symmetrical	____ 56. gloved
____ 17. faithful	____ 57. fatigued
____ 18. rosy	____ 58. triple
____ 19. under the porch	____ 59. prisoner
____ 20. belted	____ 60. cowardly
____ 21. at noon	____ 61. kind
____ 22. was stripped	____ 62. at the office
____ 23. in the house	____ 63. copper
____ 24. one hundred miles	____ 64. in the kitchen
____ 25. swordfish	____ 65. selling
____ 26. at attention	____ 66. is purchased
____ 27. raking leaves	____ 67. sour
____ 28. enormous	____ 68. daisy
____ 29. temperamental	____ 69. in the future
____ 30. dancing	____ 70. loving
____ 31. curious	____ 71. farsighted
____ 32. owl	____ 72. meter
____ 33. teacher	____ 73. thief
____ 34. was swept	____ 74. is taken
____ 35. reclining	____ 75. similar
____ 36. ancestor	____ 76. whale
____ 37. salamander	____ 77. booted
____ 38. memorizing	____ 78. in bed
____ 39. taciturn	____ 79. is traded
____ 40. lion	____ 80. merchant

As a result of the twofold division of accident, there are six ways of predicating. Using all six, name the way in which each predicate is related to its subject.

_____ 1. The summer is mild.

_____ 2. The copperhead is poisonous.

_____ 3. A crocodile has horny skin.

_____ 4. A cloud is a water-vapor mass.

_____ 5. A triangle is a geometrical figure.

_____ 6. Jean is a woman.

_____ 7. Barking is a sound.

_____ 8. A drum is an instrument.

_____ 9. Max is a dog.

_____ 10. Tom is at home.

_____ 11. Elephants have tusks.

_____ 12. The human being has a sense of humor.

_____ 13. The fox has a pointed muzzle.

_____ 14. Prudence is a virtue.

_____ 15. A silkworm can produce silk fiber.

_____ 16. The silkworm is a caterpillar.

_____ 17. The water is boiling.

_____ 18. Mary is sick.

_____ 19. Prince is a horse.

_____ 20. Bill is a social creature.

_____ 21. Patricia is an extrovert.

_____ 22. The trees are rustling.

_____ 23. The house is a building.

_____ 24. The square has four equal sides and four equal angles.

_____ 25. The potatoes are lumpy.

_____ 26. James is a man.

_____ 27. The coal is black.

_____ 28. The paper is torn.

_____ 29. A dictionary is a book.

_____ 30. Water is wet.

_____ 31. Mercury is in a liquid state.

_____ 32. The sky is threatening.

_____ 33. The elephant is an animal.

_____ 34. Mary is pretty.

_____ 35. Sam is a collie.

_____ 36. The watch is gold.

_____ 37. Pearls are jewels.

_____ 38. Hexagons have six sides and six angles.

_____ 39. The human being creates language.

_____ 40. Children are playful.

As a result of the twofold division of accident, there are six ways of predicating. Using all six, name the way in which each predicate is related to its subject.

____ 1. Butterflies are beautiful.

____ 2. Every line is without breadth, but has length.

____ 3. The human being is artistic.

____ 4. The oboe is a woodwind instrument.

____ 5. The prairie dog is squirrellike.

____ 6. My fish is a goldfish.

____ 7. The restaurant is cleaned.

____ 8. The rattlesnake is a viper.

____ 9. The trash is heavy.

____ 10. The sponge grows under water.

____ 11. Thistles have prickly leaves.

____ 12. The Scottish kilt is a skirt.

____ 13. Every point is indivisible and has position.

____ 14. The Eskimo dog has a bushy tail.

____ 15. This plant is a rose.

____ 16. The map is torn.

____ 17. An obtuse angle is greater than a right angle.

____ 18. The spoonbill is a wading bird.

____ 19. The bonfire is smoldering.

____ 20. The thermometer is rising.

____ 21. The human being is a tool-maker.

____ 22. This liquid is sulfuric acid.

____ 23. The orangutan has a hairless face.

____ 24. The wind is from the southwest.

____ 25. The pickax is a tool.

____ 26. The diameter bisects the circle.

____ 27. The insect is an animal.

____ 28. The squid has ten arms.

____ 29. The surface has only length and breadth.

____ 30. Sulfuric acid is corrosive.

____ 31. The pheasant is roosting.

____ 32. Sheba is a chimpanzee.

____ 33. The gondola is a canalboat.

____ 34. The flea is an insect.

____ 35. The equilateral triangle has three equal sides.

____ 36. The derby is a hat.

____ 37. The square is both equilateral and right-angled.

____ 38. Potassium is silver white.

____ 39. The octopus has eight arms.

____ 40. The fox is being hunted.

As a result of the twofold division of accident, there are six ways of predicating. Using all six, name the way in which each predicate is related to its subject.

____ 1. The moon is in the western sky.

____ 2. My pocket is torn.

____ 3. The saber is a sword.

____ 4. A rectilinear figure is contained by straight lines.

____ 5. The potatoes are cooked.

____ 6. This animal is a tiger.

____ 7. The mammoth had long tusks.

____ 8. Parallel lines are in the same plane but do not meet in either direction.

____ 9. The grape is a berry.

____ 10. The glacier is a large mass of ice and snow.

____ 11. The eel has a snakelike body.

____ 12. The scythe has a single-edged blade.

____ 13. The salmon are running.

____ 14. The map is a representation.

____ 15. The hold of the ship is full.

____ 16. My book is covered.

____ 17. The hollyhock has a hairy stem.

____ 18. The human being is artistic.

____ 19. The scalene triangle has three unequal sides.

____ 20. The mirror is cracked.

____ 21. The jewels are stolen.

____ 22. The rafters slope from the ridge of the roof.

____ 23. The tiger has a striped coat.

____ 24. The semicircle is contained by the diameter and its circumference.

____ 25. The palm is an inner surface.

____ 26. The kettledrum is a percussion instrument.

____ 27. The partridge is a game bird.

____ 28. The moss is near the creek.

____ 29. The raven has black feathers.

____ 30. An acute angle is less than a right angle.

____ 31. The prairie dog has a barking cry.

____ 32. The mattock is a tool.

____ 33. The human being is social.

____ 34. The hansom is a covered carriage.

____ 35. The nurse is not coming.

____ 36. Poison ivy has leaves of three leaflets.

____ 37. My dog is a pointer.

____ 38. The sky is threatening.

____ 39. The redwing is a songbird.

____ 40. The shark has a slender, rounded body.

Distinguish whether the following predicates are related to the given subject as genus, inseparable accident, or separable accident.

A. The bear

1. walks on entire foot.   _____
2. is an ursine animal.   _____
3. is a game animal.   _____
4. is a predator on domestic animals.   _____
5. has five toes on each foot.   _____
6. is a mammal.   _____
7. has small and rounded ears.   _____
8. has its den in hollow tree.   _____
9. is a carnivore.   _____

B. The striped
    skunk

1. is the size of a house cat.   _____
2. is a carnivore.   _____
3. lives in open country.   _____
4. has well-developed scent glands.   _____
5. is a valuable fur animal.   _____
6. is a mustiline animal.   _____
7. is used as a pet.   _____
8. has deep amber eyeshine.   _____

C. The raccoon

1. has five toes on each foot.   _____
2. is a procyon animal.   _____
3. dunks food in water.   _____
4. walks on entire foot.   _____
5. has yellowish white rings on tail.   _____
6. is a carnivore.   _____
7. has its den in hollow tree.   _____
8. has black mask over eyes.   _____
9. raids corn and poultry.   _____

D. The fox

1. is a carnivore.   _____
2. is the size of a small dog.   _____
3. has reddish yellow hair.   _____
4. is a canine animal.   _____
5. has a bushy tail.   _____
6. is harmful.   _____
7. is hunted by sportsmen.   _____

E. The beaver

1. is a dam-builder.   _____
2. has a family group in the lodge.   _____
3. is a rodent.   _____
4. has a naked, scaly tail.   _____
5. has its den along the bank of a stream.   _____
6. has incisor teeth.   _____
7. works in colonies to repair dams.   _____
8. has webbed hind feet.   _____
9. is a bark and twig eater.   _____
10. is a castor animal.   _____
11. is an important fur animal.   _____

A. Using the division method, outline the steps taken to arrive at the specific differences (or groupings of inseparable accidents) for the following objects. Use the format of the following example:

kimono:

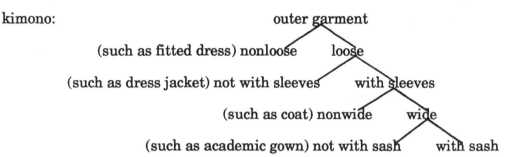

A kimono is a loose outer garment with wide sleeves and a sash.*

1. cleaver: a heavy cutting tool with a broad blade*
2. club: a heavy stick, often thinner at one end, used as a weapon*

B. Using the composition method, outline the steps taken to arrive at the specific differences (or groupings of inseparable accidents) for the following things. Use the format of the following example:

friend: a person who wills good to another, just as he wills good to himself

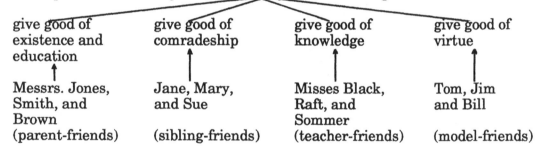

1. clown: a performer who entertains others*
2. park: an area of public land for recreation*

C. Using either method, outline the steps taken to arrive at the specific difference (or grouping of inseparable accidents) for one object of your choice.

For each of the following definitions, underline the genus. Then bracket and label the different causes composing each one.

1. bead: a small, usually round piece of glass, wood, or metal, pierced for stringing*

2. bell: a hollow, usually cuplike object, made of metal or other hard material, which rings if struck by an inside clapper*

3. gull: a water bird with large wings, slender legs, webbed feet, a strong, hooked bill, and feathers of chiefly white and gray*

4. eagle: a large, strong, flesh-eating bird of prey belonging to the falcon family, noted for its sharp vision and powerful wings*

5. needle: a small, slender piece of steel with a sharp point at one end and a hole for thread at the other, used for sewing*

6. kayak: an Eskimo canoe made of skins stretched over a frame of wood to cover it completely, except for an opening in the middle for the paddler*

7. cobra: a very poisonous snake of Asia and Africa having around the neck loose skin which is expanded into a hood when the snake is excited*

8. hoe: a garden tool with a thin, flat blade set across the end of a long handle, which is used for weeding, loosening soil, and so forth*

9. hand: the part of the human arm below the wrist, which includes the palm, fingers, and thumb and is used for grasping or gripping*

10. kettle: a metal container used for boiling or cooking things*

11. broom: a bundle of long, stiff fibers or straws fastened to a long handle and used for sweeping*

12. bulldog: a short-haired, square-jawed, heavily built dog which is known for its strong stubborn grip*

13. cabin: a small, one-story house which is built simply or crudely*

14. candle: a cylindrical mass of tallow or wax which has a wick through its center and gives light when burned*

15. bayonet: a detachable daggerlike blade placed on the muzzle end of a rifle and used for hand-to-hand fighting*

16. beach: a nearly level stretch of pebbles and sand beside the sea or lake*

17. collie: a breed of large, long-haired dog with a long, narrow head*

18. owl: a night bird of prey distinguished by a large, flat face, eyes surrounded by stiff-feathered disks; a short, hooked beak; and feathered legs with sharp talons*

For each of the following definitions, underline the genus. Then bracket and label the different causes composing each one.

1. ghoul: an evil spirit that robs graves and eats the dead flesh*

2. giant: a huge being with human form who warred with the gods*

3. raven: a large bird of the crow family; with lustrous black feathers and a straight, sharp beak; found in Europe, N. Asia, and N. America*

4. reef: a part of a sail which can be folded up and tied down to reduce the total area exposed to the wind*

5. sponge: a plantlike animal having a porous structure and a tough, fibrous skeleton; and growing exclusively under water, attached to the bottom or to other solid objects*

6. linoleum: a hard, smooth, washable floor covering made from mixing ground cork, ground wood, gums, color pigments, and oxidized linseed oil and laid on a burlap backing*

7. hinge: a joint or device on which a door, gate, or lid swings*

8. oxygen: a colorless, odorless, tasteless, gaseous chemical element, the most abundant of all elements; it is very active, being able to combine with nearly all other elements, and is essential to life processes and to combustion*

9. pagoda: a temple in the form of a pyramidal tower of several stories, usually an odd number, commonly built over a sacred relic or as a work of devotion*

10. root: the part of a plant, usually below the ground, that lacks nodes, shoots, and leaves; holds the plant in position; draws water and nourishment from the soil; and stores food*

11. ermine: a weasel of northern regions whose fur is brown in summer but white with a black-tipped tail in winter*

12. ink: a colored liquid used for writing, drawing, and so forth*

13. dish: any container, generally shallow and concave and of porcelain, earthenware, glass, or plastic, for serving or holding food*

14. chevron: an insignia consisting of a V-shaped bar or bars, worn on the sleeve of a uniform to show rank or service*

15. armor: a covering donned to guard the body against weapons*

16. borzoi: a breed of large dog which has a narrow head, long legs, and silky coat*

17. pineapple: a juicy, edible tropical fruit which resembles a pine cone*

18. squirrel: a small, tree-dwelling rodent with heavy fur and a long bushy tail*

Label the following propositions as affirmative (A) or negative (N).

____ 1. Not all diseases are infectious.

____ 2. Every nonbeliever is unable to agree with him.

____ 3. No vegetables are uncooked.

____ 4. Mary is friendly.

____ 5. Mary is unfriendly.

____ 6. Mary is non-friendly.

____ 7. Mary is not non-friendly.

____ 8. Mary is not unfriendly.

____ 9. Every airplane is not overloaded.

____ 10. Some sunsets in the tropics are spectacular.

____ 11. Not every indefinite person can be tolerated.

____ 12. Every kind of food is unable to sustain him.

____ 13. The weather is healthful.

____ 14. No weather is healthful.

____ 15. The weather is non-healthful.

____ 16. The weather is unhealthful.

____ 17. Some weather is not healthful.

____ 18. Every city is not located on a harbor.

____ 19. Some truck drivers are not non-responsible.

____ 20. Not every butterfly is able to stay alive in this climate.

____ 21. Some non-saturated solutions are unavailable.

____ 22. No newsstand is closed during the holiday.

____ 23. Not all who came were able to stay.

____ 24. None of the animals have been fed.

____ 25. Each person is unashamedly noncommittal.

Label the following propositions as affirmative (A) or negative (N).

____ 1. Every dish of ice cream is non-melted.

____ 2. None of the tomatoes has been planted.

____ 3. Not all who answered contributed any money.

____ 4. No business is open on the holiday.

____ 5. Some non-partisan citizens are unemotional.

____ 6. Not every silhouette presents a good likeness.

____ 7. Some pansies do not have non-velvety petals.

____ 8. Every marten does not have long legs.

____ 9. Some opera singers are not practicing.

____ 10. Some citizens are uninvolved.

____ 11. Some citizens are non-involved.

____ 12. No citizens are involved.

____ 13. Every citizen is involved.

____ 14. Every picture of him is unrecognizable.

____ 15. Not every traffic officer is listening to his radio.

____ 16. Some hacksaws have fine-toothed blades.

____ 17. Every jeweler has not made an inventory.

____ 18. That horse is not gentle.

____ 19. That horse is not non-gentle.

____ 20. That horse is non-gentle.

____ 21. That horse is gentle.

____ 22. Every unicorn has a single horn.

____ 23. No grapes are unfermented.

____ 24. Every unfashionable dress is unflattering on her.

____ 25. Not all protractors are on top of the desks.

Label the following propositions as universal (U), particular (P), singular (S), or indefinite (I).

____ 1. No potatoes have been peeled.

____ 2. Some books were lying in the rain.

____ 3. Every spoon is on the table.

____ 4. Every window on the second floor is not open.

____ 5. Not every employee has been paid.

____ 6. Ice skaters frequently fall.

____ 7. George came home late last night.

____ 8. The weather reports have been unfavorable.

____ 9. Breakfast cereal is found on many tables in the morning.

____ 10. George Washington was the first president of the United States.

____ 11. My newspaper has not come yet.

____ 12. No prisoners complained about the food.

____ 13. Bananas contain a high amount of potassium.

____ 14. Every flowering plant has not been purchased.

____ 15. Every musician came to the practice.

____ 16. Beagles are very friendly dogs.

____ 17. The west bridge was washed out last night.

____ 18. My new Easter dress has green and blue stripes.

____ 19. Some bridge players are ready to begin.

____ 20. Switzerland is a neutral country.

____ 21. Every toad has a rough, warty skin.

____ 22. Every peacock does not have its tail spread out.

____ 23. Furniture is cheaper at Ritz's Discount Store.

____ 24. No fern is a flowering plant.

Label the following propositions as universal (U), particular (P), singular (S), or indefinite (I).

____ 1. Some of the maps have not been spread out.

____ 2. No Dalmatian is long-haired.

____ 3. Woodchucks have coarse, red brown fur.

____ 4. Every wigwam is not abandoned.

____ 5. Every scroll is a roll of paper or parchment.

____ 6. The Arabian Desert is in Eastern Egypt.

____ 7. Some cardigans are collarless and long-sleeved.

____ 8. My picture book was left in the rain.

____ 9. This vase of flowers is arranged artistically.

____ 10. Eskimo dogs are used to pull sleds.

____ 11. Every honeysuckle plant has small, fragrant flowers.

____ 12. Every librarian has not taken an inventory.

____ 13. Merchants buy and sell goods for profit.

____ 14. No painters asked for an increase in salary.

____ 15. My dry cleaning will be ready on Tuesday.

____ 16. John F. Kennedy was a popular president.

____ 17. Dragonflies do not harm human beings.

____ 18. The baked goods have been placed on the shelves.

____ 19. Sally is at the top of her class.

____ 20. Feathers have a horny, central shaft.

____ 21. Not every frog is full-grown.

____ 22. Every student in that class is not prepared.

____ 23. Every mazurka is a Polish dance.

____ 24. Some pyramids were built by the ancient Egyptians.

Label the following propositions as universal affirmative (A), particular affirmative (I), universal negative (E), or particular negative (O).

_____ 1. No spaceship is indestructible.

_____ 2. Some businessmen are not able to meet their obligations.

_____ 3. Not every rainstorm brings a rainbow.

_____ 4. A dozen eggs are needed for the recipe.

_____ 5. Not all who mock their bonds are free.

_____ 6. Full many a flower is born to blush unseen.

_____ 7. A bird in the hand is worth two in the bush.

_____ 8. Every roof has been repaired.

_____ 9. Brave men were living before Caesar.

_____ 10. No snowshoes were provided.

_____ 11. Every child has an ice cream cone.

_____ 12. Every ship has not put out to sea.

_____ 13. No shock of corn was left in the field.

_____ 14. Some food was placed in the refrigerator.

_____ 15. Not every hamburger needs mustard.

_____ 16. Colored balloons were used for decorations.

_____ 17. Every hollyhock has large flowers in elongated spikes.

_____ 18. Every mink has valuable fur.

_____ 19. No lobster is bright red when alive.

_____ 20. Thomas Watson came home last night.

_____ 21. Some pelicans have completely webbed feet.

_____ 22. Some scrolls have not been rolled up.

_____ 23. Every Siamese cat has slanting, blue eyes.

_____ 24. No shrimp are available at the market.

Label the following propositions as universal affirmative (A), particular affirmative (I), universal negative (E), or particular negative (O).

_____ 1. Not every failure is embarrassing.

_____ 2. No elk is without antlers.

_____ 3. Every cuttlefish has ten sucker-bearing arms.

_____ 4. Some cuckoo clocks have not been wound.

_____ 5. Some jigsaw puzzles are quite difficult.

_____ 6. James Baker has a new position.

_____ 7. No kettledrum is without a parchment top.

_____ 8. Every milkweed plant has plumed seeds.

_____ 9. Every mob is a disorderly and lawless crowd.

_____ 10. Fools rush in where angels fear to tread.

_____ 11. Not every paper cutter has been sharpened.

_____ 12. Some picture windows open out on country landscapes.

_____ 13. No ostrich has useful wings.

_____ 14. Every pair of patent leather shoes was not placed on sale.

_____ 15. Every pretzel is a biscuit made from a slender roll of dough.

_____ 16. No schnauzer has a shaggy coat.

_____ 17. Good fences make good neighbors.

_____ 18. Every tepee is a cone-shaped tent of animal skins.

_____ 19. First impressions are the most lasting.

_____ 20. A penny saved is a penny earned.

_____ 21. The leopard does not change his spots.

_____ 22. Some trombones have a movable slide.

_____ 23. Not every storm has thunder and lightning.

_____ 24. No walrus is without a thick mustache.

Classify the subjects and predicates of the following propositions as distributed (D) or undistributed (U).

<u>subject/predicate</u>

_____ 1. This ax is laid to the tree trunk.

_____ 2. Every derby is a stiff felt hat.

_____ 3. No dandelion is blooming.

_____ 4. Every condor is a large vulture.

_____ 5. Not every cocoon is spun.

_____ 6. Every coconut is filled with a sweet, milky fluid.

_____ 7. Some of the coffee is not heated.

_____ 8. Some wasps are able to sting repeatedly.

_____ 9. Every walrus is mustached.

_____ 10. No umbrella is open.

_____ 11. Tobacco is used for smoking.

_____ 12. Some clocks are wound.

_____ 13. Every thistle is not cut.

_____ 14. Sugar is hard on the teeth.

_____ 15. This pumpkin is carved out.

_____ 16. Some ships are not sailing.

_____ 17. Every penguin is flightless.

_____ 18. No octopus is armless.

_____ 19. Margaret is coming home.

_____ 20. Some streets are not crooked.

_____ 21. Every kite is not flying.

_____ 22. Some sunsets are beautiful.

_____ 23. Some grasshoppers are not leaping.

Classify the subjects and predicates of the following propositions as distributed (D) or undistributed (U).

<u>subject/predicate</u>

_____ 1. No gable window faces north.

_____ 2. Life jackets are needed in an open boat.

_____ 3. Some medication does not give immediate relief.

_____ 4. Some pheasants are already nesting.

_____ 5. Every scorpion has not been caught.

_____ 6. Some tam-o'-shanters do not have a tassel.

_____ 7. This street is full of chuckholes.

_____ 8. No parakeet has a short tail.

_____ 9. Every papyrus is a tall water plant.

_____ 10. Some hammers do not have a pronged claw.

_____ 11. This line is crooked.

_____ 12. Chains are as strong as the weakest link.

_____ 13. Every market is not filled with people.

_____ 14. Some leaves have serrated margins.

_____ 15. Death is the great leveler.

_____ 16. No lily of the valley grows in bright sunlight.

_____ 17. Every mayfly is a soft-bodied insect.

_____ 18. Some nicknames are given in affection.

_____ 19. Some pretzels are not baked.

_____ 20. Every ratline is a piece of tarred rope.

_____ 21. Not every separation is painful.

_____ 22. Every stone is nonmetallic mineral matter.

_____ 23. No tweezers are sterilized.

If possible, convert the following propositions.

1. Some S is P. _____

2. Some non-S is P. _____

3. Every non-S is P. _____

4. No non-S is P. _____

5. Some S is not non-P. _____

6. Every S is P. _____

7. Not every S is non-P. _____

8. Some S is non-P. _____

9. Some men are smokers. _____

10. Every plant is living. _____

11. All snow is white. _____

12. Not all white things are swans. _____

13. No cloud is a solid. _____

14. Some children are non-talkative. _____

15. All grass is green. _____

16. All men are equal. _____

17. No glasses are broken. _____

18. Some desserts are not sweet. _____

19. Some waves are high. _____

20. Every clock is fast. _____

21. Not every acid is dangerous. _____

22. Some disciples surpass their masters. _____

23. No soldiers are cowards. _____

24. Some parents work very hard. _____

25. Every locust makes a loud noise. _____

If possible, convert the following propositions.

1. Some S is non-P. _____

2. Not every S is non-P. _____

3. Every S is P. _____

4. Some S is not non-P. _____

5. No non-S is P. _____

6. Every non-S is P. _____

7. Some non-S is P. _____

8. Some S is P. _____

9. Every fern is a non-flowering plant. _____

10. Some frogs have powerful hind legs. _____

11. No gargoyles are beautiful. _____

12. Some gems are used as jewels. _____

13. Not every ghetto is unsafe. _____

14. Every gladiolus has swordlike leaves. _____

15. Some hairpins are U-shaped. _____

16. Some photographs are not flattering. _____

17. No pigeons have slender bodies. _____

18. All pipe cleaners have tufts of yarn. _____

19. All primers help children to read. _____

20. Some reservations are public land. _____

21. No tendrils are non-supportive. _____

22. Not all trivia is recognized. _____

23. All vanilla extract is used as a flavoring. _____

24. Every wig is a false covering. _____

25. Some wood is dried out. _____

Obvert the following propositions.

1. No S is P. _____

2. Some S is not P. _____

3. No S is non-P. _____

4. Every S is P. _____

5. Some S is non-P. _____

6. Some S is P. _____

7. Some non-S is P. _____

8. Every S is non-P. _____

9. Every non-S is non-P. _____

10. No non-S is non-P. _____

11. Every geranium is planted. _____

12. Some mayflies are resting. _____

13. No hyacinth is a non-lily. _____

14. Some teeth are non-impacted. _____

15. Some gophers are not burrowing. _____

16. This jungle is not African. _____

17. Some non-bowlers are not non-cleaned. _____

18. No Dalmatian is non-short-haired. _____

19. Every pheasant is not short-tailed. _____

20. No raccoon is non-tree-climbing. _____

21. Some canals are artificial. _____

22. No canary is a non-songbird. _____

23. Some non-pockets are not non-full. _____

24. Every opossum is tree-dwelling. _____

25. No sponge is non-plantlike. _____

Obvert the following propositions.

1. No non-S is non-P. _____

2. Every non-S is non-P. _____

3. Every S is non-P. _____

4. Some non-S is P. _____

5. Some S is P. _____

6. Some S is non-P. _____

7. Every S is P. _____

8. No S is non-P. _____

9. Some S is not P. _____

10. No S is P. _____

11. No jew's-harp is non-lyre-shaped. _____

12. Every iguana is harmless. _____

13. Some hyenas are not non-cowardly. _____

14. No fig tree is non-fruit-bearing. _____

15. Some Doberman pinschers are smooth-haired. _____

16. No decanter is non-decorative. _____

17. Every cold pack is not well-wrapped. _____

18. No chariot is non-horse-drawn. _____

19. Some cashiers are not non-responsible. _____

20. This opera is not entertaining. _____

21. Some bowie knives are not double-edged. _____

22. Some caterpillars are non-crushed. _____

23. No alpaca is non-domesticated. _____

24. Some ants are wingless. _____

25. Every battlement is manned. _____

In each of the following statements an inference is made based on the process of conversion. If the inference is valid, mark (V). If it is invalid, underline the section containing the error.

1. If some praise is flattery, then all flattery is praise.

2. If all cathedrals are churches, then some churches are cathedrals.

3. If some Chinese are not white, then no white person is Chinese.

4. If not everyone who reads much is wise, then some wise persons are not those who read much.

5. If it is true that some politicians are not patriotic, then it is true that some patriotic ones are not politicians.

6. Since some drawing materials are crayons, then every crayon is drawing material.

7. No dog can apprehend a universal. Therefore none apprehending a universal is a dog.

8. If it is true that no good research scholar ignores primary sources, then it is true that some of those who ignore primary sources are not good research scholars.

9. If the good is that which is expedient, then whatever is expedient is good.

10. No free act is physically predetermined. Therefore no physically predetermined act is a free act.

11. If it is true that some gems are precious stones, then it is true that some precious stones are gems.

12. Since every loaf of bread is not expensive, then some expensive things are not loaves of bread.

13. If it is true that all carbon is combustible, then it is true that whatever is combustible is carbon.

14. If it is true that the fig is a pear-shaped fruit, then any pear-shaped fruit is a fig.

15. If the jellyfish is shaped like an umbrella, then some things shaped like an umbrella are jellyfish.

16. If it is true that some mermaids are not real sea creatures, then it is true that some real sea creatures are not mermaids.

17. If it is true that no moose is the smallest member of the deer family in North America, then it is true that some of the smallest members of the deer family in North America are not moose.

18. If the ostrich is a large, swift-running bird, then some large, swift-running birds are ostriches.

Using the rules of opposition, mark the following true (T), false (F), or unknown (U). For numbers 21 through 25, label the type of proposition before using the rules for truth and falsity.

1. If A is true, then O is ____

2. If A is true, then E is ____

3. If A is true, then I is ____

4. If A is false, then E is ____

5. If I is true, then E is ____

6. If I is false, then A is ____

7. If I is false, then O is ____

8. If I is true, then O is ____

9. If O is true, then A is ____

10. If O is false, then E is ____

11. If O is false, then I is ____

12. If O is true, then E is ____

13. If O is false, then A is ____

14. If E is true, then I is ____

15. If E is true, then A is ____

16. If E is true, then O is ____

17. If E is false, then A is ____

18. If E is true and O is true, then A is ____

19. If O is false and E is false, then A is ____

20. If I is true and O is true, then A is ____

21. If it is true that every tree is living, then
    a. No tree is living is ____
    b. Some tree is not living is ____
    c. Not every tree is living is ____

relationship: _____
contrariety _____
_____
_____

22. If it is true that every star is shining, then
    a. Not every star is shining is ____
    b. No star is shining is ____
    c. Some star is shining is ____
    d. This star is shining is ____

_____
_____
_____
_____

23. If it is false that every ship is sailing, then
    a. No ship is sailing is ____
    b. Not every ship is sailing is ____
    c. Some ships are sailing is ____
    d. Some ships are not sailing is ____
    e. Not all ships are sailing is ____
    f. This ship is sailing is ____

_____
_____
_____
_____
_____
_____

24. If it is false that some girl is dancing, then
    a. Every girl is dancing is ____
    b. No girl is dancing is ____
    c. Some girls are not dancing is ____
    d. Not every girl is dancing is ____
    e. This girl is dancing is ____

_____
_____
_____
_____
_____

25. If it is true that some rocks are not falling, then
    a. Every rock is falling is ____
    b. No rock is falling is ____
    c. Some rocks are falling is ____
    d. Not every rock is falling is ____

_____
_____
_____
_____

The propositions in the first column are marked true or false. Using the rules of opposition, mark the propositions which follow as true (T), false (F), or unknown (U). (Label the propositions first.)

(T) Some hats are cleaned.	1. Some hats are not cleaned. ____
(F) Every gremlin is angry.	2. No gremlin is angry. ____
(T) Every greyhound is slender.	3. Some greyhounds are not slender. ____
(T) Every fuchsia is a primrose.	4. No fuchsia is a primrose. ____
(T) No flute is stringed.	5. Some flutes are stringed. ____
(F) Every flamingo is non-tropical.	6. Some flamingos are non-tropical. ____
(F) Some fish are warmblooded.	7. Some fish are not warmblooded. ____
(T) Some hacksaws are fine-toothed.	8. Every hacksaw is fine-toothed. ____
(T) Some galleys are ships.	9. No galley is a ship. ____
(F) Some dodos are not extinct.	10. Every dodo is extinct. ____
(T) Some pipes are not clogged.	11. No pipe is clogged. ____
(F) No puffin is short-necked.	12. Some puffins are short-necked. ____
(T) Every penguin is flightless.	13. No penguin is flightless. ____
(T) Some oboes are woodwinds.	14. No oboe is a woodwind. ____
(T) No scaffold is permanent.	15. Some scaffolds are not permanent. ____
(T) No rattlesnake is coiled.	16. Some rattlesnakes are not coiled. ____
(F) Some pagodas are not temples.	17. No pagoda is a temple. ____
(F) No nephew is related.	18. Every nephew is related. ____
(T) No mole is above ground.	19. Some moles are above ground. ____
(F) No shark is slate gray.	20. Every shark is slate gray. ____
(F) Some skunks are not striped.	21. Every skunk is striped. ____
(F) Every swamp is dry.	22. Some swamps are dry. ____
(F) Some tepees are not tents.	23. No tepee is a tent. ____
(T) Every swallow is swift-flying.	24. No swallow is swift-flying. ____
(F) Every pillow is shaken.	25. Some pillows are not shaken. ____
(T) Some pineapples are edible.	26. Every pineapple is edible. ____
(T) Some mandolins are stringed.	27. No mandolin is stringed. ____
(F) Some hummingbirds are large.	28. Every hummingbird is large. ____
(F) Every song is displeasing.	29. No song is displeasing. ____
(F) Some mongooses are not killers.	30. No mongoose is a killer. ____
(F) Every monkey is short-tailed.	31. Some monkeys are not short-tailed. ____
(F) Every marigold is purple.	32. No marigold is purple. ____
(T) Some liquids are poured.	33. Some liquids are not poured. ____
(T) Every lobster is edible.	34. Some lobsters are edible. ____
(F) Some llamas are not domesticated.	35. Some llamas are domesticated. ____
(T) No mouse is huge.	36. Every mouse is huge. ____
(T) Some pointers are hunters.	37. Every pointer is a hunter. ____
(F) Every riddle is simple.	38. Some riddles are simple. ____
(F) No salmon is running.	39. Every salmon is running. ____
(F) Every soldier is enlisted.	40. No soldier is enlisted. ____

In each of the following statements an inference is made based on the rules of opposition. If the inference is valid, mark (V). If it is invalid, underline the section containing the error. (It will help to label each proposition first.)

1. If it is true that every S is P, then it is false that no S is P.

2. If it is true that some S is not P, then it is false that some S is P.

3. If it is false that some S is not P, then it is false that no S is P and true that every S is P.

4. If it is true that not every S is P, then it is unknown that no S is P and false that every S is P.

5. If it is false that some plants are sensitive, then it is true that some plants are not sensitive.

6. If it is false that not every pelican is a water bird, then it is true that no pelican is a water bird.

7. If it is true that no neutrons are charged particles, then it is true that some neutrons are charged particles.

8. If it is false that some starfish are without a skeleton, then it is true that no starfish is without a skeleton.

9. It is false that not every mole is underground. Therefore it is true that some moles are underground.

10. If it is true that no one is unrewarded who does his best, then it is true that some who do their best are not unrewarded.

11. If it is true that some of the dynasty were not descended from Charlemagne, then it is true that no members of the dynasty were descended from Charlemagne.

12. If it is true that not all magic is preternatural, then it is false that some magic is preternatural.

13. It is false that all particles which do not have a positive charge are neutrons. Therefore it is true that no particles which do not have a positive charge are neutrons.

14. Since it is true that no violation of the natural law will go unpunished, it is true that some violation of the natural law will not go unpunished. Therefore it is true that some violation of the natural law will go unpunished.

15. Since it is false that not all statements made by professors are true, it is true that all statements made by professors are true. It follows that some statements made by professors are true.

16. If it is true that some water is composed of hydrogen and oxygen, then it is false that no water is composed of hydrogen and oxygen. Therefore it is true that all water is composed of hydrogen and oxygen.

17. If it is true that none of those who fought against the invaders injured the sick or disabled, then it is false that some of those who fought against the invaders injured the sick or disabled.

18. If it is true that some virtuous acts are meritorious, then it is false that no virtuous act is meritorious. It also follows that every virtuous act is meritorious.

19. If it is false that some artifacts have been proved to date back to the Pliocene Age, then it is true that no artifacts have been proved to date back to the Pliocene Age and false that all artifacts have been proved to date back to the Pliocene Age. It follows that some artifacts have not been proved to date back to the Pliocene Age.

20. If it is true that some people who cannot be separated from living men first appeared only about 35,000 years ago, then it is false that no people who cannot be separated from living men first appeared only about 35,000 years ago. From this it follows that every person who cannot be separated from living men first appeared only about 35,000 years ago.

21. If it is true that all air pollution becomes more serious when weather conditions prevent the dispersal of pollutants, then it is false that not all air pollution becomes more serious when weather conditions prevent the dispersal of pollutants. From this it follows that some air pollution becomes more serious when weather conditions prevent the dispersal of pollutants.

22. If it is true that some surgeons wishing to prevent the buildup of static electricity do not wear nylon garments, then it is false that every surgeon wishing to prevent the buildup of static electricity wears nylon garments. Therefore it follows as true that some surgeons wishing to prevent the buildup of static electricity wear nylon garments.

23. If it is true that no electronic range needs utensils made of conductors, then it is also true that not every electronic range needs utensils made of conductors. Therefore it follows that every electronic range needs utensils made of conductors.

24. If it is true that all contact lenses today permit a normal tear flow, then it is false that no contact lenses today permit a normal tear flow. In addition, it is true that some contact lenses today permit a normal tear flow.

25. If it is true that some pressure exerted on a confined liquid is transmitted undiminished in all directions, then it is false that some pressure exerted on a confined liquid is not transmitted undiminished in all directions. Therefore it follows that all pressure exerted on a confined liquid is transmitted undiminished in all directions.

For the following categorical syllogisms, mark the terms, the premises, the figure, and the mood. Proceed according to the following example:

O.	Every bird lays eggs.	M---P	major		A
	Every robin is a bird.	S---M	minor		A
	∴ Every robin lays eggs.	∴ S–P		I	A

1. No Chinese is Arabian.
   Every Peking man is Chinese.
   ∴ No Peking man is Arabian.

2. No scholar ignores primary sources.
   Some historians are scholars.
   ∴ Not all historians ignore primary sources.

3. Every metal conducts electricity.
   No glass conducts electricity.
   ∴ No glass is a metal.

4. No rabbit has webbed feet.
   Every duck has webbed feet.
   ∴ No duck is a rabbit.

5. Every clock indicates time.
   Some instruments do not indicate time.
   ∴ Some instruments are not clocks.

6. Some rodents are chinchillas.
   Every rodent has four incisor teeth.
   ∴ Some things with four incisor teeth are chinchillas.

7. Every circle is a figure.
   Every circle is round.
   ∴ Some round things are figures.

8. Every dish is used.
   Some of the dishes are washed.
   ∴ Some washed things are used.

9. Everything covered with black hair is hard to see.
   Every chimpanzee is covered with black hair.
   ∴ Every chimpanzee is hard to see.

10. Some things with a stopper are decanters.
    Everything with a stopper retains liquid.
    ∴ Some things retaining liquids are decanters.

11. Every rabbit has a tail.
    No guinea pig has a tail.
    ∴ No guinea pig is a rabbit.

12. Everything with strong, large wings flies well.
    Every sea gull has strong, large wings.
    ∴ Every sea gull flies well.

13. Some things with sand are hourglasses.
    Everything with sand becomes gritty.
    ∴ Some gritty things are hourglasses.

14. Every impacted thing is hard to dislodge.
    Some teeth are impacted.
    ∴ Some teeth are hard to dislodge.

The following categorical syllogisms are either valid or invalid. If the syllogism is valid, mark (V). If it is invalid, note the rule violated.

1. Every human being is rational.
    Thomas is a human being.
    ∴ Thomas is a scholar.

2. Every human being has a rational soul.
    No horses are human beings.
    ∴ No horses have a rational soul.

3. No plant has sensation.
    The oyster has sensation.
    ∴ The oyster is not a plant.

4. Every civilized person cooks his food.
    Every civilized person wears clothes.
    ∴ Everyone who wears clothes cooks his food.

5. Every good person obeys the laws.
    These persons break the laws.
    ∴ None of these persons are good persons.

6. Some officials are democrats.
    Some democrats are progressive.
    ∴ Some officials are progressive.

7. Every Frenchman is European.
    Some artists are European.
    ∴ Some artists are Frenchmen.

8. Every tiger is striped.
    Every striped thing is noticeable.
    ∴ Every tiger is noticeable.

9. Every parakeet has a long, tapering tail.
    Every parakeet is slender.
    ∴ Some slender things have long, tapering tails.

10. Every reindeer has antlers.
    No llama has antlers.
    ∴ No llama is a reindeer.

11. Every college student has much homework.
    Some students in Los Angeles have much homework.
    ∴ Some students in Los Angeles are college students.

12. Every stringed instrument must be tuned.
    Every lute is a stringed instrument.
    ∴ Every lute must be tuned.

13. No domesticated animal is impossible to handle.
    Every llama is domesticated.
    ∴ Every llama is impossible to handle.

14. Every crustacean has a hard outer shell.
    Every lobster is a crustacean.
    ∴ Every lobster has a hard outer shell.

15. All carpenters are not industrious.
    Some carpenters are lazy.
    ∴ Some lazy persons are not industrious.

16. Every locust is a grasshopper.
    No butterflies are grasshoppers.
    ∴ Some butterflies are not locusts.

17. Every lemur is a primate.
    Some primates have long tails.
    ∴ Some lemurs have long tails.

18. Some lilies of the valley are perennial plants.
    Every perennial plant grows year after year.
    ∴ Some lilies of the valley grow year after year.

19. Some musical instruments provide fine recreation.
    Every piano is a musical instrument.
    ∴ Every piano provides fine recreation.

20. Every citrus fruit is edible.
    Every orange is edible.
    ∴ Every orange is a citrus fruit.

21. Every peacock is brightly colored.
    Every peacock does not spread out its tail.
    ∴ Some brightly colored things do not spread out their tails.

22. Some lady-slippers are orchids.
    No roses are lady-slippers.
    ∴ No roses are orchids.

23. Every jury member is sworn to hear the evidence.
    Some business men are jury members.
    ∴ Some business men are sworn to hear the evidence.

24. Every Japanese beetle is green and brown.
    Every worm is not green and brown.
    ∴ No worm is a Japanese beetle.

25. Every insect has a body with three parts.
    Every mollusk is not an insect.
    ∴ No mollusk has a body with three parts.

26. Every mole is a burrower.
    No mole is a carnivore.
    ∴ No carnivore is a burrower.

27. Some things killing poisonous snakes are domesticated.
    Every mongoose is able to kill poisonous snakes.
    ∴ Every mongoose is domesticated.

28. Every lake is an inland body of fresh water.
    No lake has a flowing river current.
    ∴ Some bodies with a flowing river current are not inland bodies of fresh water.

29. Every rodent is a gnawing mammal.
    Some prairie dogs are rodents.
    ∴ Some prairie dogs are gnawing mammals.

30. Every bulldog is heavily built.
    Some stubborn animals are heavily built.
    ∴ Some stubborn animals are bulldogs.

The following categorical syllogisms are either valid or invalid. If the syllogism is valid, mark (V). If it is invalid, note the rule violated.

1. Every kilt reaches to the knees.
   Some pleated skirts reach to the knees.
   ∴ Some pleated skirts are kilts.

2. Every gourd is a trailing or climbing plant.
   Every squash is a gourd.
   ∴ Every squash is a trailing or climbing plant.

3. Every sponge is a plantlike animal.
   No sponge grows above water.
   ∴ Some things growing above water are not plantlike animals.

4. Some mythical creations help to explain a natural phenomenon.
   Every unicorn is a mythical creation.
   ∴ Every unicorn helps to explain a natural phenomenon.

5. Every moose is a member of the deer family.
   No moose is native to Europe.
   ∴ No animal native to Europe is a member of the deer family.

6. Every mongoose is noted for its ability to kill poisonous snakes.
   No raccoon is a mongoose.
   ∴ No raccoon is noted for its ability to kill poisonous snakes.

7. Every mink has valuable fur.
   No house rat has valuable fur.
   ∴ No house rat is a mink.

8. Every mineral has a distinctive set of physical properties.
   All coal is a mineral.
   ∴ All coal has a distinctive set of physical properties.

9. Some iron is readily magnetized.
   No jade pieces are iron.
   ∴ No jade pieces are readily magnetized.

10. No iron is difficult to magnetize.
    All iron is a malleable chemical element.
    ∴ Some malleable chemical elements are not difficult to magnetize.

11. Every perennial plant grows quite easily.
    Every iris grows quite easily.
    ∴ Every iris is a perennial plant.

12. Some birds of prey are quite dangerous.
    Every falcon is a bird of prey.
    ∴ Every falcon is quite dangerous.

13. Some melodies express a musical idea.
    Whatever expresses a musical idea can be memorized.
    ∴ Some melodies can be memorized.

14. Every orangutan is a manlike ape.
    Some manlike apes have hairless faces.
    ∴ Some orangutans have hairless faces.

15. Every newt is a salamander.
    No scorpion is a salamander.
    ∴ Some scorpions are not newts.

16. Some sticklebacks are scaleless fish.
    Some sticklebacks are saltwater fish.
    ∴ Some saltwater fish are scaleless fish.

17. Every drum has a hollow cylinder or hemisphere.
    Every tambourine is a drum.
    ∴ Every tambourine has a hollow cylinder or hemisphere.

18. No reflex is a voluntary action.
    Every sneeze is a reflex.
    ∴ Every sneeze is a voluntary action.

19. Every reptile is a coldblooded vertebrate.
    Every pterodactyl is a reptile.
    ∴ Every pterodactyl is a coldblooded vertebrate.

20. Every pueblo was built by the North or South American Indian.
    Some communal villages were built by the North or South American Indian.
    ∴ Some communal villages are pueblos.

21. Every pitcher plant traps insects for food.
    No tulip traps insects for food.
    ∴ No tulip is a pitcher plant.

22. Every mole is an insect-eating animal.
    Every mole is a burrowing animal.
    ∴ Some burrowing mammals are insect-eating animals.

23. Every manatee is an aquatic mammal.
    Every aquatic mammal nurses its young.
    ∴ Every manatee nurses its young.

24. Every swivel chair has a seat which turns on a pivot.
    Some office chairs have seats which turn on a pivot.
    ∴ Some office chairs are swivel chairs.

25. Every shark is tough-skinned.
    Some tough-skinned things are difficult to kill.
    ∴ Some sharks are difficult to kill.

26. Every whale has limbs modified into flippers.
    Every dolphin has limbs modified into flippers.
    ∴ No dolphin is a whale.

27. Every whippet resembles a small greyhound.
    Every whippet is used in racing.
    ∴ Every small greyhound is used in racing.

28. No weasel is vegetarian.
    Every porcupine is vegetarian.
    ∴ No porcupine is a weasel.

29. Every igloo is built with blocks of packed snow.
    No wigwams are igloos.
    ∴ No wigwams are built with blocks of packed snow.

30. Every domesticated animal is easy to handle.
    Every guinea pig is easy to handle.
    ∴ Every guinea pig is a domesticated animal.

Write the conclusions for the following syllogisms. First find the middle term, thus finding the figure. Then follow the rules carefully.

1. Every y is z
    Every x is y.

2. No y is z.
    Every x is y.

3. No y is z.
    Some x is y.

4. No z is y.
    Every x is y.

5. No z is y.
    Some x is y.

6. Every y is z.
    Every y is x.

7. No y is z.
    Some y is x.

8. Some y is not z.
    Every y is x.

9. No y is z.
    Some x is y.

10. Every z is y.
    No x is y.

11. Every z is y.
    Some x is not y.

12. Every y is z.
    Some y is x.

13. Some y is z.
    Every y is x.

14. No y is z.
    Every y is x.

15. Every z is y.
    No x is y.

16. No liquid is a solid.
    Some milk is a liquid.

17. All water is liquid.
    Some colorless things are not liquid.

18. Every hippopotamus is thick-skinned.
    Every hippopotamus is short-legged.

19. No lotus has palmate leaves.
    Every lotus is a member of the legume family.

20. Every male moose has huge palmate antlers.
    Everything with huge palmate antlers has a weapon for defense.

21. Every mole has small eyes and ears.
    Every mole has shovellike forefeet.

22. Every star is seen as a fixed point of light.
    Venus is not seen as a fixed point of light.

23. Every viper is a venomous snake.
    Every copperhead is a viper.

24. Every rail has short wings and tail.
    Every coot is a rail.

25. No condor has plumage on its head and neck.
    Every condor has a ruff of feathers at the base of the neck.

26. Every collie has a long, narrow head.
    No beagle has a long, narrow head.

Write the conclusions for the following syllogisms. First find the middle term, thus finding the figure. Then follow the rules carefully.

1. No y is z
    Every y is x.

2. Every y is z.
    Some y is x.

3. Every z is y.
    No x is y.

4. Some y is not z.
    Every y is x.

5. Every y is z.
    Every y is x.

6. No z is y.
    Every x is y.

7. No y is z.
    Every x is y.

8. Every z is y.
    No x is y.

9. Some y is z.
    Every y is x.

10. Every z is y.
    Some x is not y.

11. No y is z.
    Some x is y.

12. No y is z.
    Some y is x.

13. No z is y.
    Some x is y.

14. No y is z.
    Some x is y.

15. Every y is z.
    Every x is y.

16. No gloves are a protective covering for the head.
    Every helmet is a protective covering for the head.

17. Every buskin is a boot worn in ancient times.
    No oxford is a boot worn in ancient times.

18. No butterfly has hard front wings.
    Every butterfly has membranous wings.

19. Every bovid mammal has a pair of hollow, unbranched horns.
    Every buffalo is a bovid mammal.

20. Every bird is an egg-laying vertebrate.
    Every penguin is a bird.

21. Every mushroom has a stalk capped with an umbrellalike top.
    No puffball has a stalk capped with an umbrellalike top.

22. Every raccoon is a flesh-eating mammal.
    Every raccoon has masklike markings across the eyes.

23. Whatever has a marsupium has a pouch for her young.
    Every female kangaroo has a marsupium.

24. No octopus has a vertebrate structure.
    Every octopus has a large head with a mouth on the undersurface.

25. Every opossum is a tree-dwelling mammal.
    Every opossum has a ratlike, prehensile tail.

26. Every ostrich has small, useless wings.
    Some ospreys do not have small, useless wings.

The following categorical syllogisms are either valid or invalid. If the syllogism is valid, mark (V). If it is invalid, note the rule violated. (It will be helpful to rewrite these syllogisms in logical form.)

1. Mrs. Jones is a good neighbor, because Mrs. Jones is very kind and every kind person is certainly a good neighbor.

2. Some bitterns, I am sure, are wading birds. It is clear, too, that no bluebird is a wading bird. Therefore no bluebird is a bittern.

3. Every religious man goes to church every Sunday. I see MacDonald going to church every Sunday, so I am sure that MacDonald is a religious man.

4. No one likes a mean individual. Gary is certainly not a mean individual, so everyone likes Gary.

5. Everyone who is unafraid of death deserves to live. As you know, every member of that army is unafraid of death. Therefore every member of that army deserves to live.

6. Aluminum is not a compound substance, for it is a metal and none of the metals is a compound substance.

7. The air is a physical body because the air gravitates and every physical body gravitates.

8. Since no modern physician believes in the practice of bleeding and Dr. Mitchell does not believe in the practice of bleeding, Dr. Mitchell is a modern physician.

9. As you say, no bagpipe is without a leather bag. You must remember that some bagpipes have one double-reed pipe. Isn't it true, then, that some things with one double-reed pipe are without a leather bag?

10. Since some burrowing mammals are carnivores and not every raccoon is a burrowing mammal, some raccoons are not carnivores.

11. We know that whatever has long claws can be very harmful. We also know that every badger has long claws. It is clear, then, that every badger can be very harmful.

12. Clearly, some who tremble are guilty and that all who are guilty should be punished. Therefore some who tremble should be punished.

13. Since some fanatics kill their best friends and Paul Morrow killed his best friend, it is clear that Paul Morrow is a fanatic.

14. Sine every human being is teachable, it follows that dogs are not teachable, for dogs are not human beings.

15. Every poor mechanic is a menace to society, for every poor mechanic fails in his responsibilities to society. Also those who are a menace to society fail in their responsibilities to society.

16. You say that the union members are not liberals. They're radicals, aren't they? And aren't the liberals radicals? Well, then how can you deny that the union members are liberals?

17. Meteorology is not a good course, for no good course is taught by anyone who is not a full professor and meteorology is not taught by a full professor.

18. Don't you know that whatever is disliked is harmful? Then you must see that some movies are harmful, for some movies are disliked.

19. Since no pain is desired and no useless thing is desired, it follows that all pain is useless.

20. No mere lapse in table manners would cause a man to be fired from his job. Now, since Tom Handley was fired from his job, we may conclude that Tom did not have just a mere lapse in table manners.

21. Tell me how you know that the cuttlefish ejects a dark brown, inklike fluid. That's easy. The cuttlefish is a mollusk and some mollusks eject a dark brown, inklike fluid.

22. I tell you that fossils are the hardened remains of plant or animal life from a previous geological period. The reason is that fossils are preserved in rock formations. Also some of the things preserved in rock formations are the hardened remains of plant or animal life from a previous geological period.

23. Anyone can see that the horse is not the same as the zebra. After all, the horse has been domesticated for drawing or carrying loads, while no zebra has been domesticated for such a purpose.

24. I wish I knew why the kettledrum is a percussion instrument. Maybe I have the answer. It must be because the kettledrum has a hollow hemisphere and a parchment top. Also some of those instruments made as I described are indeed percussion instruments.

25. No moth is a butterfly, for no moths have knobbed antennae and some butterflies do indeed have knobbed antennae.

26. It's easy to see why the muskrat is able to swim. He has both a long, flattened tail and webbed feet. Now whatever is so equipped is certainly able to swim.

27. Nutmeg is the seed from an East Indian tree, for nutmeg is a hard, aromatic seed and an East Indian tree has a hard, aromatic seed.

28. Since every puffin has a brightly colored triangular beak and the pelican is not a puffin, we can conclude that the pelican does not have a brightly colored triangular beak.

29. As you can see, the woodpecker has stiff, sharp tail feathers used for support. But no robin has such tail feathers. It is evident then that no robin is a woodpecker.

30. I'd like to classify the wolverine for you. It is known to be a stocky, ferocious mammal. But, as you well know, some mammals are carnivores. Therefore it is clear that the wolverine is a carnivore.

The following categorical syllogisms are either valid or invalid. If the syllogism is valid, mark (V). If it is invalid, note the rule violated. (It will be helpful to rewrite these syllogisms in logical form.)

1. Let me help you understand the tiger. As you know, the tiger is a large, fierce mammal. Remember too that some mammals are carnivores. Therefore it is clear that the tiger is a carnivore.

2. It is evident that the heron has a long, tapered bill. But no robin has such a bill. Therefore it is clear that no robin is a heron.

3. Since every iguana has a row of spines from neck to tail and the chameleon is not an iguana, we can conclude that the chameleon does not have a row of spines from neck to tail.

4. The chamois lives in the mountains of Europe, for the chamois is a small, goatlike antelope and living in the mountains of Europe is a small, goatlike antelope.

5. It's easy to see why the chinchilla is bred extensively. This animal yields a very expensive fur. Now whatever yields such a fur is bred extensively.

6. No cuttlefish is an octopus, for no cuttlefish has a soft, saclike body and some octopuses do indeed have soft, saclike bodies.

7. I wish I knew why the spearmint is a perennial plant. Maybe I have the answer. It must be because the spearmint is a seed plant that produces flowers and seeds from the same root structure year after year. Also some seed plants that produce flowers and seeds in such a fashion are indeed perennial plants.

8. Anyone can see that the helicopter is not the same as the jetliner. After all, the helicopter has large, motor-driven rotary blades mounted horizontally, while no jetliner has such rotary blades.

9. I tell you that the fireman's hat is a helmet. The reason is that this hat is a protective covering for the head. Also some of the protective coverings for the head are helmets.

10. Tell me how you know that chalk becomes marble when crystallized by heat and pressure. That's easy. All chalk is limestone and some limestone becomes marble when crystallized in such a fashion.

11. It is evident that the symphonic musician must be able to do more than carry a tune. Now, since Mary Lipton cannot do more than carry a tune, we may conclude that Mary Lipton is not a symphonic musician.

12. Since no pleasure is hateful and no satisfactory thing is hateful, it follows that all pleasure is a satisfactory thing.

13. Don't you know that whatever leads to suffering is harmful? Then you must see that some love affairs are harmful, for some love affairs lead to suffering.

14. Roland University is not an Ivy League university, for no Ivy League university employs beginning instructors and Roland University employs such instructors.

15. You say that the government is not communistic. This government destroys religion, doesn't it? And don't the communists destroy religion? Then how can you deny this government is communistic?

16. Every ambitious student studies many hours every evening, for every ambitious student wishes to obtain good grades. Also those who study many hours every evening wish to obtain good grades.

17. Since every artist has a sense of design, it follows that beavers do not have a sense of design, for beavers are not artists.

18. Since some obese persons eat a great deal and Jim Smith eats a great deal, it is clear that Jim Smith is an obese person.

19. Definitely, some who blush are filled with shame and all who are filled with shame suffer greatly. Therefore some who blush suffer greatly.

20. We know that whatever has a keen sense of smell can be used in tracking fugitives. We also know that every bloodhound has a keen sense of smell. It is clear, then, that every bloodhound can be used in tracking fugitives.

21. Some walruses have hind flippers which can be turned forward, while not every hair seal has hind flippers which can be turned forward. Therefore some hair seals are not walruses.

22. As you say, no bat is without membranous wings. Also remember that some bats have nocturnal habits. Isn't it true, then, that some things with nocturnal habits are without membranous wings.

23. Since no good singer ignores long hours of musical practice and that blues singer does not ignore long hours of musical practice, that blues singer is a good one.

24. Oxygen is not visible because oxygen is colorless and anything colorless is invisible.

25. The hornet lives in a social organization, for the hornet is a wasp and some wasps live in a social organization.

26. Everyone who is unafraid of hard work deserves a bonus. As you know, every member of that union is unafraid of hard work. Therefore every member of that union deserves a bonus.

27. No one complains about a kind person. No one complains about Susan, so Susan is a kind person.

28. Some antelopes, I am sure, are cud-chewing animals. It is clear, too, that no lion is a cud-chewing animal. Therefore no lion is an antelope.

29. James is a good friend, because James is concerned about my well-being and every person so concerned is a good friend.

The following hypothetical syllogisms are either valid or invalid. If the syllogism is valid, mark (V). If it is invalid, note the rule violated.

1. If a country is in debt, the people are dissatisfied.
    The people of this country are dissatisfied.
    ∴ This country is in debt.
2. If Brian practices every day, he will make the team.
    Brian is practicing every day.
    ∴ Brian will make the team.
3. If this law cannot be enforced, it should be repealed.
    This law can be enforced.
    ∴ This law should not be repealed.
4. If the president betrays his country, he should be impeached.
    The president is not betraying his country.
    ∴ He should not be impeached.
5. If the Eskimos need their sleds pulled, they will not use small dogs.
    The Eskimos do not use small dogs.
    ∴ The Eskimos need their sleds pulled.
6. If the flamingo has long legs and webbed feet, it is able to wade for its food.
    The flamingo is not able to wade for its food.
    ∴ The flamingo does not have long legs and webbed feet.
7. If less grain is produced, this commodity becomes more expensive.
    This commodity is more expensive.
    ∴ Less grain is produced.
8. If the lake is not frozen, the team cannot skate.
    The lake is not frozen.
    ∴ The team cannot skate.
9. If a dentist wants to equip his office, he must have a forceps.
    This dentist wants to equip his office.
    ∴ This dentist must have a forceps.
10. If a fox is hungry, he is not restricted to rabbits.
    This fox is not hungry.
    ∴ This fox is restricted to rabbits.
11. If the galley slaves are not chained, they will attempt to escape.
    These galley slaves are not chained.
    ∴ These galley slaves will attempt to escape.
12. If all the soldiers had been American, they would not all have run away.
    All of the soldiers did run away.
    ∴ None of the soldiers was American.
13. If all the soldiers had been American, none would have run away.
    None of the soldiers ran away.
    ∴ All of the soldiers were American.
14. If all the soldiers had been American, none would have run away.
    None of the soldiers was American.
    ∴ All of them ran away.
15. If none of the soldiers were American, all of them would have run away.
    None of the soldiers was American.
    ∴ All of the soldiers ran away.

16. If the country had one genius, it could break the spy code.
    The country can break the spy code.
    ∴ The country has one genius.

17. If potatoes contain potassium, they should not be restricted from one's diet.
    Potatoes should not be restricted from one's diet.
    ∴ Potatoes contain potassium.

18. The metronome should be used by the piano student if it helps him to maintain regular tempo as he practices. But the metronome is not used by the piano student. Therefore the metronome does not help the student to maintain regular tempo as he practices.

19. The moon accompanies the earth in its yearly revolution around the sun if it revolves around the earth once a month. But the moon does accompany the earth in its yearly revolution around the sun. Therefore the moon revolves around the earth once a month.

20. The farmer should see that the roots of his plants are well-positioned if he hopes that they will be able to draw nourishment from the soil. But the farmer does hope that his plants will be able to draw nourishment from the soil. Therefore he should see that the roots of his plants are well-positioned.

21. Have you noticed the rose window in that church? It cannot display its full beauty if the sun is not shining. You are right. The sun was not shining the other day, and the rose window's full beauty was not displayed.

22. The royal palm should be very plentiful in Florida if it grows rapidly and adapts well. That is true. As you can see, the royal palm is very plentiful in Florida. Therefore it does grow rapidly and adapts well.

23. I read about the sabot the other day. I learned that, if this shoe is made from a single piece of wood, it cannot be noiseless. I grant that. Now, will you also grant this? The sabot is noiseless. Therefore it is not made from a single piece of wood.

24. If the theory of evolution is correct, the fossils found in early geological formations will be less complex than those found in later formations. Now geologists have proved that the fossils found in early geological formations are less complex than those found in later formations. Therefore the theory of evolution is correct.

25. No arachnid is a scorpion if it does not have a tail ending in a curved, poisonous sting. Now that arachnid is a scorpion. Therefore it does have a tail ending in a curved, poisonous sting.

26. A business man's money does not make interest if it is not invested. As you can see, this business man's money is invested. Therefore his money will make interest for him.

27. The hams obtained after the yearly butchering will be preserved if they are rubbed well with salt and cured in the smokehouse. Now these hams obtained after the yearly butchering are not preserved. Therefore they were not rubbed well with salt and cured in the smokehouse.

28. No traveler in the Swiss Alps need worry if the St. Bernard dogs are near the mountains which they are climbing. As you can see, no traveler in the Swiss Alps is worrying. Therefore the St. Bernard dogs are near the mountains which they are climbing.

29. I can tell you this. If that dog is a poodle, it will look as if it has just been clipped by a barber. You are right. As you can see, that dog is not a poodle. Therefore it certainly will not look as if it has just been clipped by a barber.

30. If the mongoose has an extraordinary ability to kill poisonous snakes and rodents, it will frequently be domesticated. It is certainly true that the mongoose is frequently domesticated. Therefore it is also true that the mongoose has an extraordinary ability to kill poisonous snakes and rodents.

Expand the following abbreviated syllogisms and give the figure and mood of each of them.

1. Every X is Z because every X is Y.

2. No X is Z, for all X is Y.

3. Some X is Z since some X is Y.

4. Some X is not Z because some X is Y.

5. Some X is Z because all Y is X.

6. Some X is Z because some Y is X.

7. Some X is not Z because all Y is X.

8. Some X is not Z because some Y is X.

9. Every lyre requires tuning because every lyre is a stringed instrument.

10. None of the tulips is blooming because every tulip is too small.

11. Some of the children are not sleeping because some of them stayed up late.

12. No harness is fastened, for every harness is hanging on the wall.

13. Some sails are not furled because some sails are too wet.

14. Some gems are priceless, for some gems are extremely rare.

15. Some domesticated animals have no external tail, for no guinea pig has an external tail.

16. Some sea gull eggs did not hatch because some sea gull eggs were abandoned.

17. Some primates are active at night, for every lemur is active at night.

18. Some inexpensive things have not been sold, for none of the balloons has been sold.

19. No employee should be fired, for every employee is loyal.

20. Some members of the willow family have soft, fibrous wood, for every poplar has soft, fibrous wood.

21. Not all animals with spots are leopards because every jaguar has spots.

22. No life preservers were useful, for every one of them had been cut into shreds.

23. No member of the party attended the meeting, for no one attending the meeting is the head of a household.

Expand the following abbreviated syllogisms and give the figure and mood of each of them.

1. Some X is not Z because some Y is X.

2. Some X is not Z because all Y is X.

3. Some X is Z because some Y is X.

4. Some X is Z because all Y is X.

5. Some X is not Z because some X is Y.

6. Some X is Z since some X is Y.

7. No X is Z, for all X is Y.

8. Every X is Z because every X is Y.

9. Some tailless amphibians have powerful hind legs, for all frogs have powerful hind legs.

10. Some hounds are helpful to humankind because they are large hunting dogs.

11. No mulberry is poisonous, for no poisonous thing is an edible fruit.

12. No patch should be of worn material, for every patch is used to mend tears.

13. Not all poisonous spiders have a harmful effect on the human being because every tarantula is a poisonous spider.

14. Some animals with flexible snouts are active at night, for every tapir is active at night.

15. No tourniquet should be wasted, for every tourniquet is needed.

16. Some evening shoes have not been repaired, for none of the sandals have been repaired.

17. Some thirty-foot snakes are members of the boa family, for some anacondas are thirty-foot snakes.

18. Some tulip bulbs did not send down roots into the ground, for some tulip bulbs rotted.

19. Some griffins have no scientific basis, for no mythical animal has a scientific basis.

20. Some knights are worthy of trust, for some knights are pledged to chivalrous conduct.

21. No fox is easy to catch, for every fox is a crafty animal.

22. Some pottery coatings are not transparent, for no enamel is transparent.

Expand the enthymeme contained in each of the following paragraphs. Use the following steps:

1. Look very carefully for the main point or conclusion.
2. Find the reason or middle term for this conclusion.
3. Consider the distribution of your subjects and predicates as adequate.
4. If possible, use the first figure.

---

1. Do you know why a stack of magazines tied in a bundle will be very difficult to burn up in a trash pile? If you understand about a fire's need of oxygen, you have the answer. As you can see, the magazines have very little air, except on the outer surface. That is the reason they are so difficult to burn.

2. Two fire fighters were talking the other day about using carbon dioxide to put out fires. They said that, since this gas is heavier than air, it can sink down over a fire and shut off the supply of oxygen. They were glad it is useful.

3. Those people who remember the *Hindenburg* know why helium is used today in dirigibles and blimps. As some individuals may recall, this airship, filled with hydrogen, exploded as it was landing in New Jersey. On the other hand, helium is both very light and also safe from explosion.

4. As you know, the people in Ireland use peat as a fuel. In order to do this, they must dry out the spongy brown substance. Peat, however, is not an economical form of fuel because it still has a very high water content.

5. Have you ever seen a farmer cover his plow with a thin coating of oil before he puts it away? Do you know why he does this? You need only to remember that the plow is usually made from pig iron, which rusts easily.

6. Travelers to the tropics have often remarked that this climate is very hard on machinery. In fact, the person touring by car is amazed at the danger from rust. Then the natives only smile and wonder why the tourists do not notice the amount of moisture in the air.

7. I've often wondered why a bedroom with a large south window gets so hot. It cannot be from the glass itself, for it always feels cold. If it is not the glass, then it must be the room's opaque objects which absorb the sun's rays and then emit waves of radiant energy.

8. The brown or black matter in the soil, formed from partial decomposition of plant or animal matter, is called humus. Humus gives valuable material to the soil used for gardens. Do you see now why the leaves raked in the fall give valuable material to the gardens?

9. When water which has seeped into the crevices of huge rocks freezes, it expands in volume. For this reason, by a process called frost-wedging, frozen water is able to pry loose huge slabs from rocky hillsides.

10. Most of us have many occasions to use a thermos bottle. We know well that it is an excellent heat trap. We demonstrate this fact each time that we put hot coffee into it. Then we are grateful for its silvered glass walls with a vacuum between.

11. In solid form carbon dioxide is known as dry ice, a solid so cold that it is unsafe to handle with bare hands. It has an advantage over regular ice because of the smaller amount of it needed for cooling.

12. It is a fact that the molecules of most substances will not burn at cold temperatures. This fact is easy to understand if one remembers that these molecules are too inactive to combine with the oxygen in the air. When one knows this, one can understand why cold logs ignite slowly or why cars are hard to start on a cold morning.

Expand the enthymeme contained in each of the following paragraphs. Use the following steps:
1. Look very carefully for the main point or conclusion.
2. Find the reason or middle term for this conclusion.
3. Consider the distribution of your subjects and predicates as adequate.
4. If possible, use the first figure.

1. Did you hear that scientist say that the moon has one side which has never been seen by human beings? I couldn't understand what he meant until I heard him say that the moon rotates once as it revolves around the earth. Then I realized that the moon keeps <u>always the same side toward the earth.</u>

2. I have often wondered why the moon does not have protecting layers of atmosphere as the earth does. Its smaller size gives it less gravitational force than the earth. In fact the moon has a gravitational pull which is only one sixth that of the earth. Such a <u>limited gravity prevents the moon from holding on to even a molecule of air.</u>

3. It has been established that the sun is a burning globe of hot gases. Since this center of our solar system has a surface temperature four times that of molten steel, it is not at all like the familiar planet, earth. Because of its high temperatures, the sun cannot <u>contain any elements in a solid state.</u>

4. Did you know that the ballet dancer balancing on one toe places greater pressure on that toe than she places on both feet when standing naturally? That is hard to understand because a given ballet dancer weighs the same in both positions. Nevertheless you must remember the general principle that the smaller the area over which weight is <u>distributed, the greater the pressure.</u>

5. The other day I read that astronomical observatories at high altitudes provide greater visibility. When I told my little brother that fact, he said that the reason was to place the workers nearer the faraway stars. Personally I didn't think that answer made much difference. Then I heard that the thin, dustless air in high altitudes permits <u>greater visibility.</u>

6. It is a common fact that there are layers in the atmosphere. I had always thought that the lowest layer, the troposphere, was the only one helpful to the human being. Then I learned that the stratosphere, the second layer, contains ozone, which traps almost all of the burning, penetrating rays of the sun. Now I see that the stratosphere also is <u>very important to human life.</u>

7. Would you believe that it is the sun's heat which keeps the earth's atmosphere in motion? To understand this fact you must remember that it is the sun's heat which warms the earth and is then radiated into the air. You must also remember that the earth is warmed unevenly, resulting in differences in the air above it. Such differences <u>lead naturally to air movements or winds.</u>

8. I have noticed that areas near lakes and seas usually have a refreshing breeze. The reason is that the land absorbs more of the sun's heat during the day than the water does. When the warmed air above the land rises, the cooler air above the water flows into the space vacated by the land air. The reverse situation occurs during the night. <u>Now I see why areas near the water abound in breezes.</u>

9. Why is it that tornadoes cause large buildings to collapse? The answer lies in the fact that the whirling motion inside the tornado's cone lowers the air pressure so much that the greater pressure inside the buildings causes their walls and roofs to push out-<u>ward with great force.</u>

10. I heard the other day that the tropical Atlantic Ocean has a greater percentage of salt than the Arctic Ocean has. This is understandable if one remembers that the high temperatures and strong winds in the tropical atmosphere absorb more moisture than <u>the climatic conditions in the colder area.</u>

Expand the enthymeme contained in each of the following paragraphs. Use the following steps:

1. Look very carefully for the main point or conclusion.
2. Find the reason or middle term for this conclusion.
3. Consider the distribution of your subjects and predicates as adequate.
4. If possible, use the first figure.

1. I have heard it said that illegal immigrants add to the percentage of crimes committed in the United States. I hesitate to believe that statement because such immigrants, <u>fearing deportation, tend to avoid the notoriety resulting from a criminal offense.</u>

2. What is a possible reason that immigrants from Cuba have been so successful? Do you know that the average income of Cubans in Dade County, Florida, is $25,000? I wonder why. Perhaps it is because they have the following characteristics: They are both <u>political refugees and also too ambitious for Cuban repression.</u>

3. Recently Asians have become the fastest growing minority in the United States. In 1984 alone there were 280,000 immigrants from the Asian continent. In addition, this ethnic group is achieving economic success at an unprecedented rate. Do you suppose <u>this is because this Asian influx is largely from the educated middle class?</u>

4. People argue about whether or not the number of immigrants coming to the United States will affect adversely the American labor force. Personally I favor the position that America will continue to need immigrants to keep its economy growing. You may be surprised at my position, but I happen to know that the low birthrate in the 1960s <u>is now placing limitations on the American labor pool.</u>

5. Can you believe that even the wealthy from other countries are immigrating to the United States? What causes the rich and famous to leave their own countries and settle in a foreign land? Could it be that their very wealth is a factor? Perhaps it is because their status leads to threats of terrorism and harassment in their own <u>countries.</u>

6. Airline passengers are not complaining today when there are delays in the expected flight times. They are simply grateful that the stepped-up baggage inspections are <u>helping the international efforts against hijacking and terrorism.</u>

7. You have heard about our five-year guarantee for our Leopard sedan. You really get your money's worth when you purchase and drive one of our models. We never hesitate to guarantee our cars because we are sure that they are top quality through and <u>through.</u>

8. Every young American should think about enlisting in the army. I haven't time to tell you all the reasons why this is so. Nevertheless, just listen to the following: You obtain many educational benefits, become physically fit, and contribute to the welfare of your <u>own country.</u>

9. I'm sick and tired of taking so much medicine. Why must I take my blood pressure pills every day? I would much rather take these pills only when I'm nervous or upset. Then I remember what my doctor told me. He said that I must stabilize my circulatory <u>system by giving it regular and careful attention.</u>

10. We believe that its four tires are the most important equipment placed on your car. For this reason alone we carefully research each of our new tire models and spend long <u>hours in field-testing each of them.</u>

The following fallacies are all dependent on language. Mark the specific fallacy primarily exemplified by each one.

_____ 1. That doctor has compiled a list of poisons that children may drink at home.

_____ 2. For rent: well-lighted room for two persons with steam heat and shower.

_____ 3. The waves broke on the shore as he broke the record for the race.

_____ 4. I tell you that old man sitting over there can walk. Therefore he can both walk and sit at the same time.

_____ 5. When do the virgin maidens incense the pagan deities?

_____ 6. The president has two conservative ties for his business engagements.

_____ 7. After working all day, the dinner tasted better than ever.

_____ 8. I don't understand why my wife can't get ready on time. She gets everything else that way.

_____ 9. Nine and seven are divisible by four, because nine and seven are sixteen which is divisible by four.

_____ 10. The fathers of our country were passionate, believers in freedom.

_____ 11. Even though that bloodhound smelled out that criminal, he does not smell good.

_____ 12. Mary thought about talking with her friends for many days.

_____ 13. It is better to act justly than unjustly. But murderers die justly while martyrs die unjustly.

_____ 14. Working under great tension often can lead to high blood pressure.

_____ 15. If you are a self-starter, your boss won't be a crank.

_____ 16. Do you think? We will check on your standards.

_____ 17. If you say that Mr. Smith is a good cobbler and a bad man, it is clear that he is both good and bad at the same time.

_____ 18. Please give me the milk, man.

_____ 19. Every child is both older and younger, for each child is father of the man.

_____ 20. Time tells on a woman, while she tells all that it doesn't.

_____ 21. Bob can carry a weight of 100 pounds and one of 75 pounds. Therefore he can carry 175 pounds.

_____ 22. A friend loves only himself, for every friend loves another just as he loves himself.

_____ 23. Trade secrets: that's what women do.

_____ 24. She left the book on the table which she had just bought from the publisher.

_____ 25. That child is so good at school and so terrible at home. I now understand you when you say that he is both good and bad at once.

_____ 26. The duke yet lives that Henry shall depose.

_____ 27. The smaller is worth more than the greater, since a bird in the hand is worth two in the bush.

_____ 28. That mattress outlasted other mattresses by 3 to 1 in torture. Test in New York City.

_____ 29. That salesman said that his bookbinding is bound to please.

_____ 30. The politician moved the people as he moved from side to side.

The following fallacies are all dependent on language. Mark the specific fallacy primarily exemplified by each one.

_____ 1. Although the ballet company lined up the chairs, they were unable to line up.

_____ 2. Our manager told us today that our company serves us right.

_____ 3. My fiancé lives in a lighthouse. After I am married, I intend to spend my time in lighthouse keeping.

_____ 4. The whole is only a part, for every whole is made up of all its parts.

_____ 5. After washing and waxing, the car looked like new.

_____ 6. My bank statement revealed that I spent the $500 that I had saved. It's nice to know that I am able to save while I spend.

_____ 7. To pour out the cement, a well-shaped mold is essential.

_____ 8. If you think our secretaries are incompetent, you should see the manager.

_____ 9. A vacation is only a little more work, for it is preceded and followed by work.

_____ 10. After the plasterers dirtied the floor, they cleaned it carefully. That's quite a talent to be able to dirty and clean something at the same time.

_____ 11. After the carrier had doubled his load, he doubled on his tracks.

_____ 12. In the first part of the race that horse was the fastest of all. Then it surprised everyone by being the slowest. How could any owner enter a horse that is both the fastest and the slowest?

_____ 13. Motels for bargain. Hunters offer security.

_____ 14. After gaining all that weight last month, I worked hard to lose five pounds. It is quite a skill to be able to gain and lose at the same time.

_____ 15. That station wagon can easily slip. In your garage you will see.

_____ 16. Although he felt wanted, the criminal was lonely still.

_____ 17. The cook handed the entree to the maid that was ready to serve.

_____ 18. He managed to elbow his way through the cafeteria line by elbowing everyone in front of him.

_____ 19. Hanging on the edge of the precipice, my eyes started to water.

_____ 20. His shoes pinched his feet while he pinched out his existence.

_____ 21. New terminals click right into little. Outlets made for your phone jacks.

_____ 22. A surface has only length, for it is simply extension in two directions.

_____ 23. My brother wanted to take my piece of candy, so I let him have it.

_____ 24. After being stuffed, the cook placed the turkey in the oven.

_____ 25. As he crossed the line, he reached the marksman's line of fire.

_____ 26. I heard about the shotgun. Wedding held with great ceremony.

_____ 27. After working well for an hour, that washing machine stalled. The directions for this equipment certainly never explained to me how a machine can both work and not work.

_____ 28. That soldier rushed his comrade to the hospital as he rushed through the streets.

_____ 29. He gave the package to the postmaster that was lost in the mail.

_____ 30. I heard that man say that he is a civil servant, even if his efforts sometimes fall short.

The following fallacies are all independent of language. Mark the specific fallacy primarily exemplified by each one.

_____ 1. Jane is an introvert because she never comes to any of our parties.

_____ 2. Did you hit your employer with a monkey wrench?

_____ 3. Every human ear is pierced, for Nancy's ear is pierced and it is a human ear.

_____ 4. Our superintendent should be removed from office because he has divorced his wife.

_____ 5. That man is a criminal because he is seen with tough characters.

_____ 6. I always did as I pleased when I was small, so I know that freedom means doing as you please.

_____ 7. There should be a law against the selling of guns, for we have long needed legal protection against the unnecessary ownership of such weapons.

_____ 8. The governor will visit our city because there was a trade deficit last year.

_____ 9. You will never obtain that position because your personal record is not good.

_____ 10. Every necklace is broken in two places, for Sally's necklace is broken in two places and it is a true necklace.

_____ 11. The city will start a symphony orchestra because it has finished a ball park.

_____ 12. You should reduce because you notice that a flight of steps looks steeper.

_____ 13. I know that a fair exchange is no robbery because my father always had a fair trade in his store.

_____ 14. Diligence is the mother of good luck, for the industrious man is always successful.

_____ 15. Do you hate lectures because you always sleep through them?

_____ 16. Every massacre is justified, for Jennings' merciless killing was justified and it was a massacre.

_____ 17. Mrs. Smith will begin her housecleaning because the trees have started to bud.

_____ 18. I know that lightning never strikes the same place twice, for it has struck our barn only once.

_____ 19. That person is lazy because he is not working.

_____ 20. The best physicians in our hospital prescribe the medicine that I take for my arthritis.

_____ 21. I believe that one should put business before pleasure because a person deserves a vacation only if he has worked hard.

_____ 22. Why do you clean your house only once a month?

_____ 23. That child is a genius because he mingled with learned adults.

_____ 24. Watch that new principal. He will act as if you teachers never do anything right.

_____ 25. I understand why little things please little minds, for the slowest student in our class was content with the simplest exercises.

_____ 26. I have heard that the eagle is a very swift bird. Therefore I know that any bird which is swift must be an eagle.

_____ 27. Do you still have a closet full of expensive clothes?

_____ 28. The reason that every man has his price is that everyone is susceptible to the lure of money.

_____ 29. Everybody's business is nobody's business, for not a single person in that company was given a specific assignment. Do you know what happened? Nothing was finished.

_____ 30. Every human being is a chairman, for Arthur Manyon is the chairman and he is a human being.

The following fallacies are all independent of language. Mark the specific fallacy primarily exemplified by each one.

_____ 1. Every timepiece is broken, for my watch is broken and it is a timepiece.

_____ 2. First impressions are the most lasting, for children never forget their first impressions of school.

_____ 3. A little knowledge is a dangerous thing, for a person at the threshold of learning can get into a lot of trouble.

_____ 4. Are you still telling your doctor about your imaginary illnesses?

_____ 5. Even though that store has inferior products, it manages to sell them. Therefore I know that whatever sells must be an inferior product.

_____ 6. Since those pirate ships were searched at sea, I realize that every seagoing vessel should be searched.

_____ 7. Smoke Viceroy—the thinking man's cigarette.

_____ 8. I cannot find a job now because I dropped out of college three years ago.

_____ 9. Why do you brush your teeth only two or three times every week?

_____ 10. Absence makes the heart grow fonder, for those who are separated for a long time appreciate each other far more.

_____ 11. This deodorant was tested by the toughest judges in the world—men like you.

_____ 12. That family is quarreling because they never eat dinner together.

_____ 13. When I learned that our country saved scrap iron during the war, I realized that all scrap material should be saved.

_____ 14. Our business will succeed because it succeeded last year.

_____ 15. Every canned product should be discarded, for that dog food was discarded and it was a canned product.

_____ 16. Why do you take two coffee breaks every afternoon?

_____ 17. Idleness is the root of all evil, for the man who works only four hours out of eight is very likely to get into trouble.

_____ 18. Since those housing projects failed, I know that no housing project will succeed.

_____ 19. The school should revise its curriculum because its students are unhappy.

_____ 20. I should not get a parking ticket, for I've never had a parking ticket in this spot before.

_____ 21. Every city is corrupt, for Smithville is corrupt and it is a city.

_____ 22. No medical evidence nor scientific endorsement has proved any cigarette superior to Kent.

_____ 23. I'm sure that we have a problem with the plumbing because that new couple moved into the apartment building last month.

_____ 24. Actions speak louder than words, for the people who really do things are noticed more than those who just sit around and talk.

_____ 25. The criminals released from the city jail are soon behind bars again. Therefore it is clear to me that no criminals reform.

_____ 26. Those parents don't know how to rear their offspring because their children are seldom at home.

_____ 27. I presume that you will give to our charity, for you pledged less than $50 last year.

_____ 28. Every sailboat is unseaworthy, for the *Jupiter* is unseaworthy and it is a sailboat.

_____ 29. Why did you neglect to give your employees a bonus last year?

_____ 30. That man is a computer expert because he has a large vocabulary.

The following fallacies are either dependent or independent of language. Mark the specific fallacy primarily exemplified by each one.

_____ 1. To the housewife: save soap and waste paper.

_____ 2. Carefully placed in a garment bag she carried three dresses.

_____ 3. When the last Republican president held office, our national income was cut in half. Do you intend to vote for a Republican and have another depression?

_____ 4. The human being is both rational and irrational, for every human being is not only rational but also animal.

_____ 5. Dependence on another person is a sign of weakness. It is degrading. That's why I refuse to admit that I depend on God for anything.

_____ 6. Man is a tragic figure, not because he needs to be, but because his life is filled with tragedy.

_____ 7. Everything that exists has a determined nature. A hand is a hand; an eye is an eye. The will also has a determined nature; therefore it is not free.

_____ 8. The converse moved around many local events.

_____ 9. Professor Walker's chemical theory must be true, for the outstanding scientists have accepted it.

_____ 10. Robert Burns wrote his greatest poems during his twenties, for he cast off all moral restraints during this time.

_____ 11. Every funeral is laughable, for Smith's obsequies were laughable and they were a funeral.

_____ 12. Children of members under fourteen will be admitted at half price.

_____ 13. You know well that you had bad luck because a black cat crossed your path.

_____ 14. Every day my grandmother would say her prayers and clean her house. In this way she followed the sound advice of those who tell us to pray and work at the same time.

_____ 15. College education is a waste of time. Henry Ford was one of the richest men in the world, and he never went beyond the fourth grade.

_____ 16. Christianity is a failure because the world is enduring a period of unparalleled suffering.

_____ 17. The question is simply this: Do we want to continue to pour our money down a sewer by lending it to warring countries?

_____ 18. All regular shrimp are poisoned, for that shrimp is poisoned and it is a regular shrimp.

_____ 19. Have you heard that John won the prize because he did the most extensive research? Yes, I heard that, but I wonder if he really did that much research. Don't worry about that. He won the prize, didn't he?

_____ 20. He remembered the portrait of the loveliest girl he'd ever seen hanging in the living room.

_____ 21. There must be a global war brewing because I have never seen so much distress in the country.

_____ 22. No parrot can imitate human speech, for my Polly cannot imitate human speech and she is a parrot.

_____ 23. You assert that there is no religious freedom in Russia. But I can show you a copy of the latest Russian constitution which states explicitly that there is religious liberty in that country.

_____ 24. Don't try to tell me anything about the Church. Why only last night I read in the paper about some clergyman who was arrested for drunken driving.

_____ 25. Mr. Jones and Miss Smith are dating because they were seen together.

_____ 26. Prosecutor: Where did you hide the gun used for the murder?

_____ 27. Every man must back the labor unions. Otherwise his job will be in jeopardy.

_____ 28. Adversity makes strange bedfellows because hard times bring such different people together.

_____ 29. If the Smiths can afford a new car, it is plain to me that every working family is entitled to one.

_____ 30. Having decided to come out of his shell, he placed the shell in his gun.

The primary purpose of the theory of logical thinking is to enable the learner to become skillful in the three acts of the human mind. These operations are as follows:

1. simple apprehension, culminating in the definition
2. judgment, expressed in the categorical proposition
3. reasoning, formalized in the syllogism

Each of the above operations is developed slowly but surely in the comprehension skills which are part of the subject of reading. The following list illustrates this fact:

Logic	Reading
1. to learn the categories for definition	1. to classify various objects
2. to learn the inductive process for definition	2. to identify the main idea
3. to learn and use the four kinds of propositions	3. to make careful generalizations
4. to construct valid syllogisms	4. to make sound inferences; to predict outcomes

If the three operations of defining, judging, and reasoning are an intricate part of the reading process, then the theory of logic, which is directed toward a fine art in these three operations, can be of great service to the subject of reading.

Because of the direct connection between logic and reading, one of the purposes of this text is to make numerous applications of logical theory to the various comprehension skills. To guide this application, the following plan will be used:

1. At the beginning of each major mental operation, an overview of the connection between logic and reading will be given.
2. For the specific chapters within that operation, the particular logical principles will be applied to appropriate comprehension skills.

FIRST ACT OF THE MIND: SIMPLE APPREHENSION

A. OVERVIEW

There is a striking connection between the logical operation of simple apprehension and the initial comprehension skills of reading. This connection is easily seen in the following outline:

Logic:
Simple Apprehension to Definition

Reading:
Grasp Main Idea to Definition

from sensible singular
↓
to whatness of thing (universal level)
↓
which is clarified or defined

from supporting details
↓
to main idea
↓
which is compared/contrasted with other things for better understanding

The above general outline is further specified in the following chart, which again shows the relation between logical and comprehension skills:

SIMPLE APPREHENSION

LOGICAL SKILLS	READING SKILLS	
	WHAT	HOW
from sensible singular ↓ to whatness of thing (universal level) ↓	details ↓ main idea, topic sentence	*by induction* 1. recall details 2. find related facts 3. identify main idea
clarified or defined:	1. general or common class (similarities) 2. identifying differences (differences)	— compare two or more things
⌈categories	— categories of things	— classify various objects
predicables	1. general or common class (similarities) 2. identifying differences (differences)	1. recognize similarities 2. find differences a. *by dividing* contrast kinds under class to find identifying differences b. *by composing* find common note in individuals with same name in order to reveal identifying differences
⌊four causes	— who, what, why, materials	
	order and sequence	*by giving order and sequence* 1. sequence events 2. find order in parts, in worth 3. find order in ideas 4. make outline
expressed in words used univocally, equivocally, analogically	synonyms homonyms antonyms	

The following connection between logical and reading skills is made:

1. logic:
   the movement from the singular to the universal in induction
2. reading:
   the movement from supporting details to the main idea in the reading selection

---

The following workbook will be used for the reading exercises:

Carlisle, Joanne. *Reasoning and Reading*. Level 2. 4 vols: *Word Meaning 2, Sentence Meaning 2, Paragraph Meaning 2, Reasoning Skills* 2. Cambridge, Massachusetts: Educators Publishing Service, Inc., 1988. (Hereafter cited by name of individual volume.)

Complete the following exercises (*Paragraph Meaning 2*):
1. unity (pp. 2–3)
2. main idea (pp. 4–6)
3. topic sentence (pp. 7–10)

The following connection between logical and reading skills is made:

1. logic:
    the equivocal usage of words, which reflects the fact that words do not have one set meaning
2. reading:
    the analogical and equivocal meanings of words

Complete the following exercises (*Word Meaning 2*, pp. 28–33):
1. finding different meanings
2. words in context

The following connections between logical and reading skills are made:

1. logic:
    a. the classification of material things into ten ultimate categories
    b. the characteristics common to all or several of these categories
        1) opposition
            —through relationship
            —through contrariety
            —through privation
            —through contradiction
        2) priority
            —in time
            —in sequence, when it cannot be reversed
            —in order
            —in worth
            —in nature
        3) simultaneity (whatever comes into being at the same time)
        4) having
            —have any quality
            —have a quantity
            —have apparel
            —have parts
            —have content
            —as something acquired
            —as living with someone
        5) motion
            —motion in substance (generation or corruption)
            —motion in quantity (growth and diminution)
            —motion in quality (alteration)
            —motion from place to place (local motion)
2. reading:
    a. the classification and categories for words
    b. antonyms (opposites, usually contraries)
    c. analogies (all of the above logical topics)

Complete the following exercises (*Word Meaning 2*):
1. classification; outlining (pp. 5–8)
2. antonyms (p. 10)
3. finding categories (pp. 19–21)
4. analogies (pp. 22–27)

The following connection between logical and reading skills is made:

1. logic:
    the five predicables, which include both the genus and the specific difference
2. reading:
    the general class and identifying differences for a given subject

---

For the following paragraphs (*Paragraph Meaning 2*, p. 19, A; p. 25, A; p. 31, A) complete these tasks:

1. State the main subject.
2. Give the genus for this subject.
3. List the inseparable and separable accidents given in the paragraph.
4. If possible, add several other identifying attributes. Then mark how these attributes are predicated of the subject.

The following connection between logical and reading skills is made:

1. logic:
   —the method of division which seeks the distinctive difference for a given thing by separating it from others under the same class
   —the method of composition which seeks the distinctive difference by examining individuals with the same name to see what they have in common
2. reading:
   the method of comparison which examines two or more things to note their similarities (common class) and differences (identifying differences)

Complete the following exercises:
1. similarities and differences (*Word Meaning 2*, pp. 16–18)
2. comparison (*Paragraph Meaning 2*, pp. 27–29)

The following connection between logical and reading skills is made:

1. logic:
    the clarification or definition of a thing, which states its genus and specific difference (or grouping of inseparable accidents)
2. reading:
    —the definition of a thing, which gives its category and the detail making it different
    —synonyms, which give an easier, similar meaning

Complete the following exercises (*Word Meaning 2*):
1. synonyms (p. 9)
2. definition (pp. 34–37)

SECOND ACT OF THE MIND: JUDGMENT

A. OVERVIEW

The logician, in treating the act of judgment, explains both the proposition obtained and possible operations on this complex statement. More specifically, the logician covers the following topics:

1. the proposition
   a. actual affirmation or denial
   b. a universal or particular
   c. its types: A,I,E,O
2. the operations performed on it
   a. conversion (reversal of subject and predicate)
   b. obversion (reversal of quality of proposition)
   c. opposition (contradiction, contrariety, subcontrariety, subalternation)

The above topics are easily paralleled to the comprehension skills of reading. It must be stated immediately, however, that the primary connection is found with the proposition, rather than with its operations. This is sound pedagogy, for this emphasis permits familiarity with the basic entity first. The following chart indicates the parallel between judgment and reading skills:

LOGICAL SKILLS	READING SKILLS	
	WHAT	HOW
The Proposition		
an affirmation/ denial	declarative sentences	1. recognize declarative sentences 2. find main thought in complex sentences 3. reorder jumbled sentences 4. find phrases in sentences
a universal/ particular	words expressing quantity	—learn impact of quantifiers
its types: A, I, E, O	generalizations	—find key words in generalizations
converted, obverted, ↓ opposed	pairs of sentences	—detect equivalent sentences

The following connections between logical and reading skills are made:

1. logic:
   a. recognition of the proposition both as an affirmation/denial and as a universal/particular
   b. recognition of the types of propositions: A, I, E, O
2. reading:
   a. recognition of the sentence as a unit of thought
   b. awareness of the impact of quantifiers
   c. knowledge of key words in generalizations

Complete the following exercises (*Sentence Meaning 2*):
1. main idea; getting the point (pp. 4–7)
2. generalizations (pp. 31–35)

The following connection between logical and reading skills is made:

1. logic:
   the conversion and obversion of categorical propositions
2. reading:
   the detection of sentences with equivalent meanings

Complete the following exercises (*Sentence Meaning 2*):
1. same or different meaning (pp. 36–38)
2. conversion of generalizations (p. 32)
3. obversion of generalizations (p. 34)

No direct exercise using the rules of opposition was found in the typical elementary reading workbook. Nevertheless the following exercise may be utilized:

Complete the following tasks for the generalizations found in *Sentence Meaning 2*, p. 32:
1. Choose five generalizations.
2. Make a paragraph for each one. These paragraphs should resemble the structure of the latter section of exercise 3 of this chapter.

THIRD ACT OF THE MIND: REASONING

A. OVERVIEW

In treating the act of reasoning, the logician must cover not only the form of the syllogistic process but also the material or content used in this process. Just as the builder must study both his blueprint and the nature of his materials, so the logician must have rules concerning both the form and the content employed in his reasoning. In this introductory course, these two factors are restricted primarily to the following topics:

1. form of reasoning
   a. basic form: categorical syllogism
   b. conditional form: hypothetical syllogism
   c. truncated form: enthymeme
2. matter or content of reasoning
   a. certain (advanced study)
   b. probable (advanced study)
   c. false: fallacies

The above topics are easily paralleled to the comprehension skills of reading. This agreement can be noted in the following outline:

LOGICAL SKILLS	READING SKILLS	
	WHAT	**HOW**

1. *Categorical Form*
a. state problem
b. find middle term
 	
c. conclude according
   to rules
	
	cause and effect
	relevant information
	
	valid syllogism
		
		b. detect cause-effect relationship
		b. select relevant information for
		   problem
		c. learn common syllogistic patterns

2. *Hypothetical Form*
a. affirm antecedent
   (from cause to effect)
b. deny consequent
   (from effect to cause)
	
	inference
	
	inference
		
		a. predict or infer outcome
		
		b. find most likely reason

3. *Fallacious Content* a. note misuse of words b. note inadequate causes	 facts/opinions (from type of reason) <u>inadequate reasons</u> 1) accidental 2) general 3) partial 4) sequential 5) personal attack 6) force 7) authority 8) emotions	 b. judge opinions b. judge inadequate reasons

The following connections between logical and reading skills are made:

1. logic:
    a. understanding the structure of the categorical syllogism
    b. becoming skilled in the general and special rules of the categorical syllogism
2. reading:
    a. detecting cause–effect relationships in sentences and paragraphs
    b. selecting relevant information for given problems
    c. learning common syllogistic patterns

Complete the following exercises:
1. relationships: cause–effect (*Sentence Meaning 2*, pp. 22–23)
2. cause–effect (*Paragraph Meaning 2*, pp. 21–23)
3. relevant information (*Reasoning Skills 2*, pp. 10–12)
4. syllogisms (*Reasoning Skills 2*, pp. 23–26)

The following connection between logical and reading skills is made:

1. logic:
    the valid procedures for the hypothetical syllogism
2. reading:
    familiarity with inferential reasoning

Complete the following exercise (*Reasoning Skills 2*):
    inference (pp. 13–19)

The following connection between logical and reading skills is made:

1. logic:
   detecting the use of inadequate causes in fallacious reasoning
2. reading:
   —judging opinions from the reasons given
   —detecting inadequate causes

Complete the following exercises (*Reasoning Skills 2*):
1. fact and opinion; judging opinions (pp. 2–6)
2. cause–effect reasoning (pp. 20–22)

The correlation between logical and reading skills may be summarized as follows:

	LOGICAL SKILLS	READING SKILLS
SIMPLE APPREHENSION	The learner moves from the sensible singular to whatness of thing (universal level), which is clarified or defined.	The student moves from supporting details to main idea, which is compared/contrasted with other things to find similarities and differences.
JUDGMENT	The learner makes an affirmation or denial (judgment) which is universal or particular. Four types of judgments or propositions follow from the above possibilities: 1. universal affirmation (A) 2. particular affirmation (I) 3. universal denial (E) 4. particular denial (O) These propositions may be converted, obverted, or opposed.	The student recognizes declarative sentences, in which something is said about all or some of the subject. The student learns about quantifiers and the various kinds of generalizations. The student learns to detect equivalent or opposite sentences.

REASONING	The learner studies both the form and matter (content) of reasoning:
	
	1. *Categorical Form* (basic syllogism)
	  a. state problem
	  b. find middle term
	  c. conclude according to rules
	2. *Hypothetical Form* (conditional syllogism)
	  a. affirm antecedent (from cause to effect)
	  b. deny consequent (from effect to cause)
	3. *Fallacious Content*
	  a. note misuse of words
	  b. note inadequate causes
		The student learns syllogistic patterns, inferences, and the distinction between fact and opinion.
		
		1. *Syllogistic Pattern*
		  a. identify the problem
		  b. select relevant information for the problem
		  c. learn common syllogistic patterns
		2. *Inference*
		  a. predict or infer outcome
		  b. find most likely reason
		3. *Fact vs. Opinion*
		  a. learn various meanings of words
		  b. judge inadequate reasons

SELECTED ANSWERS

EXERCISE 1   CHAPTER 1

1. problem: Why are the tropics very hard on machinery?
   case defined: The tropics have a climate with much moisture.
   principle: Whatever climate has much moisture is very hard on machinery.
2. problem: Why are magazines tied in a bundle very difficult to burn?
   case defined: Magazines tied in a bundle have very little air.
   principle: Whatever has very little air is very difficult to burn.
3. problem: Why is carbon dioxide useful for putting out fires?
   case defined: Carbon dioxide can shut off the supply of oxygen.
   principle: Whatever can shut off the supply of oxygen is useful for putting out fires.

EXERCISE 1   CHAPTER 2

1. universal: Great care must be taken to avoid a buildup of static electricity.
   singulars: a. hanging back chain on gasoline trucks
                    b. damp floors in operating rooms
                    c. tassels on tips of airplane wings
2. universal: Heat is produced by the use of friction.
   singulars: a. rubbing cold hands together
                    b. rubbing two pieces of wood together to kindle a fire
                    c. striking tip of match on rough surface

---

EXERCISE 2   CHAPTER 3

1. equivocal   4. analogical   7. equivocal
2. univocal   5. analogical   8. analogical
3. univocal   6. univocal   9. univocal

EXERCISE 4   CHAPTER 4

1. substance   7. passion   13. relation
2. quality   8. relation   14. action
3. quality   9. substance   15. position
4. substance   10. quality   16. substance
5. relation   11. quality   17. quantity
6. position   12. quality   18. where

EXERCISE 1   CHAPTER 5

1. accident   7. genus   13. inseparable accident
2. inseparable accident   8. genus   14. genus
3. inseparable accident   9. species   15. inseparable accident
4. genus   10. accident   16. genus
5. genus   11. inseparable accident   17. accident
6. species   12. property   18. accident

---

1. a [small, usually round] *piece* of [glass, wood, or metal], [pierced] [for stringing] *

2. a [hollow, usually cuplike] *object*, [made of metal or other hard material], [which rings] [if struck by an inside clapper] *

3. a *water bird* with [large wings, slender legs, webbed feet, a strong, hooked bill, and feathers of chiefly white and gray]*

4. a [large, strong, flesh-eating] *bird of prey belonging to the falcon family*, [noted for its sharp vision and powerful wings]*

5. a [small, slender] *piece* [of steel] with a [sharp point at one end and a hole for thread at the other], [used for sewing]*

EXERCISE 1   **CHAPTER 8**

1. negative	11. negative	20. negative
2. affirmative	12. affirmative	22. negative
3. negative	18. negative	23. negative

EXERCISE 3   **CHAPTER 8**

1. universal	4. particular	7. singular
2. particular	5. particular	8. indefinite
3. universal	6. indefinite	9. indefinite

EXERCISE 5   **CHAPTER 8**

1. E	4. I	7. A
2. O	5. O	8. A
3. O	6. I	9. I

EXERCISE 1   **CHAPTER 9**

1. U-------U	4. D---------U	7. U------D
2. D-------U	5. U---------D	8. U------U
3. D-------D	6. D---------U	9. D------U

EXERCISE 3   **CHAPTER 9**

1. Some P is S.	7. —
2. Some P is non-S.	8. Some non-P is S.
3. Some P is non-S.	9. Some smokers are men.
4. No P is non-S.	10. Some living things are plants.
5. —	11. Some white things are snow.
6. Some P is S.	12. —

---

1. Every S is non-P.
2. Some S is non-P.
3. Every S is P.
4. No S is non-P.
5. Some S is not P.
6. Some S is not non-P.
7. Some non-S is not non-P.
8. No S is P.
9. No non-S is P.
10. Every non-S is P.
11. No geranium is non-planted.
12. Some mayflies are not non-resting.

---

1. invalid (I to A)
2. valid
3. invalid (O)
4. invalid (O)
5. invalid (O)
6. invalid (I to A)

---

1. false
2. false
3. true
4. unknown
5. false
6. false
7. true
8. unknown
9. false
10. false
11. true
12. unknown
13. true
14. false
15. false
16. true
17. unknown
18. false

---

1. valid
2. invalid (not false, but unknown)
3. valid
4. valid
5. valid
6. invalid (not true, but false)

---

1. Three terms only.
2. Minor premise affirmative.
3. valid
4. Conclusion follows weaker part.
5. Three terms only.
6. Two particulars do not conclude.
7. One premise negative.
8. valid
9. valid
10. valid

---

1. Every x is z.
2. No x is z.
3. Some x is not z.
4. No x is z.
5. Some x is not z.
16. Some milk is not a solid.
17. Some colorless things are not water.
18. Some short-legged things are thick-skinned.
19. Some members of the legume family do not have palmate leaves.
20. Every male moose has a weapon for defense.

---

1. Every kind person is a good neighbor.
   Mrs. Jones is a kind person.

   ∴ Mrs. Jones is a good neighbor.

   VALID

2. Some bitterns are wading birds.
   No bluebird is a wading bird.

   ∴ No bluebird is a bittern.

   MAJOR PREMISE UNIVERSAL.

3. Every religious man goes to church every Sunday.
   McDonald goes to church every Sunday.

   ∴ McDonald is a religious man.

   ONE PREMISE NEGATIVE.

4. No one likes a mean individual.
   Gary is certainly not a mean individual.

   ∴ Everyone likes Gary.

   TWO NEGATIVES DO NOT CONCLUDE.

5. Everyone who is unafraid of death deserves to live.
   Every member of that army is unafraid of death.

   ∴ Every member of that army deserves to live.

   VALID

6. No metal is a compound substance.
   Aluminum is a metal.

   ∴ Aluminum is not a compound substance.

   VALID

7. Every physical body gravitates.
   The air gravitates.

   ∴ The air is a physical body.

   ONE PREMISE NEGATIVE.

8. No modern physician believes in the practice of bleeding.
   Dr. Mitchell does not believe in the practice of bleeding.

   ∴ Dr. Mitchell is a modern physician.

   TWO NEGATIVES DO NOT CONCLUDE.

---

1. Deny the consequent.
2. valid
3. Affirm the antecedent.
4. Affirm the antecedent.

5. Deny the consequent.
6. valid
7. Deny the consequent.
8. valid

---

1. Every Y is Z.
   Every X is Y.

   ∴ Every X is Z.

2. No Y is Z.
   All X is Y.

   ∴ No X is Z.

3. Every Y is Z.
   Some X is Y.

   ∴ Some X is Z.

4. No Y is Z.
   Some X is Y.

   ∴ Some X is not Z.

9. Every stringed instrument requires tuning.
   Every lyre is a stringed instrument.

   ∴ Every lyre requires tuning.
10. Nothing small is blooming.
    Every tulip is too small.

    ∴ None of the tulips is blooming.
11. No one staying up late is sleeping.
    Some of the children stayed up late.

    ∴ Some of the children are not sleeping.
12. Nothing hanging on the wall is fastened.
    Every harness is hanging on the wall.

    ∴ No harness is fastened.

EXERCISE 4   **CHAPTER 12**

1. Whatever has very little air is very difficult to burn.
   All magazines tied in a bundle have very little air.

   ∴ All magazines tied in a bundle are very difficult to burn.
2. Whatever can shut off the supply of oxygen is useful for putting out fires.
   All carbon dioxide can shut off the supply of oxygen.

   ∴ All carbon dioxide is useful for putting out fires.
3. Whatever is very light and safe from explosion is used today in dirigibles and blimps.
   Helium is very light and safe from explosion.

   ∴ Helium is used today in dirigibles and blimps.
4. Nothing with a very high water content is an economical form of fuel.
   All peat has a very high water content.

   ∴ No peat is an economical form of fuel.
5. Whatever rusts easily should be covered with a thin coating of oil.
   The stored plow rusts easily.

   ∴ The stored plow should be covered with a thin coating of oil.

EXERCISE 1   **CHAPTER 13**

1. ambiguity
2. amphiboly
3. form of expression
4. composition
5. accent

6. ambiguity
7. amphiboly
8. ambiguity
9. division
10. accent

EXERCISE 3   **CHAPTER 13**

1. consequent
2. two questions as one
3. accident
4. ignorance of proof
5. consequent

6. absolute/ qualified
7. begging question
8. non-cause as cause
9. ignorance of proof
10. accident

---

5. My poultry are not officers.
23. Guinea-pigs never really appreciate Beethoven.
29. All gluttons, who are children of mine, are unhealthy.
33. I have never come across a mermaid at sea.
37. All your poems are uninteresting.
44. Shakespeare was clever.
49. Donkeys are not easy to swallow.
54. No heavy fish is unkind to children.
59. I cannot read any of Brown's letters.
60. I always avoid a kangaroo.

[§]Lewis Carroll, *Symbolic Logic* (London: Macmillan & Company, Ltd., 1896), pp. 132–33.

INDEX

Made in the USA
Coppell, TX
01 October 2020